ONE MAN'S SAS

One Man's SAS

LOFTY LARGE

WILLIAM KIMBER · LONDON

First published in 1987 by
WILLIAM KIMBER & CO. LIMITED
100 Jermyn Street, London, SW1Y 6EE

Typeset by Grove Graphics
and printed in Great Britain by
Redwood Burn Limited, Trowbridge

DEDICATED TO ALL TROGS. The few winners, the many losers and those, like me, surprised survivors.

To those whose guts and comradeship kept me alive.

To my wife, whose ever-ready support through many 'trials and tribulations' has made life worth living.

To many friends, whose 'memory jogging' and encouragement kept me in line.

TO THE SPECIAL MEMORY OF –

Andy	Lofty
Bernie	Lon
Big Ron	Nick
Buddha	Nuge
Jack	Paddy
Kevin	Vic
Keith	Yogi

And the best parents a man could ask for.

TROG

In the Oxford English Dictionary –
TROGLODYTE – *Cave dweller*

In the British Army –
TROG – *Abbreviation of Troglodyte*
   Term applied only to Non-Commissioned Ranks of any army or real military force. Soldiers, like cave dwellers, must sometimes live in holes in the ground to survive.

Contents

List of Illustrations

Forewarning

Whatever else I may have been accused of in my life, I have never been accused of being an author, a writer or an educated man. The story of my 'time served' with the British Army is my story, my words, my totally inadequate vocabulary. If you look for the work of a professional writer – get a book written by one. I was a professional soldier, so this is something outside my profession. I make no apologies.

Experienced soldiers will understand the omission (except where relevant to the story) of the 'blood and guts' situations. In any case, my limitations with the written word are as nothing when some of the things I have seen would defy a 'writing genius' and the disjointed brush of Picasso. What I have written is what I have seen or done myself, except where stated. No one else stood where I stood, saw what I saw, felt what I felt, or whatever. Men who were with me in this or that situation will have seen, felt or heard other things. Their story would probably sound much different to mine, but we would each recognise the other's viewpoint.

Many experiences have been left out for various reasons. Those experiences of which I have written are picked out because they were either typical of the situation or unusual in some aspect worthy of mention. My twenty-seven years in the British Army were mostly enjoyable, unforgettable years. They were made so, even under the most adverse conditions, by the men I served with. I was fortunate to always have the best men on this earth within nodding distance – not always friends but at least comrades in arms.

Those men I followed and those (much braver than I) who followed me, are the men who make me proud to have been a Trog.

CHAPTER ONE

Selection

Time. Time to think. Perhaps the best time to think, to take one's mind off the aching limbs, the searing pain of the back strap and the continual cutting of the shoulder straps. What does a man think of when he's flogging around an SAS Selection Course? Mostly, 'What the hell am I doing here?' But then, if you don't know the answer to that – there is no point in being there!

The 'forever' hard going of the Brecon Beacons, and all points nasty for miles around them. The Black Mountains, Mynydd Eppynt, Fforest Fawr, away up past Painscastle (so aptly named). Everywhere was steep up or steep down, except where there were bogs or rivers. The rain only seemed to stop when it turned to sleet or snow on the high ground. The wind always made sure everyone got their fair share. If it slackened in its icy blast at night you knew you were about to walk into a tree or over a cliff.

Think hard and think about anything – except the discomfort. Not easy for most but, perhaps, a little easier for me. Pain and discomfort I knew well. The terrible pain one gets for losing the temper against a very cool machine gunner, and the very real discomfort, both mental and physical, caused by a four hundred mile march to a prison camp, in which to spend two years as a guest of the 'Chinese Peoples' Volunteers'. Then live in 'shame' for two years because you, a young (but trying to be) professional soldier have surrendered to the enemy. Surrendered, to have your miserable life spared when you have seen your friends killed trying to do their job. A terrible feeling of having failed. Failed my country, my unit, my people. Failed myself.

The feelings of failure and shame only lifted when I was released from the prison camp, to learn that when my unit, 1st Battalion The Gloucestershire Regiment, was destroyed on the Imjin River, in Korea, we had been assessed as having done the best we could against 'overwhelming odds'.

The less than four thousand gun hands of 29 Brigade, of which the Glosters were about one quarter, had been hit by about fifty-four thousand Communist troops. The Glosters had stayed put, partly to let the other very battered battalions withdraw. Only about forty Glosters managed to escape death or capture.

Before capture I had weighed about 15 stone 7 lb (98.4 kg). When first released I weighed 9 stone 10 lb (61.7 kg), and had a partly paralysed left arm. At a shade under 6 ft 6 in (2 metres) tall I had to run around in the shower to get wet and stand twice to make a shadow. The Imjin River battle was in April 1951. I was released from the prison camp in April 1953, a few months before the Korean war ended. With twenty-one other Brits I was exchanged for over seven hundred Chinese. We were all classed as 'unfit for further military service'.

Now, here I was, after four years in Gloucester, at the Glosters Depot, where I had been medically 'downgraded' (P7 in Army terms), excused just about everything bar breathing – a most unlikely candidate for the roughest, toughest selection and training in the Army. But, as any SAS man will tell you – it's all in the mind!

So it may be, but it certainly doesn't feel like it when you are knackered out of your mind, facing a wet and icy blast, aching, sore, soaking from head to toe, and looking up another bloody great hill. Nevertheless, I felt I had the edge on most of my compatriots when it got really rough. I could always console myself that I didn't now have dysentery, a dangling useless arm or a yelling oriental gentleman trying to replace the dysentery with a bayonet. There was always the thought, 'When it gets as rough as that, I'll think again!' Not a lot of use, really, but then – it's all in the mind.

In 1955, the girl whom I had met in 1950, who had kept up our friendship by post while I served with the Wiltshire Regiment in Hong Kong, who had later bombarded Korea with my fanmail (five letters per week, of which I received about ninety over two years), agreed at last to marry me. Ann had been a great help with a difficult rehabilitation, always keeping the sense of humour at the right times. How could I face her again if I couldn't pass a Selection Course? She always had faith I would recover, be fit again. This was the proof. So it had to be done.

There was also another little matter which helped with the 'get up and go' to join the SAS. The Special Air Service was known to be a strictly operational outfit, with no time for drill or bullshit. I had joined the Army in 1946 at the tender age of fifteen, and spent eleven years in the infantry. I had been drilled to bits and nearly drowned in bullshit. None of it had done me a blind bit of good when I had been doing 'what a soldier is for'. A smart right turn doesn't dismiss a mortar shell any more than shiny brasses deflect a sniper's eye. But the good training we could have done in the time wasted on the drill square would have helped a lot!

All I had to do to opt out of the stupidities of drill, etc., was use my head and get my ass over the next hill. In 1957, the Selection Course for 22 Special Air Service Regiment was based at Dering Lines, Brecon. It was another of those wartime hutted camps, a lot of wooden huts for the troggery, a few brickbuilt buildings for administration departments, all linked together by concrete roads and paths.

The SAS Selection Detachment, which ran the Selection Courses, consisted of one captain, one sergeant and three or four trogs. Two three-ton Bedford trucks, two quarter-ton Austin Champs were its wheels. Two or three nissen huts for accommodation, another for office, stores and armoury made up the static assets. Meals were provided by a cookhouse serving other units based in Dering Lines. I found it 'shoe-string', casual but totally efficient. My first shock was seeing and feeling a loaded Bergen rucksack for the first time in my life, and realising I'd have to carry one.

There were four men on the course who had been given a second chance from previous courses, due to injuries, etc. From them we got some idea of the problems ahead. With no small amount of surprise I recognised one of the troopers on the Selection Staff as a fellow ex-prisoner of war. Bert had joined SAS almost straight from the POW camp!

The course assembled on a Saturday. We were given a quick briefing and introduction by Captain Mike Jones, the Selection Officer. Then we were given a more detailed run-down of what was expected of us – and what was not expected of us – by the sergeant. He was Paddy Nugent, one of the greatest men I've ever known. He was certainly the best instructor I ever met in the Army – as Irish as the Blarney Stone, with quick wit, a great sense of humour and a turn of speech only believed when heard.

On the Sunday we prepared our kit, then were given lessons in map reading and navigation, with much emphasis on the use of the compass. I had been involved with instructing map reading, both in the Education Centre and with the Continuation Training Platoon at Gloucester. I had also taught myself a lot about navigation at various times, but, although the lessons on that Sunday were voluntary, supposedly for those without much idea – and there were many – I joined in. There is always more to learn in such subjects. I learned a lot! Part of the Sunday lessons involved a walk up into the Brecon Beacons, which proved invaluable for getting 'switched on' to the terrain for the coming weeks.

My second shock came early on Monday morning. I had been over some rough old assault courses in my time, so, when they said we were going on the assault course I thought of the worst possible case and was ready for it. When I saw the assault course I thought they were joking. It was a doddle. One six-foot wall, a nine-foot jump over some water, a few bars and ropes – a piece of cake.

And so it was a piece of cake, for the first ten times around perhaps, then it began to notice a bit. I've no idea how many times we went round that snotty little course, Paddy Nugent lashing us with his tongue and making dire threats to lash us with about everything else!

At the end I was fit to drop, completely smashed. Some had already dropped. We were told that was just a warm-up. Sure enough it was. My next trick, as far as I can remember, was a 35-mile hike, with 50 lb on my back, all across country ('you will not use roads or bridges') which lasted nearly two days. We went from one RV (rendezvous) to another, never knowing which would be the last. I waded the River Wye twice and slept the night on the mountains, soaking wet and cold but too shattered to notice. We had to travel alone, if two men were caught walking together they risked RTU (Return to Unit); the same if we were caught on roads or bridges.

As the days went by the numbers on the course dwindled. Some men gave up and asked to be sent back to their units, others were sent back because they couldn't keep up, one or two were injured.

At last, the last exercise started. It was the endurance march, which lasted two days. The end of the first day I had my first problem. The Achilles tendon in my left ankle was pulled. Walking became difficult. The last RV of that day was in the mountains and we all had to sleep at the same place. On the last half mile to the RV I was on a grass track when a Champ came along with three of the staff in it. They tried to talk me into having a lift to the RV. Then they said I should pack up altogether – because I was limping. I walked on. There was no way I was going to pack up on the last bloody few miles.

The weather was so bad we were given a rum ration that night.

I saved mine – plus a few others who didn't like the stuff – so that, in the morning, I could deaden the pain in my ankle.

Morning came, I deadened the pain and ploughed on. The first RV was at the Storey Arms (not a pub but a café then) where we had a weapon inspection. Luckily my staggering around was taken to be because of my injured ankle. The last RV was at Talybont Reservoir, which meant crossing the Brecon Beacons again, a distance of about seven miles.

The ankle slowed me down. I was about a mile from the RV when I saw the truck pull out, heading back to camp. I checked my watch and made a note of the time. Once down to the road I got a lift in a car to Brecon, and hobbled into camp to report. At the office I told them where I was when the truck pulled out. They said, 'Prove it.' So I told them the time the truck pulled out, by my watch. I could see I had proved it.

Half an hour later we were called to the office, one at a time, to be given our results. There had been twenty-seven men on the course when it started. Six of us passed. The four who were given a second chance from previous courses, myself and one other. The six who passed were given the weekend off, and told to report back for training at 8 a.m. on Monday. The others were given rail warrants to get back to their units as soon as possible.

I felt great at that moment, couldn't wait to get back to Gloucester to tell Ann I had passed. Without bothering to shower, I put on my shoes as the boots were too painful, jumped on my bike and headed for home.

Just before I reached Crickhowell a coach coming the other way turned across the road in front of me. With nowhere to go I had to hit it. Back to the familiar sounds and smells of hospital, this time as Newport's Royal Gwent Hospital, with a badly injured left foot. The foot needed thirty-odd stitches and was put in plaster for three weeks. If I had been wearing my heavy Army boots instead of light slip-on shoes it's likely I would have got away with a bruising.

I stayed in hospital for nearly a month, and found the difference between the SAS and other units I had been with. Never, in all the time I had spent in hospital, had I ever been visited by a representative of my unit. I had seen officers, padres, sergeants and sergeant-majors visiting other men many times but never had I seen a representative of my unit while in hospital.

Though I could hardly claim to be a member of the SAS, having only passed the first part of the 'entrance exam', Captain Jones came to see me the day after I went in. Paddy Nugent, Bert and the others dropped in every few days, sometimes at very odd hours, in very muddy field kit. Thanks to the staff at the Royal Gwent they were allowed to see me any time of the day or night.

Ann travelled down from Gloucester as often as she could, so altogether I had all the help I could get. On one of his visits, Captain Jones said the Glosters were 'honking' because they had been unable to make the final transfer, and didn't know what to do about me. He said not to worry, he would 'hold the fort' until I could find out how the foot would shape up.

The surgeons were pleased with the foot when the plaster came off. Soon afterwards I was allowed to go home provided I report to the Army Medical Centre at Gloucester every two or three days to have the dressing changed and the wound checked by the Medical Officer. As soon as possible I hitched a lift to Brecon, to pick up my motor-cycle, which had been repaired.

Once I had the bike again it gave me the mobility to get over to my folks' place in the Cotswolds, a lonely cottage among the hills and woods a couple of miles from a village called Guiting Power, and about twenty miles from Gloucester. It had been our home since 1939. I knew every inch of the surrounding countryside which was now my training gound in the struggle to achieve physical fitness. Every chance I got was spent hobbling, then walking, then running around the hills, and through the woods.

Sometimes I carried a shotgun and played my favourite sport. Walking through a fir plantation, between the rows of 30-foot conifers to disturb wood-pigeons, which would take off with a clatter of wings. If they passed over the narrow gap above me, nine out of ten were dead. This called for split-second reactions and was to stand me in good stead for the future. It was probably the best training anyone could get for instinctive shooting.

My folks supported my efforts in every way they could, as always, although my mother worried I would do more harm than good when, in the early days, she accidentally saw a blood-soaked bandage. Ann and my parents between them made the task a lot easier than it might have been, but then, they had been through it all before, when I returned from Korea. The injuries were different, but at least the mind was more settled this time. Ann's parents always made us welcome too. A lot of time was spent at their place, near Tetbury, where we hoofed around the lanes and side roads every time we could.

All went well, but it was another five or six weeks before I could get the swelling down enough to get any Army boots on. Then I had to cheat a bit. Thanks to having friends in the QM Department at Gloucester, I managed to get a pair of boots two sizes too big, so I could use a bigger boot on my left foot. Captain Jones told me on the phone there was another Selection Course starting in two weeks. If I thought the foot was OK to try out, I could go down to Brecon and give it a go.

So, back to Brecon with my odd boots – which I didn't mention to the SAS staff, of course! Captain Jones asked how the foot was. I told him it was OK, so he said to try it out on the first march of the course. This I did and found it no problem, although the wound was still not properly mended and I had a bandage on it. Captain Jones asked me how it was after the first march. When I said it was OK, he said, 'Good, give it another try tomorrow.' And so on, until I had completed another Selection Course, and passed again. I 'wuz conned', but there can't have been many who had to pass the Selection Course twice to get in once.

The old shoulder problem had given me a hard time once in a while, but all those years of tedious exercise and continued practice of blotting pain from my mind had paid off. I had cleared the first hurdle and would take some stopping from now on.

A week or two of training followed, then it was off to Holding and Drafting Company at Airborne Forces Depot, Aldershot. The bullshit, and the attitude of the snivelling para NCOs in 'H' and 'D' Company came nearer to cracking me than anything on the Selection Course. Luckily for one or two at Aldershot, we had too much to lose to start throwing punches. They probably knew that as well as we did.

Away from the Glosters, very few people, even in the Army, recognised the ribbon of the United States Presidential Unit Citation which was awarded to the Glosters, and the men of the battalion who were in the Imjin River Battle. It was worn on the sleeve, just below the unit title flash, and in Airborne Forces Depot, where almost everyone had para wings under their unit title flash, the citation drew many curious glances. Standing in the queue for 'char and wads' in the NAAFI one day a group of young paras, with brand new wings, asked me what the ribbon was for. Before I could answer, one of my friends (an ex-para) said, 'That's the Blue Coffin. Haven't you seen one of those before?' 'No, what's it for?' 'It's for two thousand jumps of course. What else?'

Over the years the citation has been explained away on many occasions. Another good one I remember, 'Oh, he used to be a "Lootenant" in the Seventh Cavalry!' That one to some US Marines.

After a week or two's embarkation leave we flew out to Singapore, then by train to Kuala Lumpur, capital of Malaya, and base for 22 Special Air Service Regiment. Malaya, once part of the British Empire, had been working towards independence since World War II. The Federation of Malay States became an Independent State and elected to remain within the Commonwealth in 1957.

Japanese occupation in World War II, during which anyone who would fight against the Japanese had been armed and trained by the British, saw the emergence of the Malayan Communist Party as an effective fighting force. Its members were mostly Chinese, and less than three years after the end of World War II Mao Tse Tung's revolution in China may possibly have given them the idea of taking over Malaya and making it a communist State. As at least seven-tenths of Malaya was covered by so-called 'impenetrable jungle', the terrain was ideal for terrorist operations so, in 1948, the commies 'had a go'.

The 'go', known to us as the Malayan Emergency, lasted about ten years. During the early days the Brits had a pretty thin time, and cock-a-hoop commies paraded through Ipoh, the 'northern capital' of Malaya, with flags waving and bands playing.

In my humble opinion there were two very much overlooked factors that prevented the Malayan Emergency from becoming another commie takeover. One was the fact that the people of Malaya didn't hate the British or the British Army, an Army which does not alienate itself from civil populations. Second was the Army's old-fashioned 'close and destroy' methods, which put men on the ground instead of a preponderance of high explosives and fire-power.

Ninety per cent of winning or losing is a matter of morale in most cases. A man who has been chased off a position by a few trogs with rifles and bayonets is going to feel a damn sight more beaten than one who has sensibly withdrawn from an area being blown to bits.

The communist terrorists (CTs) turned every road and railway in Malaya into a potential death-trap by continual ambushing. But the trogs were undeterred and often turned an ambush into a death trap for the ambushers. Slowly at first, the Army gained the upper hand. Deep penetration jungle operations, part of the 'close and destroy' policy were required, and (more by accident then original intent) the SAS was reformed in 1950 to do the job.

By the time I arrived in Malaya, the CT was a pretty rare bird. Someone claimed the comparison was like a grouse shoot in Yorkshire – with only ten grouse in the county. Nevertheless, these particular 'grouse' were very good at shooting back, or even shooting first.

I think it is worth mention that the Malayan Emergency was brought to a successful conclusion as a result of Commonwealth effort. British, Gurkha and Malay trogs took the brunt of the fighting but some damn good troops from other Commonwealth countries also made their mark on the scene. The British Commonwealth is one of the very few organisations in the world to have beaten a well-organised military take over by the Communists, and in a country with terrain which greatly favoured the opposition, making the machinery of modern warfare less effective than it was in Viet Nam for instance.

When my small group of trainees arrived at Wardiburn Camp, just outside Kuala Lumpur, it was November 1957, and we were amazed to find one of the squadrons having their Christmas dinner. Then we found they were going into the jungle, on operations, for four months. This was a whole new world, there was a whole new language with it too. Not only all the old Army words, picked up in India, Egypt and many other places, to be forever mispronounced, but now a heavy dose of Malay. We were baffled by 'buckets', 'bashas', 'Kualas', 'rotan', 'attap', 'muckan' and a host of other words used in everyday conversation.

Our next move should have been a training operation, but, for some reason (I never found out), we were sent on a parachute course. The para course was run by RAF Changi, Singapore, so back down to Singapore we went, after only a few days at KL, to start something I had always wanted to do, but had some doubts in my mind as, although I didn't know it then, I have vertigo – a fear of heights.

There were two things I hated on the para course. One was the 'fan'. It was touch and go whether the fan itself or the climb up the rickety steel ladder to the platform was worse. Our introduction to the fan was a typical Para School con. One of the instructors, called 'Titch' (for obvious reasons), gave the demonstration. He was maybe seven stones, wringing wet. When he came down he floated like a bloody fairy. I thought it was no problem, and was first up the ladder. Putting on the harness, I didn't much like the look of the thirty- or forty-foot drop to the matting, but I thought of how Titch had sailed down, and threw my sixteen stone into space. I came down like a bomb and was amazed to be able to stand up afterwards, let alone walk away from it! Later I found it was wiser not to throw my sort of weight out so far off the platform. That way the fan could exert a bit of brake power!

The other contraption I detested was the 'bikini'. This was a harness used with a long tape, for getting down from jungle treetops after parachuting into trees. (An exclusively SAS method of entry into the jungle.) We were trained in the use of the bikini at the Para School, by lowering ourselves from a platform about thirty feet high. The bikini was a very cunningly devised instrument of torture. It was like a heavy canvas pair of swimming trunks, hence its name, but it had a steel ring at the front, about six inches in diameter, through which passed the tapes supporting your weight.

We had to do the training with a heavy pack, as per operations, and the torture was partly due to the pack. We started by hanging in parachute harness from the platform. The next move was to tie the tape to a secure point, then put your weight onto that by releasing the parachute harness. This move made the top of the steel ring try to push through your stomach to your back-bone. Painful but bearable. The next move was to drop the heavy pack. This caused the ring to change its direction. It now stabbed down at the 'wedding tackle' and did its best to destroy it at every move. Very, very painful. In my case, not bearable for long. I dreaded ever having to parachute into trees with that thing.

There were no balloon jumps in the Far East parachute course, we did all our jumps from a twin engine Valetta. My first jump was great. I really enjoyed it – until the ground hit me! Again my weight had something to do with it. Being nearly six foot six inches had its disadvantages too.

My first jump with equipment brought out one of the problems of being tall. Our first three jumps were 'clean fatigue' (no kit) but for the fourth jump we had a 'container' for equipment, weighing about forty pounds. For the jump from the aircraft the container was hung from two hooks on the front of the parachute harness, and held lower down by a leg strap around the right leg. The bulk of the container was from the waist to below knee level.

The exit door on the Valetta was not too high, causing me to duck as I went out. This ducking combined with the extra weight low down induced a beautiful forward somersault outside the aircraft, resulting in me wrapping myself in the parachute as it developed. Realising something was wrong, I opened my eyes and looked 'up'. (I never did a 'daylight' jump after the first two!) Where my chute should have been, all I had time to notice was the big red cross on the roof of the ambulance attending the drop. I looked 'down' and there was what appeared to be a big bundle of dirty washing wrapped around my feet.

As usually happens in a crisis, everything slowed down so I had time to think. I had been well trained, so I went through the routine. Made a quick attempt to free the main chute. When that got me nothing I pulled the reserve chute handle and started to deploy the reserve canopy. I'd only just started on that when the main chute partly freed itself, changing the situation. The words of my instructor, 'Never deploy your reserve if the main canopy can be used', came to my aid. I gave the main canopy a bit of help and it developed, slowing down my rate of descent quite well. I was tangled in the rigging lines and still upside down, but now I had time to work on that. I undid my container, and pushed it up through my legs. Its weight then pulled me horizontal. I was now on my back and could better see what to swear at.

Glancing down I could see there wasn't much time. People were running towards me with no hope of making it. Eventually only one foot was still caught in one line so I kicked the line off with the other foot. As my feet swung down they hit the ground. Good exit, lousy flight, but the best landing I'd had so far.

One funny thing about that incident which I was told about afterwards. At that stage of training there is an instructor on the DZ (Drop Zone) who has a loud hailer to talk trainees down and tell them, if they do anything wrong, what to do to put it right. We were dropping two at a time that day and I was number 2 (second out). I'm told the loud hailer patter went like this, 'OK, number one, your canopy has developed – look up! – OK, number two, your canopy has, F---ing Hell!! We heard there were a mass of complaints from the RAF married quarters which adjoined the DZ. Those loud hailers were really loud.

On all para courses at Changi a teddy bear in SAS uniform, with its own little parachute was thrown out every time the aircraft made its first drop run of the day. This was the course mascot. At the end of the course it was raffled to raise cash for a local spastic orphanage. The afternoon before the course broke up we all went to the orphanage and took the kids to the beach for a few hours. On my particular course the teddy bear was put back in to be raffled three times, and eventually given to the orphanage. We also took them a pile of sweets and various goodies. They enjoyed it and we had a good afternoon in the sea which we enjoyed too.

After successfully completing the para course we were allowed to wear on our lower sleeve a khaki parachute with no wings. As our sleeves were always rolled up in that climate I doubt if anyone ever sewed them on. We had a long way to go before we would be allowed to wear the wings of the SAS. To qualify for SAS parachute wings we had yet to pass the test of a training operation in the jungle. This involved at least a month in the jungle, being trained in basic SAS jungle patrolling.

Before going on the Training Op we were taken into the jungle near KL to be taught the rudiments of jungle movement, how to use our equipment to make shelters (bashes) and hammocks. How to make the most of our rations, and general jungle behaviour. For this introduction to the jungle we were only 'in' for two days and one night. 'In' always meant in the jungle. 'Out' always meant out of the jungle.

It was on this first visit to the jungle that I met what was to be one of my greatest enemies – attap, a useless, savage plant which grows in profusion in the jungles of Malaya. It has a clump of fronds rising from ground level, splaying out in all directions, up to twenty feet long. These have nasty thorns on the underside of the stem. But the real wicked part is like a long bullwhip. Some plants have several and they can be very long, probably up to forty or fifty feet.

The plant holds this whip like a fishing rod. It can be two or three inches thick at the butt end, tapering down to almost a hair at the lash end. The lash end can be dangling to touch the ground several yards from the base of the plant. Mixed among the other greenery of the jungle it is often almost invisible. Every six inches at the butt end down to every half inch at the lash end there are very sharp hooked thorns – in fours, around the whip – the whole of its length. It is very strong, not possible for a man to break by pulling, except perhaps at the very fine end. Maybe the last couple of inches.

Getting away from attap, once caught, is a delicate operation which takes practice – and patience. I never could see the point of catching anything which moves – just for the hell of it!

CHAPTER TWO

Malaya

A few days after our introduction to the jungle, we checked our kit for the last time, drew rations, maps, compasses, weapons, ammunition, and climbed aboard the trucks which would take us to the area we were to use for the Training Op. I don't remember how far we went by road, but I think not more than twenty miles. Then onto our flat feet. The order came to 'saddle up', we heaved our Bergens onto our backs and began the flog into the unknown.

We were carrying two weeks' rations which, by SAS standards, was not a lot. Twenty-eight days' rations was the norm when moving in. Our weapons were the standard SAS weapon of that time, the Belgian FN rifle, forerunner of the British SLR (Self Loading Rifle). Each of us carried five twenty-round magazines. The main difference between the FN and the SLR was that the FN had a three position change lever giving automatic and semi-automatic fire, whereas the SLR can only fire semi-automatic. We found the FN was too inaccurate when fired on automatic so the SLR was really just as good. The other main difference was the flash hider which, on the FN, was incorporated in the bayonet. The SLR had its flash hider as an extension of the barrel.

My Bergen probably weighed seventy pounds (I'm a big eater!) and by the time we stopped that first night I knew about every ounce of it. Jungle-marching is nothing like any other marching. We were forever climbing over fallen trees, or crawling under them, getting tangled in attap, sliding in mud, tripping over an assortment of roots, vines, sticks and stumps. There was nothing like it in the Tarzan films, or any other damned film I'd seen. Having been brought up in the woods I felt quite at home in the trees, had less trouble coping than most. Nevertheless it was very hard going.

At last, after, I think, two days' march, we reached a place which had been selected to set up a base camp. Next morning we set out on a 'light order' patrol for the day, leaving our Bergens in the base camp. The first snag was crossing a raging torrent not far from the base camp. There was a line across the river, but it was made of rotan, a type of vine used as ropes by the jungle people. (Not the Tarzan type.) I was quite used to using vines back home in UK but not to take my weight over anything dangerous, as the only vines I had ever used were extremely unreliable.

To say that, when my turn came to put my faith in that rotan, I approached the prospect with some misgivings would have been understating the case. I was bloody terrified. The river was, as mentioned, a raging torrent. The water was deep and brown – except where it was churned up into creamy spray by protruding jagged rocks. It was about forty yards wide at the crossing point, but much wider about a hundred yards downstream, where another equally nasty torrent joined it. The only consolation was nobody would hear me scream if that bloody rotan broke – the roar of the two rivers made sure of that.

My extra weight made it sag more than it did with the others. The water did its best to tear me loose, but it didn't break. Nevertheless I wasn't looking forward to the return trip that night, on our way back. After a couple of weeks patrolling from that base camp we cleared a DZ for a re-supply air-drop, which came right on the button. Then, loaded down with two weeks' rations, we marched again for a couple of days to make another base camp.

For the move to the second base camp the twenty-eight men on test were divided into six or seven patrols, each moving by a different route, accompanied or led by a staff instructor. One patrol failed to arrive at the new base and, after a wait of 24 hours, search parties were sent out. I was with the patrol which found the missing men. The instructor with the missing patrol had two bullets in his thigh (I never heard how they got there), so the immediate problem was to get him evacuated from the jungle.

The instructors decided the best move would be to get the injured man to the base camp, which was about three thousand yards distant, as the manpower was there to clear an LZ (Landing Zone) for a helicopter.

With the extra help of the patrol I was with, we made fairly good time towards the base camp, but it became obvious we were not going to make it before dark. Two of us were elected to try to get back to the base camp so things could be organised by radio, and the men could start work on the LZ at first light next morning.

We were then about two thousand yards from the base camp and had about half an hour or so of daylight left. The terrain was very rugged and the jungle, especially attap, was very dense. When darkness fell we were about four or five hundred yards from the base camp. We had no torches, being in light order, so headed for a small river which came down near the base camp. Once on the river we were able to make use of the last scraps of light to scramble up waterfalls, wade through pools to make another couple of hundred yards in the right direction. Wanting to be sure in which direction to go, we left the river and moved slowly through the undergrowth until we judged we were one hundred yards east of the river. Then I knew the base camp had to be to the south of us, hopefully within two hundred yards.

The blackness was total. The attap was thick. The air was blue. But we slowly made ground until we could find no way through at all. Absolute solid walls of brush and attap every time we tried to go south. And I mean solid. We sat down, and I lit a cigarette. Time to think, I wasn't all that experienced in the jungle, but somehow I knew solid walls don't happen. There's always a way through.

Then it clicked! When we left that morning some of the men were going to start cutting a DZ for a supply drop. We had come up against the fallen trees, or at least the tops of them. Now I knew where I was. (The other man had been with the missing patrol so had never seen this area.) We moved further east, and at last the way south was comparatively clear. Within ten minutes we were in the base camp – much to the surprise of the staff, who never expected anyone nearly two hours after dark.

Radio messages were sent that night and first thing in the morning we started enlarging the DZ into a LZ. To this end, a light aircraft came over and dropped a 'packet easy' – a one hundred pound pack containing explosives, with all the necessary fuses, detonators, etc, with which to blow trees and make a quick job of the LZ. There was one small problem, the drop missed the DZ by nearly five hundred yards and was nearly lost. It took another explosives drop to secure the first one, which was at the top of the 'highest tree in Malaya'.

The normal method of recovering 'unreachable' parachute supplies was to shoot them down with a signal pistol, which set fire to the parachute. With a 'packet easy' however it is essential to be well clear when it drops, and of course, fire is not generally a good mixer with detonators and explosives.

By mid afternoon the 'casevac' (casualty evacuation) was complete. We got back to the hard grind of real training. One of the men on the training op was an old SAS soldier who had been home on 'inter tour leave', so had to do the training op again to qualify. He was from Liverpool, so was called 'Scouse'. He was very fond of deriding my anti-leech precautions, taking great pride in showing how he didn't give a damn for leeches. I had found long ago that the best armour against infection is the good old everybody's skin. So I had gone off all things which make holes in it. Leeches seemed to think of nothing else but making holes in skin. Being specially designed for the job they are very good at getting through almost anything, to get a good fill of blood. So I took my precautions and remained not too badly bitten. Scouse on the other hand didn't even wear underpants.

We had been on a long hard patrol all day, and were returning to base camp, down a river track. The leeches were almost like blades of grass waving in the track, trying to catch a passing foot. We stopped for a break, and Scouse undid his fly to relieve himself – then he yelled – and we all gathered round. He had eleven leeches on 'it'. It looked like a bunch of grapes hanging out of his slacks. When he pulled them off he bled like a stuck pig.

It got funnier. He had to wrap a shell dressing around it to stop the bleeding, then tied the tapes up round his neck. We did the last couple of thousand yards back to camp with Scouse waddling, legs apart, threatening to shoot us all for seeing the funny side. I've seen some things in slings, but that was the ultimate sling job.

The end of the training op came, and we had to march out in patrols. They made the mistake of putting me in charge of one patrol. There were four of us, we were all starving. All were big eaters and had a job to exist on the rations we could carry. We had not yet learnt to pack the best things and leave out the rubbish.

We knew that at the first base camp a food cache had been left by the instructors, presumably to boost their rations on the next training op. The march out to the road head was a two-day flog. I worked out the angles and reckoned if we moved fast and were prepared to add about four thousand yards to our distance, we could make pigs of ourselves on the first night. I put the plan to the other three. The unanimous decision – we would eat! So we did. The tins of chicken supreme I yoffled that night were the best I'd ever had. We had a great feast, and marched out the next day feeling fed at last.

So ended a hard but very interesting experience. I think about twenty of us passed that test. I for one realised just how little we had learnt of the vast volume of jungle training. We had been taught a lot by excellent instructors, but it would take a lot more time and sweat before we were really good in the jungle.

Somewhere at about this stage in the game I lost my corporal's stripes and – as the SAS put it – was 'promoted' to trooper. In other words I was starting where all real SAS other ranks start, at the bottom. Anyone who never got promoted to trooper can hardly claim to be truly SAS. The difference in pay was partly made up by para pay which was then £2.10p per week. I always claimed para pay was reasonable for jumping – but landing was definitely worth another fiver.

After the training op we were posted to operational squadrons. I went to 'D' Squadron's 16 Troop. Before the squadron went on ops I had time to nip down to Singapore to meet Ann off a plane from UK. Ann and the wife of one of my best friends were installed in a bungalow at Petaling Jaya, a few miles from KL. Then we had a few days in which to get to know KL before the squadron went in. 'In' this time was the Triang swamps. It was a three-month operation. Our method of entry was from a briefly stopped train, at night. Not being keen on swamps I was glad to find this one was dried up for the moment, the main problem being to find any water for drinking and cooking. We pounded the area day after day in three and four-man patrols, finding practically nothing in the way of enemy signs. A few old camps, long since vacated, ancient tracks, a couple of water points nearly rotted away, nothing less then several months old.

On one occasion we returned to our base camp after a seven-day patrol and when I opened my Bergen, which had been left at base, I found a black shiny scorpion sitting just under the lid. It looked so much like a toy I thought someone was sending me up and went to take it out. Luckily my basha-mate, an old hand, saw it too and knocked my hand away just in time. It was very real all right. About six inches from nose to tail. I still had a lot to learn.

During the last month of the operation three people went down with lepto-spirosis, a fever carried by rats. One was an officer, 'Biffo', one was Nat, an Irish trooper, and the other was an Iban tracker. They were evacuated in a struggling ancient Sycamore chopper, which eventually couldn't get off the ground with three of them, and had to leave one and come back later for him. On the same op one of 16 Troop corporals was marching with a temperature of 105. There were two corporals in the troop and one of them was troop commander, I was never sure which. We also had a lance-corporal in the troop. Ranks were not high or plentiful in those days. No one worried about rank, the only thing of importance was ability to do the job.

The corporal with the temperature said it was just malaria, he would sweat it out. So he did, and carried on with his job. I was duly impressed, but didn't fancy trying it myself if the time came.

We had four Aborigine porters with the troop who carried the spare radio batteries. They and the troop signaller stayed in the base camp while the remainder went out in threes and fours on patrols which were sometimes one or two days, sometimes one or two weeks. The patrols had no radios, the only contact with the outside world was through the troop signaller.

There were four of us in the patrol I was with, led by a trooper. We did our job thoroughly, no matter how hard the going, we never gave up. The job was always done to the best of our ability. There was no movement at night. Just before dark we would stop and put up our bashas, two men to each. While we were fixing the basha a mess-tin of rice would be boiling for the evening meal. Once it was dark we lit candles and read books to pass the time. In deep jungle there is rarely enough draught at ground level to flicker the flame of a candle.

A re-supply by air came every twenty-eight days. We would all come into the troop base the day before it was due to clear a DZ. Re-supply day was often referred to as when 'The Mukan Bird Sings'. Mukan being Malay for food. Wives were allowed to send parcels to their husbands. These were collected from our homes by the regiment and came with the air-drop. Ann knew my favourite food and always sent plenty of it. Also books and magazines. There were only two married men in 16 Troop, but the amount of food and things our wives sent was enough to share with the whole troop. On one occasion our two parcels had a parachute all to themselves.

The troop was a mobile library. We all went in with at least two books which were passed around. More came on the air-drops. If we ever came into contact with another troop there was always a big book-swapping session. A selection of newspapers, magazines and books were always sent on air-drops by one of those unsung heroines of the WVS (Women's Voluntary Service) who organised a library, games room, reading room set-up in our base at KL. Though very seldom heard of, the WVS did a lot of good work behind the scenes, being much appreciated by the troops on operations.

We always got one day's 'fresh' rations on the air-drop. Usually steak, potatoes, other vegetables, and fresh fruit. We also got new boots and new OG (Olive Green) shirt and slacks. Other items of military clothing and equipment were also sent on request. 16 Troop, while I was with it, always made the most of the air-drop, having a beano of food on air-drop days. The next morning at first light we moved base camp to a fresh area, often 10,000 yards or more distant. So that which could not be consumed or carried was destroyed by burning. Anything which wouldn't burn was buried.

Some troops moved base camp immediately after taking their air-drop, which meant a lot of good food was wasted, as a man can only carry so much. I didn't think our one day per month 'rest' was overdoing it. The operational situation at the time didn't put us on the defensive, or there may have been good reason for moving after an air-drop.

After the Triang operation, we had about ten days in KL, then came a week of relaxation and training at a beach near Port Dickson, on the west coast. The snag was, we had to parachute onto a beach near there.

It was the briefing for the jump which caused all the problems. They said it was a small beach, with an area of jagged coral at one end, and a mangrove swamp at the other. We were jumping from a Hastings and I was near the end of the port stick, which made me worry about landing in the coral. There was little or no chat about the problem, but it was very apparent afterwards that everyone in the squadron was thinking along the same lines.

Standing in the aircraft as we approached the drop I noticed both sticks were getting more and more bunched as we at the back crept forward. When the green for 'go' came on, there was a pause at the front end as they made sure of missing the mangrove swamp. Meanwhile the back of the stick was pushing hard to get out before the coral got under us.

The result was obvious, we came out of the aircraft on one another's backs in a big fast-moving 'bus queue'. How I got out the door I'll never know. The RAF dispatchers were on their backsides beyond the doors and I was running before I got near the exit. There were no real injuries, but a lot of 'strop burns' from contact with other people's deploying parachutes, also a lot of bruises and a few cuts. No one was anywhere near the mangrove swamp or the coral. The whole lot was in a big heap in the middle of the beach.

There was, however, a problem. The Commanding Officer of 22 SAS had not been with the unit very long. He had come to watch the drop, the first he had seen involving SAS troops. He was not impressed. Coming from the Parachute Brigade he was well used to seeing good, clean, regulation jumping. This 'absolute shambles' he had just seen was obviously the way the SAS always did their parachuting, and it was not good enough!

A really horrific bout of para training was going to be the answer. In the event it didn't come off – thank goodness. Hardly anyone in the SAS liked parachuting, we looked upon it as a necessary bind. Another means of getting from A to B, no more, no less. One of the things I noticed about the regiment, no one was ever afraid to say they didn't like certain aspects of their military situation. Parachuting being a good example. No one who hated it was afraid to say so.

After Port Dickson, the squadron went in again, I can't remember where, but for two or three months, maybe four. Again, although it was supposed to be a 'hot' area, we found nothing of note. A lot of sweat, a lot of hard patrolling produced the usual big round zero. The opposition were getting very scarce by mid-1958. The only things of note I can remember of that op was one of my friends getting hit so bad by hornets that we had to stay put for a day during one patrol to give the swelling time to go down so he could open his eyes. Another very good friend of mine had an argument with a phosphorous grenade. We used them as smoke grenades sometimes to help the Air Force find our little hole in the jungle.

On this occasion Don threw the grenade OK but it hit a branch and was catapulted back at him. With 'E' Type acceleration he nearly got clear but a dollop of phosphorus landed on his head and set fire to his hair. He dived in the nearby river and scrubbed his head until it stopped smoking, then came out of the water to where we were all laughing at him. A minute or two later someone noticed Don's hair was smoking again, so back into the river he went for another scrubbing. The same thing happened several times during the following half hour. I wouldn't mind betting if anyone looked with horror above Don's head now – he'd get a very worried look in his eye.

On the 'night of the tigers', as I always remember it, the troop was moving base camp from one area to another and, for some reason, we stopped one night in a 'saddle' between two high ridges. We had seen tiger tracks and I had caught a glimpse of one once. I only knew I'd seen a tiger when we found its fresh tracks where I had seen the flash of golden movement.

That night on the saddle I'll never forget. The tigers started roaring about midnight. We had all been asleep, but the first shattering roar from about one hundred yards away had everyone wide awake. That was answered by other roars and growls from all around. At the time I didn't know that tigers hunted in packs. For some reason I never thought of them attacking us, even when they were only a few yards away. As always in the jungle at night, it was inky black. I could hear and smell tigers, but couldn't even see my hand in front of my face. I felt distinctly nervous but not particularly frightened.

We had an Iban tracker with the troop; he was so terrified he left his basha and sought human companionship. That nearly cost him his life as his groping hands landed on one of my friends who was lying there cuddling a shotgun. Their combined yells made me think at first someone was being taken for supper, but there was nothing anyone could do. We were all completely blind in that darkness. Our bashas were about twenty yards apart, many of us sleeping alone in one-man bashas – as I was at that time – so all we could do was wait. My greatest fear that night was not from the tigers, but that someone would start shooting. Eventually the big cats moved off, their growls and roars faded down the valley. All was well, sleep came quickly again.

The SAS operated in Malayan 'tiger country' for about eight years. Mostly in small patrols of three or four, sometimes only two men, and obviously one man moving on his own, sometimes for many hours. Yet I have never heard of any SAS man being attacked by a tiger.

On one operation I managed to frighten myself quite well one night. My basha was about twenty yards from any others, and I was on my own, reading by candlelight. We must have just had an air-drop as I had some empty cans in a box just outside the basha. Hearing the cans rattle, I turned to see what caused it, and just caught sight of something moving quickly into the darkness.

Grabbing my torch I shone the beam in the direction the 'thing' had gone. A pair of large 'catty' eyes shone from a few yards away. They were on something with a furry, black-spotted body, which looked quite big through the network of leaves and twigs. I immediately thought 'leopard', and for no reason I can think of I made that squeaking noise which is used for calling your pet cat. The animal immediately came towards me and in my rush to grab my parang or rifle I dropped the torch and knocked over the candle.

Then I sat there in inky black silence holding the parang or rifle, I can't remember which, feeling sure the beast was about to land on me, straining every nerve for any sound which might give it away. Eventually, being still in one piece and unattacked, I plucked up the courage to fumble for the torch. There was nothing to be seen. Not even under my hammock!

Next morning the old hands told me it was probably a civet cat, a quite harmless denizen of the jungle, not very big as jungle cats go, but a lot bigger than your average UK moggy.

Every time we came out of the jungle we went on the ranges to fire off all the ammunition we had carried on ops. Some of the men were really good with their personal weapons. All were good but some were brilliant. Keith, in particular, who was a good leading scout, always carried a 'pump gun' (pump action 12 gauge shotgun). On a rough 30-metre range one day, we were walking in turn across a rickety plank over a lot of mud and, somewhere in the middle of the plank, someone would give the order, we would turn to our left and fire at four 'figure' targets. In the case of the shotguns they were firing one round at each target.

Keith's turn came. At his first shot his hat slipped off the back of his head, and rolled slowly down his back. He hit all four targets dead centre then caught his hat with a hand behind his back before it could fall in the mud. If I had done that I would have waited for the applause. Keith just walked on as if nothing had happened.

On operations our weapons were stripped and cleaned thoroughly every night. All the woodwork was taken off, cleaned and oiled with linseed oil. The weapons were never more than arm's length from us until they were handed back to the armoury after an operation. We never washed with soap, shaved or cleaned our teeth on operations, as the smell of soap or toothpaste carries for miles in the jungle. Wading rivers and marching for hours in pouring rain kept us clean. It rained every evening, so if we felt dirty we stripped and stood in the downpour to get a shower. Our weapons, on the other hand, were spotlessly clean and gleaming all the time.

Before leaving the jungle we had to shave off our beards, put on a clean shirt and slacks and try to appear a bit 'soldier-like'. After one op I retained a big bushy moustache. When I got home Ann ran away from me, saying, 'Keep away, you look like Uncle Fred'. Poor Uncle Fred had been dead ten years, so I wasn't flattered enough to keep the shrubbery, and have never tried since.

Life out of the jungle was pretty good, as we tried to catch up in about ten days for the months on ops. Soon after she arrived in Malaya, Ann was very startled when she saw the local grass cutter at our window one day. She had never seen such an apparition. He was a Tamil, and very black. Like most of his compatriots he chewed betel nuts, so his mouth – teeth and all – were bright scarlet. He had a huge grass cutting knife over his shoulder and had no shirt on. He just appeared there – while we were having breakfast – grinning from ear to ear.

The Aborigines who came on ops with us as porters carried their own food, which they obviously liked. Their food seemed to consist of rice and a lot of small, dried fish, which stunk to high heaven. Being in the tail-end patrol on troop moves I often marched for days in the steady hum of 'Ikon Bilis', which is what they called it (small fish).

On my first op with 'D' Squadron my basha-mate shocked me by swapping a perfectly good tin of bully beef from our joint rations for a fistful of ikon bilis. I thought the heat had got to him – or the smell! He was an old hand, a damn good jungle cook. From that handful of stinking little fish he made one of the best meals I've ever had. Forever after that meal the smell of the Abo's rations never bothered me in the same way. Towards the end of every march, when our one daily meal was nearly due, I found the smell positively mouth-watering.

Late in 1958, 'D' Squadron went on what was to be its last operation in Malaya. None of us knew it at the time of course. There had been ideas of some squadron personnel taking their exams for the Army Certificate of Education 1st Class. To this end we were taking a lot of study material into the jungle with us so we could study at night instead of reading books. We were on the trucks, having just drawn our weapons from the armoury, all ready to go when someone called me off the truck and told me to report to the squadron office.

The squadron commander was there. He told me I would not be going on operations, I had to study for my 1st Class Education Certificate. I said I could do it in the jungle, but there was to be no argument. The squadron went and I stayed. Ann was surprised to see me back home. She had only seen me off a few hours before, and didn't expect me back for about four months.

The exam was in three weeks' time, so I had three weeks to prepare. There were three of us from the regiment lined up for the exams, and four days a week we went to school again, at an Army Education Centre in a camp near KL.

Finding myself with no possible reason to 'skive' I decided to report to the Medical Officer with a problem which had worried me on ops. I had noticed all physical exertion became more difficult towards the end of a long op. No one else seemed to deteriorate physically as I did, so I felt something was not right. I had never had to slow up on ops but it became progressively more difficult to keep up the pace.

I was given a thorough going-over: chest specialist, x-rays, the works. Nothing. The SAS MO, Captain Adlington, however, never gave up. He had me in again for yet another check-up. This time we went down to basic diet on ops. He had me list everything I carried in my rucksack. In ten minutes he solved the problem. I carried no sugar whatsoever. I didn't eat sweets or chocolate. I drank Oxo, never tea or coffee. I ate curry and rice, cheese and hard-tack biscuits. Nothing else. After that I took good care to have a brew of tea or coffee with sugar every day. When Ann found out she wouldn't let me have tea or coffee without sugar again. That was hard going too!

Just before the exam the squadron all came back to KL. There was something new coming up, but no one knew where or what. A squadron doesn't suddenly get brought out, cutting an operation short, for nothing. The exam came, and I passed the required subjects. The squadron was training hard in the meantime. The week after the exam we moved out of KL, down to Singapore onto an aircraft for a destination unknown. There was much speculation about which war we were going to.

The Chinese Nationalists were in some aggro over the 'off-shore islands'. But that area was discounted as we could see no possibilities for us in that situation. A couple of places in Africa were gently simmering. Again nothing seemed to fit. After we left Singapore we knew by the direction of our flight we were not going further east.

We landed at Colombo, in Ceylon, changed aircraft and took off again, flying north-west. A couple of hours in the air and the word came round we were heading for a place called Muscat and Oman. No one seemed to know much about the place. That seemed strange to us, with all the travel experience in the squadron. We landed at Mesiera, an RAF base on a small island, and changed aircraft again, this time to a Beverly, which could land and take off on short, rough landing strips.

CHAPTER THREE

Northern Oman

So to the Sultanate of Muscat and Oman, an Arab country on the neck of the Persian Gulf, opposite Persia and Pakistan. The Beverly thundered its way over strange jagged mountains and bare open desert to land in a cloud of dust near Bait el Falage, an old whitewashed fort and a few mud huts.

Oman in those days was a long way behind the times in almost everything. It was nothing like the modern, bustling state it is today. There was, I believe, only about one mile of tarmac road in the country. All other roads were dirt tracks. I don't remember seeing any motor vehicles, apart from our military trucks and a few belonging to the Sultan's Armed Forces. All transport, as far as I could see, was by camel or donkey.

The scene anywhere in Oman was just as it had been in biblical times except for one very apparent detail. Almost all males aged twelve or more carried a rifle of some kind. Many of them were old Martini Henry rifles of ·45 or ·50 calibre, supposedly very good at long range. There were also quite a lot of Enfield ·303 rifles about, the same weapon as used by the British Army until a year or two previously.

The men wore mostly white clothes, as per biblical times. The women were covered from head to toe in black, sometimes relieved by the odd touch of dark red. Only their hands and eyes were ever seen by anyone outside their own family. Most of them wore heavy silver jewellery, bracelets, earrings and nose rings. Most of the men wore a heavy cartridge belt, usually full of ammunition for their rifle, with a huge curved knife (kunji) in a heavy, ornately embossed silver sheath at the front, low, and in the centre of their stomach. The richer or more powerful the man, the larger and more decorative the kunji. I don't remember any local currency other than Austrian 'Maria Theresa' dollars, large silver coins. How they came to be in use in Oman I have no idea.

Our camp, which had been partly set up already by an Engineer detachment, but was still practically nothing, was about ten miles

north of Muttrah, a sea port. Muscat, the capital, was a little further
south down the coast, two or three miles beyond Muttrah. The
buildings in both towns were not, I believe, of more than two
storeys. They were of mud and rock construction, with flat roofs and
small windows, many without glass but with wooden shutters. All
'streets', except the main through road, were very narrow alleys,
being only two or three metres wide.

The old whitewashed fort about a quarter mile from our camp was
nothing to do with the military scene. I've no idea of its use at the
time, but the plain red flag of the Sultan flew above its tower. (The
rebels of the day were said to use a white flag – very handy if you
are not sure whether or not to surrender!)

Our first job was to erect a few tents in which to sleep and eat.
We also put up a perimeter fence of rolled barbed wire. Then a
squadron briefing. The squadron commander, Major John Watts,
gave us a quick rundown on the country, and why we were there.
It appeared there was a British agreement, donkeys years old, to aid
the Sultan any time he asked. He had asked.

It was the usual internal problem, with the rebels being armed
and trained out of the country, then coming back to stir it. Enemy
strength was a bit vague. It was estimated at between two thousand
and five thousand. Five hundred 'well-trained' troops, in uniform,
the remainder being mountain tribesmen, well armed, with a savage
reputation. A British infantry unit had had a go at them and came
off second best, but that didn't mean a lot, knowing how the
infantry went on. The enemy held a big lump of high ground called
Jebel Akhdar, a plateau with mostly sheer cliffs all around it, sitting
at about six or seven thousand feet, with parts rising to ten thousand
feet or more.

It may seem strange to anyone outside the SAS but it is a fact that
after we were given the 'gen' on the enemy situation, there was not
one of the forty-odd gun hands present who doubted our ability to
crack the job. The squadron was by no means fully up to strength,
and reports I have seen mentioning the 'sixty men' of 'D' Squadron
forgot to mention the sixty included cooks, drivers, clerks, stores
people and signallers. I was with 16 Troop and we operated with 17
Troop, which I well remember gave us a combined strength of
twenty-one men (all ranks).

Once we were settled in and organised at Bait-el-Falage, we
started training again. I had done no marching for a bit, due to the
education caper, so I found it hard going. Mostly, though, we had

to get switched on to shooting at distances of more than thirty yards.
A lot of ammunition was used, but it was well worth it.

About a week after our arrival in the country we set off to get on
with the job. 16 and 17 Troops went to the north of the Jebel, 18
and 19 Troops went to the south side. After about one hundred
miles of driving on very rough tracks, we arrived at the end of a wadi
(valley), at a small village where the trucks could go no further. All
around were great cliffs, rising thousands of feet. Our troop
commander, Captain Rory Walker, chatted up the villagers and
managed to get a guide who claimed he could lead us to the top of
the mountain. That night we set out with the guide, marching in
light order, to have a go at the mountain. We expected to meet
opposition, and by the time we were nearing the top I was praying
someone would start a war, so I could drop down for a rest. I was
shattered, all that classroom time caught up on me.

Somewhere near the top we came to a sheer cliff of about two
hundred feet and found steps had been carved in the rock. We heard
later they had been carved there by the Persians, two thousand years
ago, when the mountain had last fallen to an enemy force. Not long
after the steps we found ourselves on the plateau. Not a shot had
been fired. We had caught the opposition off guard. The guide went
down on his knees and gave thanks to Allah. I think he was the most
surprised to have reached the top.

Marching had kept us warm, now we realised how cold it was at
7,000 feet. There was still a lot of time before daylight, three or four
hours in fact, so we posted sentries and went to sleep. At least, we
tried to sleep, but there was a strong, icy wind which didn't help.
Nor did the fact that we were in tropical clothing, shirt and slacks.
Luckily we had carried our Dennison smocks (camouflage paratroop
smock) and these now saved us from some of the cold. Mine was a
bit small for me, but I got legs and all inside it that night. Some of
us had ice in our water bottles by morning. Daylight came at last,
soon to be followed by a blazing hot sun, for which we were truly
thankful.

Jebel means mountain, Jebel Akhdar means Green Mountain,
but don't get the idea we found grass or normal trees on that
plateau. There was very little greenery to be seen anywhere. There
were odd bits of very low shrubbery, less than knee height. There
were more camel thorn trees than are usual in the desert but these
were not plentiful, or even big.

The plateau was not flat by any means. It had its own hills and valleys, cliffs and open spaces. The hills where we reached the plateau on the north side were often several hundred feet high, easily defended but easily shot at from good positions on other hills all around. The valleys varied from shallow depressions with gentle slopes, to huge cracks in the plateau with sheer rock cliffs going down several thousand feet, almost to sea level. These 'cracks' were really wadis, caused by water over the centuries, sometimes a hundred feet wide, sometimes half a mile.

The plateau is about twenty-five miles long, its width varies from a mile or two to a maximum of about ten miles. Like most mountains in that part of the world it has a predominantly rocky landscape. Rocks of all sizes everywhere, from gravel size to ten-storey house size. There was sandy earth on most of the flat areas but it was well cluttered with rocks, some loose and some embedded, not moveable. The rocks were all shades of grey, sandy, brown and almost black. Some were multi-coloured. A man could lie down almost anywhere and not be seen from twenty or thirty metres. On the other hand, a man walking could often be seen from several miles.

As with most areas of the Middle East, an arid, dry landscape is ensured by the daily deployment of vast herds of goats which nibble away anything showing the slightest hint of green. Whether or not the herds of goats and their child shepherds we saw near the top of Jebel Akhdar returned each night to their villages, some 8,000 feet below, I have no idea. But if they did it's a mystery where they all got the energy.

Before going up onto the Jebel we were told it was 'green' and there was fruit up there. It was a standing joke among the trogs that the only fruit we saw on the Jebel was a certain officer (not SAS) who came up much later in the campaign.

As soon as it was light we went off in patrols to check the immediate area. No contact was made with the opposition. The area seemed dead. It was then decided we would stick to what we had taken so easily and extend our foothold as and when we could. To this end, 17 Troop headed back down to collect their packs, we could obviously not exist without our full kit and rations, especially at that altitude. There was the small problem, of course, that it would leave 16 Troop on their own until the next morning. Ten or eleven men had their limitations against an attack by possibly a hundred or two. Or more.

Anyway, nothing ventured – who dares and all that, we looked to our weapons, did what we could to improve our position and made the most of the sunshine. By midday the sunshine was getting a bit much and we were looking for shade.

We were wearing khaki drill trousers, and on looking around I decided they were definitely the wrong colour for the terrain. Something would have to be done to tone them down a bit. Our smocks were ideal, so at least we were halfway to being bad aiming marks. An old soldier once told me, 'Half the battle is not to be seen, the other half is not to be easily seen through a gun sight – you can't always achieve both, but if you don't get one right you're a cert for the boneyard.'

Towards evening a couple of patrols went out but found nothing. Before dusk we built a huge fire to help us through the night. We put the fire in a small hollow so that after dark the embers would not be seen from anywhere around. Darkness fell and we closed in around the hollow, nothing had been seen all day, we felt reasonably secure. It was important that we get as much sleep as possible while we had the chance, so we lay in a close circle around the hot embers, with one man on sentry, and all within arm's length of the next man.

My turn on sentry was around midnight. I moved to the machine-gun, which was the sentry post and began to study the shadows and darker shadows which made up the local scenery. After about twenty minutes some shadows started to move. I looked away immediately, checked other possible danger points, then looked past the shadows which had changed. They had moved, and were still moving. Again I checked all other possibilities, again nothing.

Only one area was wrong. Bringing the machine-gun to bear on the approaching danger, I kicked the nearest sleeping man who immediately rolled over into a firing position. Seeing I had started the 'stand to', I watched the shadows, which were now an approaching mass about fifty or sixty yards away. A brand new sliver of moon glinted off a rifle barrel in the approaching unknown, so I slipped the catch to 'automatic', practised a sweep low across the front of the mass and took up first pressure on the trigger. By this time the whole troop was lined up on the target all ready to roll it out. All except two that is, who were watching the opposite direction, in case of other shadows starting to move.

Being the sentry and having the machine-gun lined up, it was my ball to open, but something was wrong. It was all too easy. No attack would come in a heap of a target like this. Captain Walker thought the same obviously, when the oncoming crowd was at about thirty yards range he whispered, 'Hold your fire', and instructed the Arab guide to challenge them.

At the first shout the mass stopped dead. One small sign or sound of weapons being prepared and we would have wiped them out. The Arabic went back and fourth a few seconds, then a quick interpretation. Captain Walker said, 'It's OK, they are this bloke's people.'

We had been instructed by the Sultan of Oman to kill everything on the Jebel. There was nothing up there except enemies. Kill every man, woman, child, camel, donkey and chicken. The people obviously knew about these instructions and thought we would carry them out. The 'mass' turned out to be about a dozen donkeys being led by four men. They were very surprised to find us there and, as they were really there illegally, being forbidden to travel over the mountain, were very grateful their lives had been spared.

With the help of our guide we soon made friends, and found that these tribesmen regularly used that route over the mountains as it saved two or three days' hard travel between their village and the nearest town. Captain Walker quickly saw the possibilities of this chance encounter and enlisted the help of the men and their donkeys to bring up supplies until something better could be organised. Without those people and their hardy mountain donkeys we would have been very lucky to have retained our flimsy toehold on the plateau in the early stages.

No one in Middle East Command had expected us to get to the top of the plateau so quickly, there was no supply system prepared in advance. As usual, things were to come down to the sheer luck and ability of the man on the ground. A signal had been sent to Squadron HQ telling them we were on the plateau. Major Watts didn't question the signal, but when he passed on the information to HQ Persian Gulf they asked him to check again. I have heard John Watts then replied to the effect that if his troops said they were somewhere – then that's where they were.

In the morning 17 Troop reached the top with all their kit, a Gloster Meteor reconnaissance jet flew over and around our position, having a good look, presumably to check we were really where we said we were.

The first two or three days at the top we managed to find a small amount of water in holes in the rock. When that ran out the donkeys came into their own, bringing water and rations up the mountain.

After 17 Troop reached the top with their kit, 16 Troop did the trip down that day, then spent the following night flogging slowly up again. It was a hell of a climb and took all night. On the climb up with our kit, 16 Troop had the dubious job of escorting a small donkey train; about six friendly tribesmen were each in charge of a donkey which was heavily laden with rations and jerricans of water. Half a dozen of us were each allotted a tribesman and donkey, with orders to make sure they reached the top with the supplies intact.

We started the climb in daylight about an hour before sunset. Just before dusk I found myself lagging further and further behind the column. My donkey handler seemed to be having a lot of trouble with the donkey and its load.

Twice the load had slipped around under the animal and we had to reload it. Several times the donkey stopped, stubbornly refusing to move. By then I had realised my Arab companion was the 'village idiot'. We couldn't speak to each other because of the language problem. I knew no Arabic, he knew no English. Eventually the donkey turned around and set off downhill. Its handler stood and laughed insanely, so I dropped my pack and managed to catch the beast, bringing it back to where the handler stood, still laughing.

Thoughts of being diplomatic flashed through my mind. We had been warned not to antagonise the locals, we needed all the friends we could get. The thoughts of being diplomatic flashed straight out of my mind, even quicker than my knife came out. The point dented the skin of his throat just under his chin, I pointed at the donkey, then at the track upwards. I also probably looked a bit upset.

The village idiot laughed until he drooled. By this time he was up on his toes, and I was expecting to see blood. Reason mostly prevailed. My bluff had been called. The knife returned to its sheath, the laughter grew louder.

Reason didn't quite prevail. Unreasonably, I vented my frustration on the poor dumb animal, aiming a punch at its head. As I threw the punch the donkey happened to shake its head, so where it landed I don't know, but the animal went down like it had been shot.

The laughter stopped. The donkey struggled to its feet, looking in better shape than I had ever seen it. The handler stared at me open-mouthed for a few seconds, then without so much as a smirk he went to work on the load, putting it straight, tightening the girth. Within a minute we were on our way up the hill, the donkey more than willing and the handler pushing it, with occasional fearful, backward glances.

It was the luckiest punch I've ever thrown. Hole in one. All
problems solved. We soon caught up with the troop. That climb
with full kit was a memorable, nasty, long, flogging struggle against
gravity but at least we now had the bare necessities of life with which
to face the odds.

Our sleeping bags were the big old-fashioned heavy duty, semi-
waterproof, 'airborne' things which weighed a ton, well, about twenty
pounds I would think. They were carried strapped to the outside of our
packs, usually underneath, and their bulk was almost as much
problem as their weight but we were damned glad of them during the
terrible cold nights of the next few weeks. Once both troops were really
on the plateau with all our kit we started to push south and east. There
was no point in trying to take on heavy odds on their ground. What we
wanted was ground of our own and hope we could pull them onto it. So
there was no mad rush to make contact.

We heard of our first casualty with some anger. 18 and 19 Troops
on the south side had hit some opposition who had managed to kill
'Duke' Swindells. Duke was well known and well liked. There was
now a feeling that a mad rush to hit them might be a good idea.
Rory Walker kept his cool – things progressed as planned.

The 16 Troop sergeant, 'Herbie', took a six-man patrol forward
about two thousand yards to set up an observation post. They were
there all day and just before dusk were attacked by thirty or forty
enemy. The opposition came in a fast 'fire and movement' attack
but got their just deserts from Herbie's patrol, losing about ten men.
Our patrol withdrew according to plan, but there was no follow-up.
In the morning we all went forward, expecting to have to fight to
retake the position, but found the opposition had had enough, not
even taking the position the night before.

Captain Walker decided to move the whole set-up forward to a
hill we named Cassino. It dominated a considerable amount of real
estate and was readily adaptable for defence by our small force. We
had just about taken up our fire positions on Cassino, and were
getting sorted out with our building programme for sangars (rock
walls instead of trenches where it was impossible to dig) when I
heard a sound which has always made me nervous, since April 1951:
the hollow clang of a mortar being fired. Everyone heard it and all
movement stopped. Someone said, 'It's only a "woozer" ' (our
nickname for the tribesmen's ancient Martini Henry rifles). I said,
'Shut up – and listen.' Then we heard the shell, high above,
swishing down towards us.

It exploded with a crash about two hundred yards south. The mortar coughed again. We were flat on the deck. This one exploded about two hundred yards north. We were bracketed. According to all my training and experience we were about to get a pasting. We waited, and waited. Nothing happened. That was it. What sort of enemy fires a good ranging bracket – then stops. I thought I knew. An enemy who is waiting for the right moment, which meant he was waiting for someone else to get into an attack position. I felt quite certain the enemy was about to launch a full scale attack. Happily, it was one of the many times in my life when I was wrong.

The same thing happened again the next day. Between five and six o'clock in the evening, two or three ranging bombs, then nothing. We called it the 'Six-Five Special' – after a well known UK television programme of the time.

They fired their two or three bombs at us almost every evening. After the first time, we went out to find where the mortar had been fired from, and found the position. Also, we found – from bits of rubbish left at the position – it was an 81mm mortar. This meant it was a better weapon than any we had available. The troops on the south side of the Jebel had our 3-inch mortar group with them, but the 3-inch mortar hasn't the range of an 81mm. On the north side we had nothing except our personal weapons, (FN rifles) and Bren light machine-guns. We did have one ·303 bolt action sniper rifle in each troop, but they were, I thought, more a liability than an asset.

We asked for something with which to hit back at defensive positions and were sent some '94' grenades. These can be fired off the muzzle of a rifle by using ballastite cartridges, but, although quite powerful for their size, have a maximum range of about 100 metres. There was also a big snag. The ones we got came with ·303 cartridges, so were useless with our 7·62mm FNs. At a push they could be used with the sniper rifles, if we were prepared to sacrifice any accuracy in future sniper work.

Quite often the opposition fired ineffectively at Cassino from long range. They were certainly not living up to their reputation of 'savage fighters', nor did they appear to be well trained.

The nearest the enemy came to causing us a problem was when they crept up onto what we called 'Herbie's Hump'. It was the position where Herbie's six-man patrol had our first contact. The Hump was about two hundred metres or less east of our nearest positions on Cassino, and although lower than our position we could not see over it. The side facing us was a sheer cliff of about thirty feet, the other side was a gentle slope with large rocks and bushes on it. The cliff was about forty metres long with sharply sloping ends. My sangar was at the east end of Cassino, facing Herbie's Hump and nearest to it. There were two of us in the sangar.

The second afternoon we spent on Cassino about a dozen or so enemy opened fire on us from the Hump with ·303 rifles and two light machine-guns. A considerable amount of spiteful ammunition splattered among us. We were not on 'stand-to', just resting, so it caught us a bit off balance; no one had twigged the enemy's approach. I grabbed my rifle and felt for grenades as I tried to get a look at the attackers. There was a lot of fire hitting my immediate area.

Uppermost in my mind was the fact that the last time I had taken on this type of weapon, at this range, I had come off a very definite second best. Nevertheless all experience is good for something (usually) and my experience told me this machine-gunner was a totally different kettle of fish from the cool, calculating bastard who had nailed me in Korea. His bursts of fire were too long to be accurate, and he sounded more like a man in a hurry to get rid of ammunition.

Another difference was the weapon I now held ready for action, confidence seemed to flow from the familiar feel of the lethal wood and steel of the FN. On top of that there were no exploding mortars or grenades. No scrambling, panting, wide-eyed tommy gunners. (I hoped!) I wasn't bleary-eyed, tired out, battered, or green.

He was mine for the taking, even before I'd spotted him. Easing up to peer through the dust and smoke I could see the black magazine showing plainly against the background of a light-coloured hat or shemag as he fired from between some rocks on the rim. The sights of the FN lined up on him, everything was right, I squeezed off the shot, and missed. The puff of white smoke off the rock a foot or so to the left surprised me. It had looked so bloody easy. He didn't like it though, my second shot was too late to catch him.

The FN sights raked along the rim to the left, a slight movement, another shot. Probably another miss, then the enemy fire ceased. I raised up to look for a target, there were none. I felt cheated, staring at the now empty enemy position with dust and smoke still hanging over it. Knowing they were gone. Knowing I had taken my big chance for revenge and blown it. No excuses, I should have made that shot count. My great chance to get a bit even with machine-gunners who picked on me. Shit!

We had no casualties. Enemy fire had been heavy but wild, only lasting about twenty or thirty seconds before they 'bugged out'.

At that stage of the operation we were not sure of the enemy's tactics or capabilities. The attack could have been an attempt to pull us off our defensive position in a follow-up of the attackers – only to fall into a classic trap sprung by a larger hidden force. Their knowledge of local terrain would indicate this type of tactic as a possibility. Later experience makes me feel there was no trap. They were just trying us, 'testing the water'. We didn't 'bite' anyway.

They did a repeat performance from the Hump an evening or two later, but it was over so quick I didn't even get a shot at them that time. I wanted a clear target again but couldn't find one. Again there were no casualties on Cassino. After that the enemy confined themselves to longer range, even less effective fire, and of course the 'Six-Five Special'.

A few hours after the first attack from Herbie's Hump, one of our people who had been away at the time, on a patrol somewhere to the west, arrived back on Cassino. Covered in dust and sweat, he thankfully unslung his heavy belt, laid down his rifle and said, 'It's all go, innit!' A voice from the next sangar said, 'Don't bloody bet on it, mate, a couple hours ago it was all coming back!'

Had the enemy known there were so few of us I think our troubles may have been considerably greater, but we patrolled very actively day and night. The daylight patrols were either within reach of assistance from Cassino or were back along the Jebel to our original position and the supply route, ground which we called 'ours'. At night we patrolled anywhere, mostly forward towards the enemy positions. Even if the enemy didn't see or hear us at night their scouts and patrols must have found our tracks all over the place.

Although we didn't know it at the time, Radio Cairo was conducting a propaganda war against us, claiming the heroes on the other side were wiping us out in hundreds – if not thousands! So it is quite likely the enemy thought they were up against a huge military force. This would have been much easier for them to believe than the plain truth. Otherwise even a couple of them with rifles could have closed down our supply line quite easily, we had no one to defend it! Cassino was virtually isolated, well within their reach and capabilities. We had no 'ground-to-air' radio facility to handle close air support, and there was no chance of a relief force getting through to us within several days (even had such a force existed!).

It would be quite unfair and untrue to say the tribesmen of Jebel

Akhdar were useless fighters. They were many in numbers and there were undoubtedly brave men among them. Before we arrived on the scene they had a ferocious reputation. We knew that on one occasion they had charged down the lower slope of the Jebel to attack a position which contained artillery. The charge had been so fast that one of the guns firing at them had depressed its aim too low and destroyed its own emplacement. It had taken air strikes and armour to chase the rebels from towns on the plain, near the Jebel, and push them back into the mountains. Since then everyone who had tried to pursue them had retired with a bloody nose. There was quite an impressive casualty list.

They had shown guts enough at times but they were, after all, civilians. Good old boys who would carry a gun and have a go at anyone who had the temerity to get on 'their Jebel'. They could not however be expected to cope with the SAS, which had a high proportion of hardened, well-trained, experienced professionals who didn't give a damn for anything except doing the job. To add to the rebels' problems they were also led and advised by civilians. Badly led and badly advised.

We also had our problems, overshadowing every move we made. The whole scene would have been closed down much quicker except for our 'softly, softly' approach to the operation, necessitated by strict orders to avoid casualties as a top priority! Yes, just think about it. Send men to do a job which, on the face of it, looks almost suicidal – and, at the same time, order them not to risk casualties. Sounds like the big political 'umbrella'. Anyone who gets his men or himself killed must have disobeyed orders – therefore don't blame us!

The pressure was heaviest on our field commanders, especially John Watts as squadron commander, ultimately responsible in the field. Rory Walker also had the problem of often holding us back when experience and better judgement (his and ours) said, 'Do it!'

It was almost like trying to play a game of chess – or draughts – without losing a piece. There were many times when members of 16 or 17 Troop wanted to pull some kind of trick on the opposition. Seldom was anything allowed, although I believe an attempt was made to capture the enemy mortar by a small fast-moving night patrol. The idea being to catch them 'red-handed' so to speak when they fired their evening shots. It didn't come off though. The enemy had enough sense to fire from many different places.

After a lot of studying of Herbie's Hump, the day after the

Para course at RAF Changi, Singapore. Author seated extreme right, front row. February 1958.

16 Troop, 'D' Squadron, plus mortar NCO Jebel Akhdar, Christmas 1958. Just after the 'Akbat' raid.

Rest stop on the way down the Jebel Akhdar, Oman, 1959.

(*Left*) Oops! Mine damage. (*Right*) Duke's Grave.

second blitz from there, I had the bright idea of using a small ledge on the cliff facing Cassino as a base from which to throw grenades among future attackers. The snag was, whoever did it would have to lie concealed there in the heat of the sun all day as there was no way of reaching it undetected in daylight.

Mentioning the idea to George started an argument between us as to who should try it. We had to fix it all with Rory, so decided he could nominate which of us went. The other would do cover with a rifle, from my sangar. Rory listened to the plan, thought about it for all of three seconds, then told us to forget it. 'The sun must have got you already!'

To help with the supply problem some Army donkeys were brought in from Somalia. They were small and not much use compared to the big local donkeys which were almost as big as mules. They were only allowed to be loaded with 50 lb, whereas we trogs – with only 'two wheel drive' – were expected to carry twice that, and more. Some of us went down to collect a batch of donkeys and stores. One of the men got kicked while trying to feed a donkey. We started to go off them at that point. By the time we reached our base at the top we had exhausted ourselves, carrying our heavy loads and dragging the reluctant mokes.

We had strict orders that no donkey would be shot unless it went lame. Just before we reached our base there was the familiar 'double tap' of two fast shots from an FN, and a donkey fell dead. The man whom it had kicked stood there with a smoking rifle saying, 'It limped, the bastard limped, I saw it limp!'

So we had our first fresh meat for several weeks. It was a great treat after all that time on tinned rations. In fact, our rations at that time were some of the worst I have ever had to exist on (barring POW 'rations' in Korea!). All our rations were what the Army calls '24 Hour Packs'. They were not designed to be the only source of food for a period of several weeks.

To make matters worse we were getting only one type of pack sent to us, so we had no variation to our diet. The same food day after day for weeks can become very boring. I would have three or four biscuits with a small tin of cheese and jam from a tube in the morning, then put the whole day's ration into a sort of 'biscuit stew' in the evening. We had no rice or potatoes, and no bread, so the few biscuits in the ration pack formed the bulk of our daily food.

Soon afterwards we got our first re-supply by air. It was a fiasco. All the more so after being familiar with the near perfect air-drops

by the great combination we had in Malaya – RAF Valettas and
Bristol Freighters with the men of 55 Company RASC handling the
drops.

This was totally different. Our DZ was not a wee hole in the trees
which needed a lot of finding, but a damn great patch of open
ground big enough for ten football pitches. The aircraft was a
Hastings and it dropped its load from about 2,000 feet, when it
should have been down to 500 feet. Those parachutes which worked,
drifted off into the distance, and once over the edge of the plateau
were lost to us forever. The packs which broke loose came down like
bombs all over the place. Nothing in them was usable.

A few days later we had another drop. In the meantime one of our
mortars was being sent to us from the south side, so we had ordered
mortar ammunition. The drop came in lower this time, about 1,000
feet. The packs, however, broke away in great order. Having seen
the first effort we were all well clear of the DZ. A good thing too!

Whoever packed that lot had really worked on it. The High
Explosive (HE) mortar shells were in the same packs as the
phosphorous shells. When those packs 'whistled in' the phosphorous
shells were smashed, so the phosphorous set fire to everything all
around. The HE shells got hot and began exploding when they felt
like it.

We salvaged what we could. A few brave souls rushed in and out
of the exploding DZ trying to get the mail, the decent rations (the
rum ration?) and anything else they could. Like most of the others,
I got behind a good size rock, lit a cigarette and waited for the
shrapnel to stop screeching past before venturing out into that lot.

I don't know what signal Rory Walker sent about the air-drops,
but something sparked someone, somewhere. After that disaster,
things improved rapidly.

Having located the enemy's main defence line, Captain Walker
decided to try out our other air support, a squadron of ground attack
fighters based at Sharjah, in what is now the United Arab Emirates.
We had no ground-to-air radio links at that stage, so things were a
bit tricky once the aircraft were overhead. Enter now a clown, yes,
even in the SAS (did I say 'even'? At times it was full of them!). The
clown had already proved himself by eating a whole troop's bread
ration – 'by mistake'? That wouldn't have been so bad but it was
the first bread we had seen (or didn't see!) for several weeks.

We had received an air-drop earlier and the marker panels for this
had supposedly been brought in by the clown. We had laid out the

marker panels for the air-strike just in front of our positions, on the north-east side of Cassino. The panels were in the shape of an arrow, pointing in the direction of the enemy position we wanted hit. The jet pilots would have been told the bearing from our arrow to the target, and the approximate distance.

We were having a brew of tea when the jets came on the scene. They were Venoms, a twin fuselage jet fighter, the Naval version of the more common Vampire. We watched them circling, getting the lie of the land. Then I saw something was wrong. I was likely the only one there who had been attacked by jet fighters before, and I recognised the pattern of flight. They were stacking up to hit Cassino.

I yelled a warning to the others and grabbed a towel, or something white, stood up and waved like mad. The men around me followed suit quickly. I watched the rocket pods on the first aircraft. The first puff of smoke would see me in my sangar.

It never came. The two Venoms screamed over our heads and away. We heard afterwards the leading pilot couldn't believe his eyes when he saw – with his thumb on the button – his target waving at him! Realising there had been a bog-up, the Venoms returned to their base without firing a shot.

We looked to our set-up for the reasons, and found them. The sun was dropping in the west, our arrow on the north-east side of the position was now in shadow, not easily seen from the air. It was an easily made mistake which could have cost us. But there was worse. The clown had not collected the air-drop panels. The wind had blown them into a rough arrow pointing at Cassino, and the bearing from those panels to us was almost the same as from us to the target.

We still had a lot to learn, but would we have time at this rate? Rory Walker made sure we all knew the whys and wherefores of that lesson. I know it's a lesson I will never forget.

To help with our firepower problems some ·30 calibre Browning machine-guns were borrowed from the Lifeguards. They had plenty to spare, as most of their armoured cars had been blown up on the roads and tracks around the foot of the Jebel (by mines originally supplied to Saudi Arabia by the Americans!). Also a couple of 3.5-inch rocket launchers were brought up to our position. I think we had two or three ·30 calibre Brownings and a couple of lads from the Lifeguards came with them, to help out. With these extra weapons an attack on the enemy's strongpoint now became a better proposition. A company of infantry from the locally raised Northern

Frontier Regiment arrived to defend Cassino, giving us a base to work from and releasing both troops for offensive operations.

The enemy positions were about four thousand yards from Cassino, so a 'step-up' operation was needed to give us plenty of time to cope with them during darkness. Halfway between us and the enemy was a ridge we called Middle Wallop. They had fired at us from there with rifles and machine-guns. Their 81mm mortar had been positioned behind it on several occasions, to fire its few evening shells. To the left of Middle Wallop and a bit further from us were twin peaks we called 'Sabrina' (in honour of a certain well-known TV personality). The enemy often patrolled Sabrina and I believe they had a permanent observation post (OP) somewhere there.

The enemy's main defence line was a natural fortress: a cliff about 50 feet high, maybe more, which barred the way to the main plateau. There was a gap in the middle of the cliff, about 25 yards wide, partly blocked by huge boulders. It was obviously the front door to the fortifications, heavily guarded by at least fifty enemy who were in the honeycomb of caves all around it. The proper name of the fortified cliff was Akhbat el Zhufar. We called it 'The Akbat'.

We spent a lot of time scanning the whole area through binoculars, watching enemy movements and trying to find where there were obstacles barring our way. It was very difficult to assess the ground at any distance as it was so broken and disrupted with jumbles of loose rock, in piles many feet high and deep fissures where they were least expected. Some of the wadis were over a mile deep, with sheer cliffs from top to bottom.

The view from Cassino was vast. On a clear day, which was most days, we could see right across the coastal plain to the north-east, right out onto the blue water of the Persian Gulf. Through binoculars we sometimes saw ships out there and envied their crews the good food and plentiful 'liquid refreshment'. The coast was about fifty miles away. To the south and west the sands of the 'empty quarter' stretched away into infinity. It looked very empty at that distance.

The main part of the Jebel was roughly east of us. Almost every day heavy bombers, RAF Shackletons similar to the famous Lancaster of World War II, would appear at a great height and drop huge bombs on one particular area, miles away along the top of the Jebel. Using our binoculars we could see the bomb leave the aircraft and watch it fall to explode with a great pall of dust and white smoke on what appeared to be a bare area of mountain top.

There was much speculation about what the Air Force were trying to achieve. Some thought it was just a bombing range. Others thought the target was Saiq, the rebel headquarters. I remember a discussion when one voice said, 'It can't be Saiq they're bombing or we would be able to see the houses, where the bombs are landing.' Another voice answered, 'Not if they've been dropping those bloody things on it for the last fortnight.' In fact the bombers (we were told later) were trying to destroy an area where the rebels were supposed to be storing a lot of military hardware in huge caves. Also the rebel leaders were supposed to have their headquarters there.

In case of casualties we had to find a place where a helicopter could land and – most important – take off again. The one ancient Sycamore available had a casualty lifting ceiling of 7,000 feet, and I remember being on a patrol to check on LZ situations about 2,000 feet below where we were operating. So I presume we were at about 9,000 feet on Cassino.

On one patrol a swarm of locusts came onto us and we had quite a time covered from head to toe in the damn things. They seemed to like the look of our smocks and KD. My KD slacks were now covered in patches of black boot polish to cut down the 'glare', but it didn't stop the locusts.

All of us had badly chapped lips from the wind, the cold night and the burning hot sun by day. Our boots, which had rubber soles, were worn down so that the screws which had held the soles on were like football boot studs with rubber washers under them. The toe caps were mostly worn away and some of us had our toes showing through. After six weeks a re-supply of boots was most welcome. To say the going was 'rough' was quite an understatement.

We were all impatient to have a real go at the opposition. Our respect for their much-vaunted abilities and superior numbers had dwindled to zero. It was high time they were given a short sharp lesson.

CHAPTER FOUR

'Akbat' and Tanuf Slab

Captain Rory Walker worked on all the information we could gather from patrolling and observation. He made a plan, put it before the usual SAS 'Chinese Parliament' – so we could all get our 'cribs' out of the way at the start – then, with a few changes to allow more or less time for this and that, we went ahead with it. As with all good plans, there was scope for changes as it went. We all knew our jobs. What to do in the case of this or that going wrong. In the event so much went wrong and so much went right it worked anyway.

It was decided 17 Troop would make a diversionary attack in the area of Sabrina. 16 Troop would scale the cliff of the Akbat and hit the main strongpoint from the rear. The overall plan being to badly shake or destroy enemy morale. There was no question of it being more than a raid, as we had not the men to hold such a large feature and fortification, even if we could take it.

As we had no radios, apart from the morse set to Squadron HQ, everything depended on timing for support and diversionary fire. The machine-guns were to engage the enemy positions at the time we were hoping to be scaling the cliff, to cover any noise we might make. A rocket launcher would also be used to hit the main strongpoint just as we reached the cliff.

Because we had no real maps of the area (Captain Walker had the one map, which was a white sheet covering nearly all of Northern Oman) route planning on the final approach was impossible. There was so much 'dead ground' (real estate out of sight) between us and the Akbat we had to make do with more hope than certainty.

On the first night both troops and the machine-guns moved forward to take Middle Wallop. There was no opposition but we did almost get a big enemy patrol (which had fired at Cassino, now held by the Company of Omani Northern Frontier Regiment). We heard their running feet a few yards away in the darkness as they headed back for their defence line.

Before daylight 16 Troop had moved forward to a position directly in front of the enemy's 'front door', and about 600 yards from it. We lay in the open all day, watching the enemy and hoping their patrols didn't stumble upon us. As soon as it was dark we started the final approach, leaving our signaller and the two-man rocket launcher crew to do their work from that position.

About four hundred yards was covered quickly and fairly quietly. Then we came to a deep ravine. The ravine had steep sides and was about eighty feet deep. It took some time to find a way down. So long in fact we knew our timing was going to be out. As we reached the bottom and contemplated a stiff climb up the other side we heard 17 Troop's diversionary attack going in to the north.

At first I didn't recognise the sound of firing. The sound was strange and startling. Weird in fact. Perhaps because we were in a deep ravine the crash of rifle and machine-gun fire, echoing from a thousand rock faces, passing high above us in the night, made a weird swishing sound. It started slowly, swish, swish, swish, then built up rapidly into a long, shuddering ssshhhhh, like a strong, fast-approaching wind. Eerie.

Then, just as we were starting to climb the far side, rockets started exploding just up the ravine. We realised they were our own rockets, falling short by two hundred yards. Some re-thinking had to be done. The timings had to be altered. Captain Walker gave me a message to take back to the signaller. Also a verbal message for the rocket launcher crew.

The night was inky black, except for a few stars, but I knew I could find the three we had left behind. The only problem was, they weren't expecting anyone. I hoped they were all together and one hadn't wandered off a few yards so I'd bump into him before schedule. All went well, the timings were re-arranged through SHQ to 17 Troop signaller with the machine-guns.

I galloped back to the ravine and we all started off once more. Soon after leaving the ravine we came to the Akhbat cliff. We had spotted a place which might be scaled and moved along until we found it.

Captain Walker, who always insisted on doing leading scout on troop moves, tied the rope around his waist and started to climb. The first thing we noticed was that the rock crumbled under his feet and hands, making for a tricky climb. About fifteen feet up he was stuck, couldn't go up, and had to be helped down.

After a quick whispered discussion it was decided to move north, to try nearer the main strongpoint. I volunteered to re-coil the rope while the rest moved out – fast. The rope was snagged in the rocks and took a few seconds to organise. With the rope safely hung around me I took off after the troop. Ahead of me I heard a few shots, nothing came my way so I kept going, along the bottom of the cliff.

That re-organising of the climbing rope, although taking valuable seconds to complete properly and causing me to be suddenly alone in the dark on the very spot where two short hours before, through binoculars, I had seen a twelve man patrol of the enemy moving slowly along at full alert, was one of the best moves I've ever made. Not only was it coiled so as to be ready for its intended purpose but its tidiness ensured my spare magazines and grenades were still at maximum availability. A fact to be thankful for soon after. At the base of the cliff there was a well-worn track which, although undulating in places was fairly free of loose rocks, making little problem for quiet, fast movement by starlight.

Sometimes weaving between huge boulders, sometimes in the wide open I rushed on for what seemed to be quite a distance, all the time expecting to catch up to the troop, who, I thought, would be waiting for the rope. It did cross my mind there was a possibility of catching up with the wrong people, or perhaps meeting them. Trust in one's comrades, their expertise in this type of work and our 'codes of practice' become paramount on such occasions.

By the time I caught up I was beginning to think I'd missed them somewhere. I asked where Rory was, thinking he would need the rope. I was directed up between some rocks and ran quickly up through the gap. Coming out into an open space I heard the unmistakable sound of a grenade being thrown. I immediately hit the deck, not knowing who or what was where.

The grenade bounced and clattered on rock then exploded. I heard Rory say, 'Give them a phosphorous!' A couple of seconds later the sound of the 'phos' being thrown. When it exploded I saw it was in a cave entrance, then all hell broke loose.

I saw Scouse (not he of the leeches), one of our Bren gunners stand up in front of me, so I joined him. We stood about six feet apart, firing back at every gun flash. There were plenty. Most of the fire was coming from above us. Although feeling sure I would be hit – there seemed no way they could all miss – there was no time for the luxury of fear, anger or other straightfoward sensations, we were far too busy. Realising whoever else of our people were in there with us were away to our right, about twenty metres, I knew that everywhere else was 'open season'.

Scouse raked the thickest areas of muzzle flashes with automatic

fire; I fired a single shots at the nearer enemy muzzle flashes, taking
the nearer ones at about 20 to 30 metres first when possible. At least
two were only about ten metres from us but they only fired one or
two shots each before the return fire closed them down.

At no time during the raid did I see a clear target. All one sees
during a night action, once firing commences, is muzzle flashes and
grenade bursts. The trick is to keep one eye closed for as long as
possible – if it's a short sharp job – to prevent temporary blindness
caused by the gun flashes. On this particular occasion, being right
in among the opposition, it was another luxury I couldn't afford.
Blurred shadows, a couple of half-seen, split-second silhouettes and
a glinting cartridge belt is all I remember.

A shot hit the Bren magazine and Scouse did the fastest magazine
change I've ever seen. I went down on one knee, to make a smaller
target, and noticed the return fire had slackened.

A shot came from a cave to my left, so I tossed a grenade over
the wall at the front of it, fired a few more shots at nothing in
particular, then heard Herbie, the troop sergeant, calling us off.
Scouse and I were only too glad to leave by then, as everyone else
seemed to have gone – opposition and all.

Well, most of the opposition. In the comparative silence which
followed the gunfire there arose those never forgotten sounds of
such places: sounds of choking, groaning, retching and babbling;
voices of men crying out in agony and fear; someone thrashing
about on the ground a few yards away, making a gasping, bubbling
sound.

Over to the right, where Rory's voice had called for the
phosphorous grenade, another voice now sounded, vaguely
familiar. It was pleading and incoherent. I stopped in my tracks,
then started back in the direction of that voice. After a few steps I
stopped, listening, then called the man's name. No answer, so I
started to go further. Herbie rushed up behind me and grabbed my
arm, 'Get to hell out of it, Lofty!'

Still not sure, I said, 'Are all ours out?' 'Yes,' he said and gave
me a shove in the right direction.

Good old Herbie, always on the ball. He always knew where
everyone was, even in the midst of chaos. Four of us had been in
the middle of that lot, and I didn't even know what was going on
– didn't have an invite. Not a scratch between us, it was quite
remarkable. For comparison it was like standing in a street of tall
houses, being shot at from all the windows at once.

As we pulled back with the rest of the troop I saw a big 'cave' at a lower level, and suggested a grenade would make it safer to turn our backs on.

Rory agreed and said, 'Make it a phosphorous though.' So I did. It wasn't a cave but a great stack of brushwood. The grenade turned it into a huge bonfire which lit up the whole area.

It was only then I realised where we had been: into the front door of the great Akbat strongpoint. I should have known – it was the only break in the cliff.

Now, thanks to that last grenade, we walked away from our handiwork lit up like broad daylight. Not a shot was fired from the great fortress. We walked in a straggling group across at least 50 yards of open sandy ground, making perfect targets for anyone in the fortification less than 100 yards behind us. There was only one answer, the whole garrison had fled in panic.

Any shred of respect for local fighting qualities evaporated that night. They might be great at long range, where they rarely did any harm anyway, but close quarters – our favourite – they didn't want to know. Irrespective of numbers or reputation they were now definitely on a loser. We knew it, and I expect they did too.

During what was left of the night, and an hour or two of daylight, we hoofed back to Cassino, collecting our three men, then the machine-gun crews on the way. We took each day as it came on operations, never knowing what day of the week it was, or even the date, so it was with some surprise, when we reached Cassino, I found it was Christmas Day. So the Akbat raid went from Christmas Eve to Christmas Day 1958.

Somewhere in Bahrein or Sharjah we had an SAS representative looking after our interests at that end of the air-drop scene. He was a humble trooper, or maybe corporal, and – after himself, naturally – he always put his mates first. So it came to pass on Christmas Day we drank his health in lots of lovely whisky, rum, brandy and vodka which, originally destined to grace the bar of an officers' mess, had accidentally found itself with the wrong air-drop label and thereby saved from waste. Sweeny, you played a blinder.

Someone at HQ Persian Gulf also came through on the right line. We received on the same air-drop tinned roast chicken. It worked out one tin between two men. Half a chicken each – Happy Christmas.

The Akbat raid had worked out well, but could hardly be claimed as going 'according to plan' as far as 16 Troop were concerned. We had achieved our aim by playing it off the cuff as we went. The rest of the plan had apparently worked like clockwork. 17 Troop achieved their objectives against light resistance. The machine-gunners had come in on cue as required, in spite of the re-arranged schedule, and we had no casualties.

One thing had gone seriously wrong. Our 3·5 rockets, which should have had a maximum range of 900 yards were pushed to make 400 yards. Had 16 Troop moved a little further north to find a way across the ravine we would have been hit by our own rockets, which were falling 200 yards short of the target. Also, several rockets had failed to fire from the launcher. Others had failed to explode on impact. Whether it was the altitude or sub-standard foreign rockets caused the problem, I never did hear.

Christmas Day we ate and slept; Christmas night we sat around a good fire in a hollow behind Cassino and sampled the good spirit. During the celebrations the opposition regained enough of their composure to give Cassino rather a lot of mortar shells combined with a steady raking of machine-gun fire. After a few minutes the NFR fired a red signal flare down our side of Cassino. It was the agreed signal showing they needed mortar support fire to calm down the opposition. Our mortar position was about 300 yards from the hollow where the party was in full swing.

Nothing happened. No mortar support was forthcoming, so a second red flare came sailing down the hillside, then a third and a fourth. Meanwhile the streams of tracer bullets coming over the top of Cassino increased if anything. Being mostly ·50 calibre, they went a long way across the sky before burning out. More flares were sent towards the mortar position, until some of them set fire to a lot of grass and scrub on our side of the hill.

The NFR were yelling for our mortar crew to return the fire. Still nothing happened. After several minutes I ran down the hill to the mortar position to see if all was well. One of the crew was sat with his back against the mortar fast asleep. I awoke him and said, 'They want you to do something about those bloody mortars.' He said, 'What bloody mortars? – I haven't heard anything!' So I said, 'Well, look behind you – half the bloody mountain's on fire.'

Before I got back to the camp-fire our mortar was hurling shells back at the opposition who were soon finished for the night. The party, of course, carried on regardless.

Rory Walker was not the greatest piper by a long chalk, but he had his bagpipes there that night, doing his best to terrorise the

natives – or us! He was to hit the headlines a few years later
when he played his pipes outside the besieged British Embassy in
Jakarta, Indonesia. I hope he had improved by then.

A few days after the Akbat raid we marched down the way we had
come up, leaving the NFR company and our mortar crew to hold
Cassino while we had a much needed break. Such was the
reputation of the opposition, the NFR would not have stayed on
their own, otherwise the mortar crew could have come with us.
Shortly after we left the north side, 'A' Squadron, 22 SAS, took over
the Cassino position, having been rushed from Malaya to give us a
hand.

We returned to Bait el Falage, near Muscat, for a few days' rest.
While there, one or two of us went to see Duke's grave. The only
way to the only Christian cemetery in those days was by sea. As the
cemetery was just up off a beach surrounded by sheer cliffs, George,
myself and one or two others hired a boat with an outboard engine
(and a driver who knew the cemetery) to make the trip. It being hot,
and we being thirsty, we took along a crate of canned beer.

We found the cemetery OK, and as all the other graves were very
old we found Duke's easily. There were no stones to mark his grave,
just a mound of earth, so we gathered some rocks and built a
surround. Then put a couple of big rocks at each end. Someone
found a stone cup, half buried in the sand, so we put that on top of
the grave. Having no flowers we decided we would fill it with beer.
It wasn't very big, held about half a pint, was in the shape of the
FA Cup, minus handles. George poured the beer, filling the cup, we
thought it was likely more fitting than flowers – knowing Duke.

We wandered around the cemetery for a few minutes, looking at
the names on the ancient headstones, then George gave a yell.
'Who's drunk Duke's beer?!' No one had been near the grave since
we poured the beer. Looking at that empty cup I felt the hair prickle
on the back of my neck! We stared at each other for a few seconds,
knowing no one had drunk it, hoping someone would say they had!

I poured more beer into the cup and we left almost right away.
The cup was probably carved from porous rock, and the place was
like an oven anyway. Nevertheless, it was good to think Duke had
enjoyed his beer.

In the few days we were resting, I bought a camera with lots of
film to take on the next operation. We fired our weapons quite a bit,
zeroing them to our liking. We would have done a lot of swimming
but the beach was thick with jellyfish. George said they were

harmless, and dived in through them – only to come up yelling about ten yards out. They had quite a nasty sting, so we then had the problem of getting George back through them. We eventually got some branches and swept a gap, through which he made a mad dash.

The next time we went to the beach we saw a shark fin cutting through the water about 50 yards, out; that was me – and a lot of others – finished with swimming in that area.

Our next operation was on the south side of the Jebel Akhdar Plateau. A place called Tanuf gave its name to a monstrous slab of rock, two or three miles long, which appeared to be leaning on the mountain. The Tanuf Slab was where Duke had been killed, but there was no real problem as we now had the measure of the opposition.

The usual hard, hard climb, loaded down with kit and we reached the top of the slab. It was not as high as Cassino by a long way, but the opposition were very touchy about its occupation as they knew it was closer to the main part of the plateau and made a good base from which to chip our way upward and forward. Right at the top of the slab we organised a good defensive position, which was promptly mortared from a position high up and far away, beyond the reach of our 3-inch mortars. Our sangar walls were strengthened and grew upwards rapidly.

The day after that they gave us a short pasting with a ·50 calibre machine-gun. Our ·30 calibre machine-guns couldn't compete range wise. The sangar walls all thickened some more before nightfall. No one was hurt by all this show of firepower. We knew someone would get hurt when we closed with the opposition though. We were also very confident it would not be us!

As far as I remember, the squadron commander went up the Tanuf Slab with us, then had to go down again for one of those conferences which always seem to bug good field commanders. On his return to the squadron position he brought some mail. After the mail was doled out he called me over. He was still showing signs of the hard climb back up the Slab. (No helicopters for mere squadron commanders in those days!)

His first words took me by surprise. 'Why haven't you written to your wife?' I told him I had written at least two letters while we were at Bait el Falage, soon after Christmas. The Major looked decidedly suspicious. 'She hadn't had a letter since you left Malaya, so you'll bloody well write now – and give me the letter when you've finished!' With that he handed me a writing pad, envelope and stamp.

I don't know what had happened to the several letters I had sent Ann from Oman, but there was no point in arguing over it. I wrote a letter, handed it to the squadron commander, who said it would be sent out at the first opportunity. I retired to my sangar, feeling a bloody fool but anxious over Ann's worries if she had not received any mail since I left.

Later I found the situation had been made worse by one of Ann's friends getting one or two letters every week from her husband. The fact that he was a signaller in base all the time was, of course, lost on the two wives.

During the hours of daylight we were on constant watch with binoculars. Every movement by the enemy was carefully watched, very often when they thought they were too far away to be seen. On one of these occasions we watched several of the enemy carrying something we couldn't identify into a cave about 3,000 yards away. It was obvious they were not doing something for the benefit of our health so, as we had just been joined by a RAF Forward Air Controller it was a good chance to try him out. He could speak to the jet pilots when they were overhead and direct their attack.

The RAF type was a pilot from the Venom Squadron, so had the great advantage of knowing the pilots he was directing. He was also an ex-member of the Rhodesian SAS (our 'C' Squadron), so fitted well with us. His head was shaved down to the wood and his code name was 'Goldilocks'. Very fitting.

The Venoms were sent for. In the meantime our Commanding Officer, Lt-Colonel Deane-Drummond, who had arrived in the helicopter to have a look at the position, was about to leave. The jets were in contact with Goldilocks just as the chopper started to take off.

At that moment we found out what the opposition had been carrying into that cave. A ·50 calibre opened up, trying to hit the chopper as it lifted off. The chopper dropped down the mountainside unharmed, out of the line of fire. So the ·50 laced the position with long, stringy bursts for a minute or so.

Goldilocks now came into his own. His mates were circling way up out of sight to the south, and he got busy with the target description. The flight leader came hurtling over us and fired a marker burst from his 20 mm cannon, which struck way above the cave. Goldilocks corrected from that burst, and the second jet put his shells around the cave. The first jet came back and fired one rocket which struck about ten feet above the cave. The second jet came screaming over us and placed his rocket straight in the cave mouth. It was great to watch. Those people must have thought the return fire was fantastically fast and effective. They would never know it was on its way before they had even fired.

A day or two after that incident we moved off the Tanuf Slab towards the main plateau. We only moved a couple of thousand yards. The main purpose of the move was to keep the opposition on their toes, also check out the ground and any natural obstacles between us and the villages on the plateau, which were the enemy's main bases and supply areas.

We reached a very rough, jagged rock area in the early hours and got into defensive positions. Soon after settling down, before daylight, the opposition fired a couple of ranging shells with an 81mm mortar. These fell about three hundred yards south of us. A few minutes later they began firing again, at a slow rate, putting down twenty-five shells in the area of their ranging shots. Realising they had made another cock-up, I went to sleep before they finished, something I thought I could never do with mortar shells swishing overhead.

On this operation Rory Walker, who had led the troop so well and was very well liked by everyone, had been put on another job, co-ordinating air supply from the sharp end.

From our new forward base it was planned to do a reconnaissance onto the plateau. The squadron commander, John Watts, picked three of us from 16 Troop to accompany him on a patrol through the enemy defences. 17 Troop and the rest of 16 Troop were to provide 'step-up' for the first part of the patrol and give us cover if we had problems getting through.

About 1,000 yards forward from our start line, just before parting with our step-up group, we had a head-on contact with a strong enemy force. A bright moon, which I had found disquieting with the prospect of climbing towards it through enemy positions, had in fact the opposite effect when meeting the enemy in the open. They had their backs to the moon, therefore when we met they were easily seen as black shadows. Perhaps our leading scouts opened fire too soon to obtain maximum effect, but at least we had the drop on them and they withdrew.

We had been moving parallel to the enemy defence line, at about 400 yards' range, and now came under fire from their forward positions. Looking at all those muzzle flashes, I realised we would have had some problems getting through undetected, even in a small group. Although there were obviously a lot of people firing at us, there was comparatively very little fire actually coming our way. It was more like being a spectator at someone else's battle, with the odd few shots accidentally crackling around us. As usual the rockery of all types in the area magnified the sound, gave an uproar of echoes and, causing ricochets galore, added that savage screech to the overall row.

A couple of our Bren-gunners and a rocket launcher crew returned the fire on enemy machine-gun positions. I don't think any rifles were fired by our people after the initial contact. Sharing a large rock with a friend, we peered round our respective corners. I estimated the nearest enemy position to be at least 300 metres from us. He obviously thought the same. 'Too far to bother,' was his verdict.

After a minute or so the enemy fire slackened enough for us to sit on our rock in comfort, awaiting a decision for our next move. It was not long in coming. The enemy were pretty thick on the ground in that sector, so John Watts decided to call off our patrol for the time being, as they were now all 'stirred up' and would be extra alert. This was very likely another of those cases where the squadron commander's decision was heavily influenced by our 'top priority'. No casualties!

The patrol move through enemy lines at that stage was not crucial to the operation. Had things been different, it's likely a dummy frontal attack on an enemy who was obviously jittery and couldn't hit a barn at night, would have caused ample confusion for us to have slipped through with little risk. Personally, I would rather have gone through the defences with a gun in one hand and a grenade in the other, so to speak, than try to tiptoe through their kitchen.

The group commenced withdrawal to more friendly territory. All firing on our part ceased, as it would show our movement. We checked for casualties and found one man was missing.

There was no confusion at the time, although we were still not actually being fired upon, but in an area where a fair amount of enemy rifle and machine-gun ammunition was banging and screeching around, or crackling overhead. While the main party returned to our forward base, sweeping the area for the missing man as they went, four or five of us began sweeping the area to our furthest point of movement that night.

(*Top*) Tanuf Slab, Jebel Akhdar, Northern Oman, January 1959. This sangar was nicknamed 'Fort Knox'. It grew rapidly in size and strength every time we took enemy fire, until two men could easily pass each other when walking in opposite directions around the top of the wall. The low ground (wadi) in the background to the right, is roughly 5,000 to 6,000 feet lower than the sangar and 7–10 miles distant. This particular sangar was the highest of our positions on Tanuf Slab. Note my wife's photo in bottom left corner.

(*Centre*) Same sangar viewed from front. Note discarded 3-inch mortar bomb carriers lying in foreground. Others had been used, built into sangar to form rifle and machine-gun embrasures, two, three or four through each embrasure. Note standing man's leg visible through wall.

(*Below left*) One of the many .50 calibre Brownings captured at Saiq. From the hoard found by Miley and myself.

(*Below right*) Donkeyborne supplies unloaded. Donkey wallopers and escort resting before return to Tanuf. Tanuf Slab, about 100 metres from sangar position seen in the top photograph, down lee-side of hill. Note same background 5–6,000 feet below.

16 Troop less Troop Commander and author (who took the photograph), Jebel Akhdar, 1959.

Author, just before the final push to Saiq.

Searching for one man – who could have been wounded, unconscious or dead – in an area covered in man-sized rocks, at night, is a rather hopeless task. The moon and stars came to our aid on this occasion but made me, at least, feel rather exposed to the opposition.

We formed a line and moved slowly over the areas of possibility, feeling in the darker shadows, staring hard at suspect shapes. The opposition settled down to the occasional raking of the area with machine-gun fire which, although having its nuisance value, was also very handy as it indicated there were none of their people in the area. After half an hour or so of fruitless search Herbie called us off and we commenced our move back to the forward base, still in our search line.

About halfway back we met two men coming out to meet us. The missing man had been found. It had all been a mistake, no one had really been missing. A waste of time, perhaps, but it had brought out the problems of searching ground under those conditions – and the importance of being 100 per cent sure of where everyone was. There was no one to blame, it was just one of those mistakes which can happen in a noisy, dark situation.

The squadron stayed in that forward position for a couple of days but, as far as I know, or remember, we were not bothered by enemy activity. There may have been the usual hopeless, long range sniping but nothing of note. A day or two later we all withdrew from the Jebel, marching back down to Tanuf for a few hours' break. Something was in the air. We would find out soon enough.

CHAPTER FIVE

Akhdar – Final Assault

Our next trick was rather complicated. 'A' Squadron joined us from the north side. Both squadrons were to be used in an all-out assault to finish the job. Perhaps I missed something along the way, but I don't remember knowing the name of the place or area where we were going to do this final assault. I knew it was several miles southeast of Tanuf and we were fairly well briefed on the route to be taken up the Jebel.

A couple of 'D' Squadron people had done a sneaky recce of the lower part of the route and had studied the climb in some detail from out on the desert, but they couldn't take any risk of alerting the enemy to our interest in the area. So there was a lot of problems which could not be solved in advance. We studied air photos of the route but none I saw showed the view from directly above.

I heard later that the local donkey wallopers who were being used to help with supplies on the south side were sworn to secrecy, on pain of death, not to breathe a word about where they were to take the next lot of supplies. This ensured the enemy would know all about it. But, of course, the donkey wallopers had been given the wrong location.

We spent a day checking and zero firing weapons. Checking all our kit, ammunition, grenades, rockets, rations, everything down to the smallest detail. 16 Troop, under Herbie's direction, ran through all our contact drills and immediate action drills.

Our main load was ammunition. I remember having two 3·5 rockets, four 90 (Energa) grenades (now issued with correct cartridges). Eight No 36 grenades, six No 80 (white phosphorous) grenades. Five 20-round magazines of rifle ammunition, plus 100 rounds in bandoliers. One 250-round box of ·30 calibre machine-gun ammunition.

Hanging on the back of a truck I found one of those spring balance weighing hooks and, just for curiosity, weighed my kit. My Bergen rucksack, loaded and ready to go, weighed 98 lb. My belt weighed 22 lb – 120 lb total. I don't remember if that included

66

my rifle. It probably didn't, as I don't remember putting it with either belt or Bergen. Everyone had similar loads to carry. We wondered what the night would bring in the way of 'uphill'. Any opposition we met would be welcome, as an excuse to unload some weight.

Final checks were made and we climbed aboard trucks. There were about fifteen or twenty vehicles in the convoy, which headed north from Tanuf, on the rough dirt road and tracks along the base of the Jebel. The trucks were well sandbagged as protection against mines. 16 Troop were in the leading truck. It was still broad daylight. We were clearly visible to the watching eyes on the Jebel. At the back of the convoy, the last vehicle was the water tanker. In the passenger seat of the tanker sat Bill, an SAS medic corporal who had already been blown up twice on mines, once while in an ammunition truck half full of mortar shells. So Bill travelled in the safest place in respect of mines. Just before dusk we saw a great mushroom of smoke and dust go up at the back of the convoy. A few seconds later the thunderous bang of an anti-tank mine reached our ears.

The convoy stopped, and John Watts rushed back to the rear to check the problem. A few minutes later he came back and said, 'You're not going to believe this.' Poor old Bill was only badly shaken having gone out through the observation hatch of the cab on the water tanker.

How could they always pick on Bill? The whole convoy had trampled over that mine, but it waited specially for Bill's water tanker. There was no real mystery about the mine. It was likely a 'Ratchet' mine, which allows so many vehicles to pass over it before detonating. Very handy for mining busy tracks and allowing the minelayer to be long gone before anything happens. Nevertheless, Bill's attraction for mines was phenomenal!

After dusk the convoy turned around, and, without lights, rushed southwards, through Tanuf and on into the desert, parallel with the Jebel. At the right spot we turned off the track and headed straight for the foot of the Jebel. Reaching the steep slope up from the desert, the trucks stopped, we piled out, dragged our heavy loads onto our backs and strung out in single file by troops, to make the climb of our lives.

There was no real track at the point we went up. We had seen air photos of the route, taken by a Gloster Meteor recce jet. The only photos I had seen were what are called 'nose-face' photos, taken by the nose cameras of an aircraft flying straight at the area to be photographed. So we had at least seen a view of the route, as seen from about 2,000 feet high over the desert as the aircraft flew towards the Jebel.

We knew we had to find our way more or less straight up the side of the Jebel, a climb of roughly 8,000 feet. The actual climb involved more than is apparent at first sight, as the air photos had not shown 'dead ground'. Somewhere about halfway up we had to climb down about 200 feet, almost sheer. Ropes had to be used, as climbing down in almost total darkness can be tricky. We couldn't see the bottom, or what sheer drops were below us.

Going up was not so bad, but the weight we were carrying began to tell about 2,000 feet from the top. Men began to collapse in their tracks. I saw two fall flat on their faces, unconscious before they hit the ground. Those of us who could kept going. We stopped for nothing. I personally could think of nothing except those machine-guns at the top – and the ball they would have when daylight came if we didn't get to them first.

Men who fell got to their feet again and staggered on. There is no greater spur to keep going than the thought of a gut full of ·50 calibre if you don't. When I reached the 'top' it was a false crest. Another sheer drop lay before us, but the main plateau was a relatively easy climb from the bottom of it. We could see the top of the plateau against the sky. It appeared to be not more than five or six hundred feet higher than our false crest, although it was difficult to judge in the dark as we were not sure how far away it was.

The cliff was only 40 or 50 feet but the first five or six of us to arrive hadn't a rope between us. The last 2,000 feet had been a matter of every man for himself, heading for the lowest point on the skyline ahead, as instructed.

There were no officers present with the first few at the top, but the decision was to consolidate at that false crest until more men arrived. It was obvious to everyone that the false crest had to be the enemy defence line, as it had a commanding view of the slopes we had climbed, as well as the final slope of the plateau.

Our surroundings were, of course, very dim outlines against the night sky. Distances were difficult to assess. We worked to build sangars in almost total darkness, and as silently as possible. Picking up loose rocks from all around I suddenly noticed I had got shit on my hands. I realised I was using rocks which had been used as covers by someone 'cat crapping'. I spread the word and almost immediately someone found a ·50 calibre machine-gun. It was on an anti-aircraft mounting, loaded and ready to go. There was no sign of the crew, so we carried on preparing our defences as more men arrived in ones, twos and threes.

Where there's one gun, there are usually more not far away. As our strength increased, men went silently searching among the great rocks and jagged outcrops all around. Someone with a rope had arrived, so we fixed the rope to get down the cliff and, as all of 'D' Squadron were now ready to go, 17, 18 and 19 Troops went on ahead leaving us to give covering fire if required, solve the problem of the machine-gun crew and any other problems in the enemy defence line.

Daylight started to creep across the landscape and we soon found the caves. They were on the cliff side of the ridge which formed the false crest, facing the main Jebel. Two of 16 Troop, George and Alex, went to sort out the lower cave. My patrol commander, Miley, and I approached the caves nearer the gun position. We waited for the daylight to strengthen, then moved in. The first two caves, not being deep, were easily checked. The third went well into the rock face. It was my turn to make the entry so I went in fast, prepared (I hoped) for anything. Nothing in the outer chamber, but the roof was low at the back and it looked like an inner chamber might yield something. I signalled Miley to go through as he was much smaller and would be able to cope better in the confined space. He did a fast check and found nothing except grass which looked like it was used as a bed.

As we came out of the cave a few shots rang out, then a grenade blew, so we knew Alex and George had found the gun crew. Alex had been climbing down to the cave and had almost reached the ledge in front of it, unable to use his rifle, when one of the enemy came out to stretch himself. Alex has always claimed George waited to the last split second before firing – just to give him a hard time!

With that one out of the way Alex pulled himself onto the ledge and put a grenade into the cave. That took care of the other occupants, the problem was solved.

That we had caught the opposition asleep, with no sentries or lookouts posted, no forward listening posts and – as we found later – pretty thin on the ground, was more proof of bad leadership. Presumably the main rebel force had been bluffed into the wrong defensive area by our tales to the donkey wallopers and deceitful daylight moves by the convoy of troop carriers, but it would have to be a very naive soldier who didn't have a 50 per cent stand-to during the hours of darkness when the enemy was obviously up to some new 'skulduggery'.

Our move up the almost sheer side of the Jebel had been much too noisy for our liking. We had sacrificed silence for speed. Although we had kept as quiet as possible there is no way a man can climb over loose rocks and shale, heave himself up rock slabs (and fall down a few) in almost total darkness with a heavy load and at the same time be both fast and quiet.

Alerted by the row Alex and George had made, another machine-gun crew got busy on us from about five or six hundred yards away. Luckily it was only a light machine-gun and its fire was almost ineffective. Nevertheless, being subjected to a hail of machine-gun fire in that terrain is a very noisy and off-putting experience. The bullets crackled overhead, banged ferociously against rocks and ricocheted noisily all over the place.

After the first few seconds some of our people were standing in the open, looking for the enemy gun position through binoculars. This was very off-putting to the gunner, who obviously could not see where all his fire was going. He started making wild 'corrections' which took most of the heat off us. We very quickly located him, near the top of a castle-like, sheer-sided pile of rock, above and to the east of our position. None of us had as yet fired a shot in that direction.

A half belt of ·30 calibre return fire by a couple of 16 Troop more or less cleared that problem, so that the enemy were reduced to the occasional nervous burst of fire when they thought no one was looking (that's how it seemed to us anyway). There were, I believe, a few other machine-gun positions put out of action by members of 'D' Squadron that night and early morning, but I saw nothing of them.

Daylight had shown us the edge of the main plateau was about eight hundred metres away and about six or seven hundred feet higher than our position. There was a flattish wadi between the foot of our cliff and where the last climb started, about two hundred metres away. From there a track showed clearly, climbing away up over the shoulder of the comparatively rolling hillside of the plateau.

Rory Walker had arrived, with a back pack like a young mountain. He decided to press on in company with his old troop. But his load was just too much for him to keep up as we belted off up onto the main plateau. Seeing the situation, I volunteered to stay back to keep an eye on him rather than see him left on his own, looking rather small and alone in the vastness of enemy territory. He caught up with me and we went on together awhile. Before clearing the last crest we stopped for a breather.

Looking back down to our last position, we could see 'A' Squadron had just started down the rope. What happened next was really comical. Two of their people were at the bottom of the rope, one was halfway down and another was just starting down, when that machine-gun fired another nervous, ineffective burst. One of the men at the bottom of the rope tried to go back up, the one at the middle tried to go back up, the one at the top slid down and demolished the lot at the bottom.

Then they started shooting in various directions. Rory and I looked at each other, then both slid around the rocks we were leaning against, to put them between us and 'A' Squadron.

Goldilocks must have been around somewhere as, soon after that, the Venoms appeared and blasted the machine-gun into eternal silence. The Venoms then attacked other positions along the enemy defence line, east and west of where we crossed it. Whether they were just hitting likely places or were being directed onto enemy positions I don't know. It is most likely they were being directed onto enemy positions found by 'A' Squadron as I had never seen them waste ammunition before. It was the last time I remember seeing the Venoms on that operation. The tearing roar of the rockets, their exploding crash, the crackling and crash of cannon fire and the occasional, rather pathetic sound of answering machine-gun fire along with the scream of the jets spoilt the calm silence of a beautiful morning, peculiar to high, wild places.

Rory and I plodded on and soon found 'D' Squadron, who were getting patrols organised to look for a fight. So far the expected battle had been a big fizzle. Rory did his thing with the air-drop markers and smoke grenades. The RAF came in right on the button with the first air drop. I have always felt sure those several supply drops that morning were more to do with winning that campaign than any other single factor.

The enemy listened to Radio Cairo, who claimed every other week that another British airborne brigade had been wiped out in Northern Oman. I can imagine the enemy lapping up all this heroic crap but knowing in their hearts they had not wiped out anything. Then the moment of truth when the sky over the plateau was thick with parachutes, load after load. To an enemy unfamiliar with

airborne operations it would have been obvious to all who weren't
real close to the air-drop that those airborne brigades Radio Cairo
thought they had wiped out were now arriving – en masse! So they
all ran away – and lived happily ever after – much to our disgust
after all the effort we had put into getting close to them.

Of course, at the time of the supply drop, we didn't know all that,
and were expecting a real battle to develop any minute. The crew
of one Hastings aircraft complained bitterly they were being shot at,
so off we went on patrols to find the culprits.

George, myself and a Bren gunner found a long cliff full of caves
– where we thought the ·50 calibre had fired from. We spent a
hairy half-hour going from one cave to the next, checking them out.
Checking a cave is a particularly tricky business. Anyone in the cave
has the obvious advantage of waiting comfortably in the dark
watching for the visitor to show up clearly in the entrance. There is
no way to enter a cave without making a beautiful target of yourself,
except by using explosives or smoke, or waiting for a very dark
night.

Then there is the problem of adjusting one's eyes to the darkness.
By the time your eyes are of any real use the opposition has had
about two minutes in which to fill you full of nasty little holes. We
didn't have the time to wait for a dark night.

There were at least thirty cave entrances to check, along a cliff
about 300 metres long. Explosives and smoke were a possibility but
we still had a war to fight and would likely need our grenades much
more urgently before it was finished. So, as usual, we leaned on
hard experience, fast reactions, teamwork and good old Lady Luck.
Experience has shown that a fast, awkward moving target is very
difficult to hit, especially when it arrives suddenly, even when half
expected.

The gamble on our side was (partly) that the first enemy shots
would not hit us, whereas our fast reaction to any gun flash would
– if not disabling the enemy – at least put us on more equal terms
for the vital split seconds which decided who lived and who didn't.

George and I took it in turn. That was the other part of the
gamble. Russian roulette with a different twist. Which one would
the fountain bless? Where there were defensive walls just inside the
cave entrance we would throw a grenade-size rock as we went in.

The Bren gunner's job was vital and tricky. Ideally he should be
in a position to fire into the cave if the first man was hit so that the
second man could pull his wounded comrade clear, or solve the

problem before the enemy gained the initiative. The Bren gunner was also responsible for the suppression of any interference from other quarters while his mates were busy. On this occasion our Bren gunner could not move too far forward without being at risk from other uncleared caves so he used the same tactics as a 'winger' on the football field, positioning himself to bounce them in off the 'far post'. In fact, with big caves that is by far the best method, when your own men are in trouble at the entrance. The machine-gun fire hitting the side wall sends a hail of ricochets and rock fragments into the cave and at the same time creates a pall of dust and smoke to cover the recovery of wounded and the follow-up grenading.

The caves we found that day varied considerably: some were very big at the entrance (10 to 15 feet high and 10 to 20 feet wide); others had a small entrance (4 or 5 feet square) but were quite big inside. Several had been recently used. Some had not been entered for perhaps years.

The first thing we checked for was recent tracks, human footprints in the dust. Some were so well used there was no dust in the entrance. Most of these had a defensive sangar at the entrance and another a few metres inside the cave. Very sweat-making! – hard on the adrenalin pump!

We would wait a few seconds listening for any tell-tale sound, sniffing for smoke or smell of scent; a final check that the other two were in position, then rush through the opening or dive over the wall or maybe roll across the floor towards a handy-looking bit of cover, depending on the set-up and what our nerves told us. There was another worry in our minds. We could barge in on a perfectly innocent shepherd family, hiding from the war. We had discussed this possibility briefly before starting and decided we would cross that bridge when we reached it, but in any case no chances were to be taken. 'If in doubt – lash out!'

We found nothing, and returned to the squadron position to find no one else had found anything either. About this stage in the game we heard 'A' Squadron had taken casualties following us up the mountain. A sniper had hit a grenade or rocket on a man's belt, killing him and the man behind him, and seriously wounding another man. We were jarred off to think there had to be casualties in the regiment when we had achieved so much without serious resistance.

I don't know if it was that day or the next that 'D' Squadron again moved out to look for the enemy. The first village we came to was named Habib. The houses were mostly very small, with only two or three small rooms, all at ground level. They were all built with mud and rock walls. Some had been patched with corrugated iron or tin sheets. I don't remember much about the roofs but I'm pretty sure they were mostly thatched or corrugated tin and almost flat. The buildings were crowded together in a small area about the size of a football field or smaller, as if huddling together for protection from the savage, jagged rockery all around. Their windows and doors were all very small, most windows being little more than slits in the walls. Very few had any glass in them, not because of the war, as there was no war damage that I could see, but because no glass had ever been put in them. Some had rough wooden shutters, others had nothing or were stuffed with sacking.

A few men were sent to have a quick check around the village but not many buildings were entered. We had no wish to enter people's homes if there was no reason, no threat to us. Most of the doors were closed but not locked, almost all were held shut by a rock or piece of wood leaning against the outside, as if to say, 'There's no one inside.' A few houses did not appear to have a door, just an empty black doorway. I personally saw none of our people enter a house. An empty house – or an empty village – has a certain feel about it. I had no 'tingles', no quickening of the pulse when I stepped into the village street.

My soldier's instincts told me there was no danger. Unexplainable. I didn't even think about it at the time but, long afterwards, thinking back, strange.

I crouched in a couple of doorways to check the interiors, not the way to operate if there is the slightest suspicion of danger. The reason for crouching was to let light enter through the doorway, which was the main source of interior light. That way I didn't have to enter the building and step clear of the doorway. Afterwards it seemed all the more remarkable when remembering it was the first village we had entered in enemy territory. It was completely deserted except for a big old brahma bull we found locked in a shed. He looked a bit hungry so we let him out to forage.

We had received '24-hour' pack rations on the air-drop. These were in a cardboard box which contained three separate meal packs, each marked with its intended place in the day: 'Breakfast', 'Snack' and 'Main Meal'. We were sitting well spread along a narrow 'street' in Habib, having a meal break. The bull came wandering up the 'street' and picked up an empty 'Snack' pack. I took a photo of it (since lost) with the word 'Snack' showing clearly like a speech balloon in a cartoon. It seemed to like 'compo' hard tack biscuits better though.

From Habib we moved on to Saiq, the main village on the Jebel, headquarters of the enemy. The move from the air-drop site to Habib was done in column, due to the terrain, but soon after leaving Habib we came to a wide open area covered in loose rocks and very low scrub. Expecting to hit heavy enemy resistance any minute the squadron spread out into a wide skirmish line with everyone right on his toes and ready for the first signs of trouble. I don't remember seeing anything of 'A' Squadron after leaving the air-drop site, so I don't know where they went. As far as I know, the forty-odd gun hands of 'D' Squadron were on their own.

I do remember someone saying, 'If they're ever going to hit us, it's got to be in the next thousand yards.' The further we went out across that comparatively open area the more I felt we were walking towards a helluva barney. By habit looking ahead for my next bit of cover, noting its position, then gazing all around – with a quick glance over my shoulder for good measure, reaching the rock or small depression I'd noted for cover, looking ahead for the next – and so on. We were all doing the same, looking for possible gun positions, any sign of movement, a glint of sun on metal. We looked for low mounds or slight depressions in the ground around us which would favour fast safe movement on all fours – or our bellies – if the need arose. It's too damn late to start looking once the good old brown has hit the fan. Our ears strained for the first crackle and screech of machine-gun fire, or the muffled bark of a mortar.

Nothing happened. Where were the five hundred well trained rebel troops? Where were the two thousand or more of savage mountain tribesmen? Surely someone would have to have a go at just forty of us?

Dirty, unshaven, our sweaty hands holding rifles or machine-guns, every now and then shoving a thumb under the cutting pack straps to ease the weight and prevent an arm from going numb, we plodded on. I think we all subconsciously wiped from our minds the maximum possible odds we could come up against. Allowing for a couple of thousand away on other business we could still be faced by odds of over sixty to one, but we had decided long ago the odds were never likely to be much more than ten to one, so there would be no problem.

No odds materialised. No one interfered with our walk in the sunshine. Nothing happened.

I think I can claim to be the first 'invading' soldier to see Saiq from the ground. I happened to be 'left winger' of 'D' Squadron when we approached the village, and stopped the squadron when I reported. John Watts came over to where I stood, on the edge of the wadi cliff, about 300 yards from the village. He said, 'That's Saiq, for sure.' Then he issued orders for the final approach and securing of the village.

Saiq too had been completely abandoned. Not a living thing in the place. I could 'feel' eyes though, from the rough and rugged ground surrounding us. The village was bigger than Habib, boasting several two storey buildings. It had been damaged by air attack during the last few months but not many buildings were badly damaged. The damage could all have been done by three or four rockets and a few dozen cannon shells. It was known that the rebel leaders had made it their headquarters, supposedly having bomb-proof caves somewhere north of the village. These had been the target for the heavy bombers which had, as far as I could see, not touched the village.

I was not involved in the house to house check through the village so did not see it all at close quarters, being one of two men sent to cover one of the routes out of the village. We saw no one, just a few chickens. Once the place had been checked we set up base (threw down our packs and got a radio working) on the south side of the wadi, opposite the village. The wadi was about fifty metres wide at that point, and only about twenty feet deep. We set up a loose defensive area with half-hearted sangars. There was no real need to entrench ourselves. If an enemy turned up, we would do the attacking, we would have to – to keep the initiative. In such small numbers, against heavy odds we could not turn ourselves into a compact target to be mortared and machine-gunned. There was natural cover everywhere around us, so we used it.

Patrols of two and three men were sent in all directions to check for signs of the enemy. Booby traps were a possibility, as were ambushes and mines, or combinations of all three. Miley and I checked a deep wadi just below the village. It looked well used and we soon found a large cave. Going through our familiar 'caving' routine we were soon inside, and getting our eyes accustomed to the darkness discovered we had hit the jackpot. The cave was full of weapons.

I don't remember the quantity of all the weapons, but I do remember counting twelve Bren guns, each with its box of magazines. There were a lot of ·50 calibre machine-guns, one or two mortars, and a lot of ammunition for everything. In the middle of the main chamber there was a pile of blankets, which suddenly moved. We were both on our nerve ends, moving very carefully, half expecting a hoard like this to be booby-trapped. When the blankets moved we both dropped and were in the aim at the point of movement.

A little whimpering sound came from the blankets. Miley stepped forward and quickly snatched the top blankets away. Imagine our complete amazement to find ourselves staring into the tearful eyes of a two-year-old girl. I quickly went past and checked the rest of the cave. Miley just stared at the kid. I don't think he realised his rifle muzzle was about six inches from her face. He was waiting for me to finish the check. When I found nothing he moved the rifle and clicked the safety on.

We got out of the cave, Miley carrying the child. A supply drop was just coming in by the village. The child was obviously terrified of the aircraft. We calmed her down and gave her some sweets from the rations we carried. By the time we had climbed up out of the wadi she had, as children do, accepted the new situation, laughing and pointing at the coloured parachutes floating down nearby.

Up on the flat ground again we met Bob, a corporal in 18 Troop. We had a quick conference and it was decided the best thing for all concerned was for the child to be returned to her mother as soon as possible. Bob said he thought he had seen some civilians about 600 yards down the slope, south of the village. We went about 200 yards in that direction, Miley carrying the child.

At the top of the slope we stopped. It was decided Bob and Miley would leave their rifles with me and take the child to the bottom of the slope where there was rough ground, huge rocks, a few scrub trees. I complained there was little I could do to cover them at that range but they thought it was a risk which had to be taken.

When Bob and Miley were about 200 yards from me, a woman ran from behind a big rock, then ran back out of sight again. Bob and Miley went another hundred yards towards where the woman had shown herself, then stopped. Bob lifted the child up in the air, then put her down gently on a big flat rock. They then turned and walked slowly back up the slope. When they were halfway back to me a woman ran from behind the big rock, collected the child and bolted back again.

As Bob and Miley rejoined me, we could see several people now standing beyond the rock, looking towards us. We waved to them, then walked back towards Saiq. Ten minutes after we arrived back at the squadron position, a dozen people, women and old men, came to us from down the slope. They were welcomed, offered water and food.

Within twenty minutes forty people had come up the slope, were with us, and looking very relieved it was all over. They had had a hard time, with the ever present threat of air attack. The village had been strafed several times over the past months. It seems no-one learned much from Hermann Goering's experience. Governments and top brass alike still think people can be subdued by air power.

The facts of life are much different. People are more likely to be alienated by air attacks. The only way to take ground is to put upon it a man in the right uniform, with a gun in his hand. Bombs cannot discriminate as a soldier can – between an enemy soldier and a little girl for instance.

Some of the civilians went out into the countryside to bring in others who had been too frightened to return to their homes. By evening the people were allowed to return to the village. We were beginning to realise there was to be no final showdown. The enemy had been defeated with a minimum of bloodshed.

Just north of the village, about 400 yards up the wadi, was a big cave with a small entrance. It was the bombproof hideaway of one of the rebel leaders. Our patrol was given the task of searching it and keeping everyone well away from it. The cave contained a lot of paper records which, we heard afterwards, incriminated a lot of people who had been playing both ends against the middle. It also contained weapons, ammunition and money (Austrian 'Maria Theresa' dollars) as well as rich household effects.

We were rather amused at the way the locals tried to get our permission to enter the cave. First an old man came and pleaded almost tearfully for us to let him enter. Then another old man who walked imperiously with a stick. He glared at us and tried to push past us, demanding to be allowed into the cave. Finally flourishing his stick in our faces, ranting and raving, almost frothing at the mouth. Then stamping off back to the village with many backward glances and cutting motions with the stick. I think he could easily have bitten a wire nail in half.

Our next callers were two typical 'mothers-in-law'. Smiling at first, but soon working up to screaming obvious abuse and even trying physically to push into the cave. They had obviously twigged we were harmless to civilians who didn't carry guns. Their shrill ranting could easily have changed my mind though!

The last try was the best. Just before dusk three people appeared, approaching up the wadi. The larger of the three figures, a woman, sat on a rock about one hundred metres from us. After a short conference, which we couldn't hear, the other two came to us and signalled they wanted into the cave. They were two young teenage girls, reasonably smooth, all big eyes and flashing teeth. We had to laugh at their antics to get past us, but they were no Mata Haris, just two good looking kids who had been elected to crack the problem.

When they got no change, they giggled at one another and looked back towards the black-clad lady on the rock, who screamed something at them which obviously meant 'keep trying'. When they still failed to get past us they sobered up quite a bit and went back to mum, or whoever she was, where they got a good ticking off by the sound of it, then the whole party withdrew, slowly towards the village in the gathering dusk.

There were more tries the next day with at least one old man and two or three women who came at different times, alone. No one cracked it while we were there, but full marks for trying.

A few days after taking the villages 'D' Squadron marched down off the Jebel. We had been told as soon as the fighting was finished we would be sent back to UK. The operations in Malaya were now over, and the regiment was to be based in UK for the first time. But the plans of mice and men, etc. We were fated to remain in Oman a further five or six weeks. The squadron did what was called 'flag marches'. A typical bloody waste of energy, plodding to and fro over the Jebel in a so-called show of strength. It pleased the brass no doubt, but the troggery, who continually pull the top brass's chestnuts out of the fire by their sheer guts and determination are not at all keen on flogging up 'empty' mountains. Especially ones they have just 'emptied'. There would have been a lot more people impressed if the vast army of brass had waddled its way up and down a few times instead of doing it all by helicopter. They might just have appreciated what it was like to nip up 8,000 feet on a dark night in about six hours with over 100 lb of kit. Don't know what I'm bitching about anyway, I got myself a stomach infection and never did the 'flag marches'. Instead, I was employed at Bait el Falage, helping with the trucks, issuing petrol, etc. A lousy job, in a lousy place – but still better than flogging up empty mountains!

A British cemetery was organised at our camp, to take the bodies of our men killed on operations. While it was being built someone pinched the truck I was using to shift petrol, and left it parked in the cemetery. I collected the truck, and as I approached the gateway coming out, a child ran through the opening in front of me causing me to swerve and hit the gatepost. The gatepost was made of concrete, about two feet thick, but the impact toppled it. The truck was hardly marked.

The 'A' Squadron set-up, which was running the base, decided I had to be charged over the cemetery gate affair. So, next day, I was on the mat. No one had asked me anything about the accident so I had no chance to explain anything. 'A' Squadron sergeant-major marched me in with great glee. The charge was read. It was a cock-up! I was charged with 'taking an army vehicle without permission'. After checking with the MT Office, they were all at sea as to what to do and eventually told me to get out of the office. That was the last I heard of it.

By the time we left Muscat and Oman we were all damn glad to go. Not because of the operations, but because of the stupidities which followed them.

One thing which may puzzle the reader who has any knowledge of military formations and minor tactics is the fact that we often operated in twos and threes, although the basic patrol is based on four men. In fact, the four-man patrol has been proved many times to be the ideal group for most SAS operations. In Northern Oman we were organised in four-man patrols, and those patrols, as far as I know, remained the same through the operation. But the SAS is such that through training and operational experience almost any two or three men can work extremely well together, especially men from the same squadron. So, when you are up against long odds the tendency is to use smaller groups (of two or three), on jobs they can cope with, so as to give a wider spread, cover more ground, do more jobs. Of the men named in the Oman operation only Miley and I were in the same patrol.

In the situation where I was left lagging behind, a long way, with the village idiot and his donkey, for instance, other members of 16 Troop kept an eye on our progress and, often, on looking up to the skyline above, I would see the welcome sight of one of them watching to check there was no problem. They would give a wave of a hand to say all was well with my surroundings, which they could obviously see much better than I could. An answering wave and they would disappear, then someone would appear much further up the mountain a few minutes later. This was not pre-arranged, just common sense.

Most of 'D' Squadron people, including the squadron commander, had occasion to move around on their own during the operation, both in daylight and in darkness. Sometimes there was a calculated risk, usually the risk was negligible. The where, when and how is a matter of professional know-how.

CHAPTER SIX

The World at Large

The operations in Oman had lasted from November 1958 to January 1959. During that time my wife, whom I had left at our home in Malaya, had no idea where we had gone. Duke's death somehow got into the national press, so those we had left in Malaya knew we were in a shooting war, but only that it was somewhere in the Middle East – which covered a multitude of sins.

Rumours that four of us had been killed, including John Watts and myself, were quickly stamped on by HQ 22 SAS in KL, but not before Ann had suffered some aggro. After several weeks, Ann was told I would not be returning to Malaya so she was to pack all our household kit and prepare to return to UK. Packing-cases were supplied. My friend and his wife, who then lived next door, helped with the packing. Having been put off flying by a rough ride on the last leg of her flight out to Singapore, Ann opted for a sea passage home and really enjoyed it!

'D' Squadron returned to UK in March 1959, and enjoyed a couple of weeks' leave. Our new base was at Merebrook Camp, Malvern. It was a rather tatty old wartime camp, of the usual pattern: a few brick-built administration buildings, a lot of wooden huts.

The first day after returning from leave we did a twelve-mile route march with 50 lb of kit in our rucksacks. We marched on roads. Practically the whole squadron was crippled with blisters and other problems. It struck us all as rather stupid that we who could cope with some of the roughest terrain in the world, with no one (that I know of) falling sick or raising a blister, could be destroyed by a bit of a walk on roads. We didn't even walk up the Malvern Hills; the route march was all on fairly level roads, east of Malvern. Later, when we tackled the Welsh mountains with heavier packs over much greater distances we came into our own again. I don't think any of us will ever forget the disaster of marching on roads.

At Malvern we were inundated with a plague of clowns. It wasn't so much their numbers as the positions of power they held. They caused a lot of problems, some of which dogged the SAS for years afterwards. The most memorable of these problems was known as 'bubbling RVs'. No, not a rendezvous in a bubble bath. If you were 'bubbled', you were betrayed to the enemy. If, on exercise, your RV was 'bubbled' the 'enemy' would be in ambush there. Then you usually spent the rest of the exercise being interrogated, and having a hard time in general.

Because we were mostly very experienced under field conditions we were not easily captured on exercises, so some clown – or clowns – decided it would be a good idea to get us captured, partly to get us the experience of quite nasty interrogation, partly to give the interrogation teams more work.

The troggery learns those lessons quickly, and takes a long time to forget them! For years after that period no SAS patrol would give its correct position on exercises. Elaborate evasion tactics were used in relation to all RVs. Troops and patrols made a habit of fixing RVs at least 1,000 yards from any which were sent by radio. An RV which was known to HQ was always avoided like the plague. It got so even our own people couldn't find us.

One clown came to North Africa with the squadron, on our first desert training session. He couldn't really navigate but was a good pretender. We spent all one morning driving in a straight line out into the desert, everyone eating the dust of the truck in front. Then we spent all afternoon driving in a straight line back to base, again eating dust. I think he was afraid of getting lost.

Another clown who came with us at the same time insisted we should have our kit laid out on our beds when we were in base for a day or two. He actually charged a friend of mine for having his PT shoes the wrong way around on his bed. Heard a good story about that one after he went back to his unit. According to the tale, he was in charge of some missiles somewhere in West Germany, and when an inspecting team arrived unexpectedly one day, they found he had all his missiles aimed on a back bearing. They were pointing at Paris or somewhere like that. For which the clown got the boot from the Army. Probably wishful thinking, but it makes a happy ending for a lot of people.

As far as I remember, it was at Malvern 'the crab' first appeared. It was, I believe, 'A' Squadron's answer to our 'one-legged chicken'. The 'one-legged chicken' was what was stamped on all military equipment, leaving the well-known broad arrow everywhere it went. It only lasted a few months before being superseded by 'the crab', whose source I know not.

The 'one-legged chicken' had many notable achievements, one of which was when its tracks were found leading into the Operations Centre, into the Ops Officers' Office and into that holy of holies – the Top Secret Safe. Where it laid an egg (real, large, brown and broken) with the word 'oops!' chalked alongside. It had achieved that escapade in the dead of night – much to the horror of those responsible for the security of the Ops Centre and all its contents.

There were many types of crab at first. They all consisted of a simple drawing, an oval shape with six or eight legs, with a word or name in the middle. The difference being only in what was written. The challenge of the crab was to appear, large or small, in the most unusual or embarrassing places. It didn't leave tracks – just appeared. Like the 'one-legged chicken', the crab often pointed out cracks in the security system by appearing where there was no way it could. A few crab examples are worth mention.

The regiment went to Hildesheim in Germany for training. Being too crippled at the time to parachute at night, I was sent on the advance party, by train and sea. We had a lot of time to kill between trains in London, and were in a mixture of recumbent postures on a platform at Liverpool Street Station.

Someone got bored. Crabs started to appear. The Military Police on duty at the station took exception to 'The next train from this platform will be the "Sex Crab" to Reading', etc. So two burly MP sergeants came stamping over to us to find the culprit. Needless to say, no culprits were found, but those two nearly had a fit when they noticed their boots after they walked away. On each of their highly polished toe-caps was a miniature crab.

At Hildesheim we were based in a barracks occupied by an artillery unit. In the barracks there was a fairly tall aerial mast, about one hundred feet high, I think. As daylight broke one morning, a huge cardboard box was to be seen at the top of the aerial. On each of its four sides was painted a huge crab.

Years later, talking to the gent who had been our RSM at Hildesheim, he told me that when he first saw it he grabbed the first SAS soldier he saw and sent him up there to get the box down. The man did so, without the slightest hesitation. It wasn't until after he had disappeared into the mess hall that the RSM realised it was probably the very man who had put it up there. There weren't many who would climb a thing like that.

One of the most famous crabs was on the end of a runway at Bahrein airport. It was so big, pilots claimed they could see it from eighty miles away on their approach to Bahrein.

Higher authority, often the target of the crab, eventually managed to fade it out – or perhaps it got 'demobbed'.

The regiment spent about a year at Malvern. It was a year of catching up on all those skills which are so much taken for granted now, but which up to that time had not been essential to the operational requirement, so had mostly not been touched. There were suddenly courses galore. No troop was ever at full strength, there were always several members away on courses of one kind or another. Although most of us could drive, very few had British driving licences so a massive driver training programme was instigated to put that situation to rights.

Long, flogging exercises in Wales seemed to fill in all the gaps. We hoofed from one end of Wales to the other, and back again carrying vast loads as usual, but now aggravated by extra radios, a lot more machine-guns (Brens and ·30 calibre Brownings) with piles of ammunition.

Parachuting became an ever present threat to the smooth running of everything else. Being a very bad parachutist, I could never see the sense in jumping just for the sake of it. My landings were always hard and fast. I had what I called my dish-cloth technique. I landed like a dish-cloth – splatt! There was no chance of doing the much vaunted parachute roll. I did all the things I had been trained to do. It never seemed to make any difference. I rolled all right but there was nothing controlled about it.

My first injury came in 1959 at Weston-on-the-Green, near Oxford. It was another jump for nothing of course. As I descended faster than most there was always the danger of pulling one of the other people in on top of my chute. It had happened before but at a height where things could be sorted out. This time I knew nothing about it. People who saw it happen say my parachute was completely collapsed by someone crashing down on it about fifty feet from the ground. All I remember was thinking, 'Here comes another fast landing.'

I was knocked unconscious by the landing and when I came to, the man who had collapsed my canopy was bent over me apologising. That was the first I knew of anything wrong with the landing. Nothing was broken but I had badly torn a lot of muscle in my stomach, groin and thighs. I walked off the DZ with a burning sensation where the muscles were damaged, and didn't get the full effect until it had all gone stiff during the truck ride back to Malvern.

The MO gave me the next day off, then I did my best to join in with training as I didn't want to miss out on anything. That injury played me up for months, whereas if I had rested it in the first place it's likely it would have mended in a week or two. On the other hand, if we hadn't done that stupid jump for nothing!

My second parachuting injury came after the regiment moved to Hereford in 1960. We had an aircraft available for a day or two, using an old airfield at Madley, near Hereford, for the aircraft and jumping onto the Lugg Meadows, east of Hereford. On my second jump I had an extra fast landing, ploughing up the turf as usual, but also busting two rivets out of my steel helmet. This time it was only concussion, and, although I never knew it at the time, a hairline fracture to the base of the skull. I was over the concussion after a couple of days but suffered loss of memory on occasion for a long time afterwards.

One of those memory lapses was worrying. I had gone into town to buy something, driving my car as usual. I returned home, as I thought, only realising something was wrong when I found the drive gates closed, different curtains at the windows – and realised I didn't live there any more. I drove away, parked and sat there trying to remember where we lived. We had moved several months – maybe a year – previously. I knew who I was and everything else, except where my home was.

After half an hour of searching my pockets, the car and my memory I hit on a plan. I decided I would get my address from the duty clerk at the camp. Luckily for me it all came back as I crossed the old Wye Bridge. Only my wife ever knew about that one.

I was knocked unconscious on several parachute jumps before I was saved by the introduction of the PX parachute in 1962 or 1963. I think the old X-type parachute just about kept me upright, whereas the PX actually slowed me down as well.

The regiment moved from Malvern to Hereford in 1960. Before we made the move Ann had become so pregnant we had to exchange the bike for a car. It always amazed me that she, who never batted an eyelid at speeds in excess of 100 mph on a motor-cycle, got into a right panic at anything over 30 mph in a car!

Soon after the move to Hereford, 'D' Squadron went to Kenya for two or three months. We were based at Nanyuki, which, although on the equator, is elevated enough to be quite pleasant, temperature-wise.

Kenya had been the scene of some particularly nasty terrorist activities during the 1950s, when the Mau Mau uprising took place. By the time we went there, however, the problem had been solved more or less to everyone's satisfaction and 'peace had been declared'. Nevertheless, a few of the hardcore terrorists, mostly those wanted for murder and other atrocities committed during the Mau Mau troubles, were still known to be semi-active and hiding in the bush, notably in the denser bush and jungle on the Aberdare mountains. There was very little chance of our making any contact with the terrorists on our training but it did give an extra kick to things when we were working in the Aberdares.

One of the first things I remember at Nanyuki was the flu epidemic. Asian flu had struck in the UK. Two of the squadron had it when we flew out to Kenya. A week after being shut in an aircraft with them we all had it! All training came to a grinding halt.

During that week or two, while the squadron was more or less laid up, I went on a snake hunt around the camp perimeter. The MO had said he would be interested in any snakes we might find. I found a snake and, with help from a friend, caught it and took it to the MO. He was not too grateful, as it turned out to be a rather large puff adder, reputed to be very dangerous in the venom department.

'D' Squadron was very fortunate to have in Kenya one of the best squadron commanders, Major John Slim, whose forward thinking and strong faith in the men he commanded was to make a long lasting impression on the whole regiment.

We threw away the book on jungle experience gained in Malaya and started with a clean sheet. We tried new ideas in the African jungle, some of which were old ideas not usable in the Malayan jungle. Nothing was taken for granted. The squadron didn't waste any time in Kenya. Some things worked, some didn't, but mostly we finished up knowing which would and which wouldn't.

We tried marching through bush on the slopes of Mount Kenya at night. Part of our route was through fairly open bush, part was through quite dense jungle. A lot of heavy, ground-shaking animals were disturbed that night, but I have no idea what they were. One small incident, however, put me off night movement in thick jungle. We were moving fairly quickly so were not very quiet at the time. I was leading scout. Suddenly the ground gave way under my feet and I fell forward. Luckily for me the sling on the machine-gun I was carrying caught on something and I hung onto the gun. When the other people reached me I was dangling in space over a good forty-foot drop to jagged rocks. It was a ravine about twelve feet wide with a tiny stream at the bottom.

Every morning when we were in camp we had PT (physical training) before breakfast. Half was normal Army PT, the second half was always unarmed combat training. Morning PT became interesting.

In a bomb crater, on the slopes of Mount Kenya, we built a 'house' with sandbags and this, as far as I know, was the first ever CQB (Close Quarter Battle) House for 22 SAS. Although the 'Grant Tyler' methods with which we were trained in Kenya have long since been superseded by continually improving, better methods, it was a good start to CQB shooting and was the start of the regiment's ability to successfully go into places like the famous embassy in London.

The Aberdare forest in Kenya was one of the worst jungle areas I have ever seen. The trees are often not dense enough to keep out the hot sun. Attap, the curse of Malayan jungles, was not present but was more than made up for by – would anyone believe? – blackberry brambles and monster stinging-nettles! We seemed to wade through oceans of tearing, stinging mixture of them.

There is also a lot of uphill in the Aberdares. 16 Troop never claimed to be the world's lightest sleepers, but very little moved near us at night without all or most of us knowing about it. We were all a bit shamefaced one morning in the Aberdares though. Two or three elephants had walked through our deep jungle camp in the night – and no one had heard a thing. The great footprints were there for all to see in the morning. Someone claimed it was those bloody nettles had drugged us.

Most of us came face to face with big wildlife at some time or another in Kenya. None of us seemed to get the urge to shoot them though. I was leading scout for the troop most of the time. All leading scouts carried Bren guns, because of the possibilities of upsetting the wildlife. Our reasonably quiet movement caused us to come up on the animals rather unexpectedly but, as far as I know, there was never any cause to use weapons. If the animal didn't back off after a few seconds of 'eyeball to eyeball', we walked quietly around them. There seemed to be a sort of mutual respect. It was cowardly on my part really, as it's easy to walk round huge unarmed animals when you have a relatively powerful machine-gun in your hands.

The more I saw of the wildlife in Africa the less respect I had for the so-called 'big game' hunters. The animals are so easy to shoot, it's pathetic that anyone could take pleasure from it. A mother elephant running foward to put herself between her calf and possible danger can be a bit unnerving, but we had to respect the normal maternal instincts. Just standing still, making no threat, is usually enough to satisfy the great animal there is no danger.

There is only one 'big game' worth shooting, and that's the one who shoots back. For voicing those sentiments and stating it would be more difficult – and raise more interesting reactions – to shoot cows in a field back home, two of us were politely requested to leave the bar of the Equator Hotel, near Nanyuki. The bar was about half full of 'big game' wounders at the time. I think the management were worried about damages.

A couple of weeks before the squadron was due to return to UK from Kenya, a message came saying Ann was having problems having our first child, so I was flown home right away. In the event, there was no problem with the birth, but the doc said it was because I had arrived home. For all the help I was, I think he was joking.

So now I had a son, and a lance-corporal stripe (which had somehow arrived in Kenya). Things were getting more complicated.

Although we were based in Hereford, we hardly saw the place. 'B' Squadron had been disbanded after the regiment reached Malvern, so now there were only two operational squadrons. The two 'Sabre' Squadrons rarely saw each other. It was very seldom we were both in base at the same time. In fact, as I remember it, it was very seldom any of us were in the Hereford Base.

During one of our many exercises in Wales there was a small 'happening' which I cannot leave to be lost in the mists of time. We were using a military establishment at Towyn in North Wales, as an exercise base and interrogation centre. The place was also the base of a boys' regiment (artillery I believe) and on the day of one of their passing out parades, when all the proud mums and dads had come to watch their smart lads on parade, one of our lot made a bid for freedom from the interrogation centre.

Imagine the distraction for the proud parents as this dishevelled, unshaven apparition, smartly turned out in his underpants (known in the Army as 'drawers dracula'), sprinted across the parade ground, hotly pursued by several irate gentlemen dressed in 'Eastern Bloc' uniforms (red stars and all!) waving Russian sub-machine guns. I would have hated the job of explaining that lot.

In that period between returning to UK in 1959 and about

mid-1962 we spent all our time living out of rucksacks or suitcases. As an example of this continual bouncing from one job or place to another, I have always remembered the first seven or eight months of 1962. In those few months I saw thirteen foreign countries, and later that year I went to Scotland for the first time in my life.

Some of the training we did was a dreary flog but most was interesting, often challenging. One such challenging session was our first exercise in Denmark. In my case it was more so as it was the first big exercise I had as a patrol commander, and with very little time to prepare as I only arrived back in Hereford the day before we left for Denmark.

Four of us had been sent to the Snowdon area in North Wales to advise and help train the Staffordshire Regiment in mountain warfare. We arrived back in Hereford expecting a few days with our families. I was sent for by the squadron commander and told I would be taking a patrol to Denmark the next day.

There followed an intensive briefing with piles of maps, air photos and sketches. The next day we flew to Sylt, an island off the Danish coast. The following night we parachuted onto the mainland. It was one of the few times when my blind faith in the RAF was shaken. There were five of us in the patrol, a Marine Commando had been sent with us for some obscure reason. ('Obscure' because he was a frogman, and my target was nowhere near any water!) Perhaps the navigator mistook metres for feet, I don't know, but we were dropped from three hundred feet. Only two of the patrol had released their equipment before we hit the ground. Luckily for us the Drop Zone was covered in thick springy heather so no one came to much harm. A few bruises and a bit of a shaking was all. Being a supreme coward I had released my kit just in time. When you are jumping into a black void and can't see a damn thing there's no sense in taking chances.

The main purpose of the exercise was to test the Danish defences, who certainly made life difficult. But, with a liberal helping of good luck, we managed to hit our target right on the button and get clean away. Not all the patrols were as lucky and some spent a few days not enjoying some very nasty interrogation. The interrogators were Brits, specially sent over for the job. They were – to say the least – most unkind. The training was for them as well as us, and they made the most of it.

One of the most memorable training stints was in Oman. The one thing which stood out above all others to make that trip memorable was Charlie, a gifted trooper in 16 Troop. We were based at Ibri in Northern Oman, and the accent was on desert training with vehicles. The vehicle we used on that trip were mostly Austin K9 one-ton trucks, plus a few Morris 'Commercials', which were also one-tonners.

We perfected our desert navigation techniques and learnt how to get vehicles over any desert terrain. The training was hard work but very enjoyable, as can be imagined. It was all very hit and miss at first, but after hours spent digging out trucks we soon learnt how to recognise soft sand and how to cope with it.

Sharing our camp at Ibri was an 'old' sergeant, or staff sergeant, in the Royal Engineers. His job was to drive along all the roads in his area every day, in a specially equipped but very battered Land-Rover, checking for mines and lifting any he found.

How he got away with it I've no idea. The detection part of the equipment was held out in front of the Land-Rover, about twelve feet from the radiator on tubular steel poles, when it passed over a mine it flashed a warning light in the vehicle. But the Engineer bloke drove at about thirty to forty miles per hour. There was no way he could stop in twelve feet. A lot of our people claimed he was only twenty-one – it was his job which gave him white hair and made him look forty-odd! His two or three rows of World War II campaign ribbons must have meant something though.

I don't know where he was the morning one of our trucks drove out of the camp and hit a mine, twenty metres from the gate. One of our people, a passenger in the cab, thought they had a tyre blow (so he claimed), until he saw the three-foot deep crater in the road and bits of wheel, etc., scattered around the area. Being only about forty metres away, cleaning my teeth, I got showered in gravel and nearly swallowed my toothbrush. A few trucks were blown up on mines laid by the local rebels, but no one was seriously injured so all it did was add a bit of spice to the trip.

Charlie has been called a genius. He was – at the very least – a superb mechanic. His mechanical exploits on that trip to Oman were legendary in the SAS. I can't pretend I knew what he did, or how Charlie solved our problems but we all saw him perform – what were to us – miracles. He had less desert experience than most of us, so had not had to solve these problems before.

One of the first things he showed us was that because water cannot be compressed, a one-ton truck could be jacked up on a full jerrican of water. This helped us a lot as solid, strong load spreaders to put under a jack in soft sand are not easily found in the areas where they are most required. We tried it with full jerricans of petrol, or at least Charlie did, while we stood at a very safe distance. It worked, but, because petrol can be compressed, the jerrican looked a bit sick afterwards. Not recommended! The jerrican has to be opened with extreme care if the petrol is required later.

In the intense heat of the desert the trucks were continually stopping owing to lack of petrol reaching the carburettor. At least, that's what Charlie decided. After a day or two wrestling with the problem he decided drastic action was the only answer. We were a couple of hundred miles from base and Charlie had only his toolbox to work from. Somehow he drilled the filler cap on one of the Austins, and fitted an air valve. Then rigged an air line from the spare wheel so that air pressure went to the fuel tank and pushed the fuel through faster to the engine. He did other things, I suppose, to make it work, and it did. Charlie's modified truck had no more problems.

The only problem was spare wheels. The more distance we put in, the more punctures we had, so Charlie decided the system needed a re-think. His eventual solution was to pressurise the fuel tanks by pumping air directly into them. We watched from the safety of a distant sand dune as Charlie went to work. We saw him drive the truck madly around, this way and that, for a while to test it. Then he came over to us. His pressurised fuel tank had changed shape. It was now very rounded, bulging as if about to explode. Charlie assured us it was all safe enough, and proceeded to modify all the troop vehicles. It worked really well and only needed more air twice every day during constant travel. That was easy compared to breaking down every ten to fifteen minutes.

Charlie's real stroke of genius came at the end of that trip to Oman. His endless search for better ways to do this or that made life a little uncertain at times, occasionally landed us all in trouble but was well loaded on the credit side.

We were to be flown out to Bahrein aboard a RAF Beverly from a patch of desert near Ibri. The Beverly was an awkward-looking four-engined aircraft which always appeared (to me at least) to defy all the laws of gravity and aerodynamics, but it could land or take off almost anywhere. Our Beverly landed OK, then taxied to where we were waiting to climb aboard. As was normal practice, three engines where shut down and one left running, so as to start the others when required. The engine which had been left running suddenly gave a couple of 'splutters', then stopped.

There was a sudden great silence. We realised, without being told, there was no way that Beverly could start itself. The aircrew said they would radio for a starter to be flown from Bahrein, but it would be unlikely to reach us before the next day. Breakdowns and delays never happened coming out, but we were quite used to problems when returning to UK, so we resigned ourselves to another night in the desert.

Charlie had a chat to the RAF flight engineer, then rushed off in a Land-Rover. Word spread that Charlie had an idea. I had a quick vision of the aircrew standing around the burning wreck – but quickly dismissed it as pessimistic thinking. Charlie returned with a lot of telephone wire plus a 'few odds and ends'. He and the flight engineer climbed into the aircraft.

After a few minutes Charlie emerged and got to work on two Land-Rovers, wire going in all directions. Then, with the ends of a lot of wire in both hands, he climbed back into the aircraft. A few minutes later he appeared in the doorway and signalled the drivers to start the Land-Rovers. They started up and revved the engines hard. When he was satisfied with the noise Charlie turned and gave the 'thumbs up' to the flight engineer, somewhere inside the aircraft. The next thing, an engine turned over, fired, and started. The engine noise was nearly drowned by the cheering.

Part of our training for desert vehicle-borne operations was taking part in a squadron exercise, which involved all patrols making an RV somewhere a long way out in the desert, then moving as a squadron to put in a night attack on the Fahud Bowl. The Fahud Bowl is a large circle of rocky hills, the remains of a volcano, sand on the inside, sand on the outside, several miles across.

The 'navigators' among us, notably a couple of the troop sergeants, were, I considered, smack on target as we started our approach from perhaps forty or fifty miles out in the desert. We maintained a good speed over mostly gravel plain. All was going according to plan when the clown running the show (not the squadron commander, who was elsewhere) suddenly decided he could see the black jagged outline of Fahud away to the left of our approach bearing.

The squadron came to a halt. There was a quick 'Chinese Parliament' with all the good navigators insisting on maintaining our previous direction and the clown insisting we turn towards the black outline on the horizon. The clown, of course, won.

The incident was long remembered as 'the time so-and-so tried to put in a squadron attack on a cloud bank'. Nevertheless, that particular clown impressed me a great deal that night – by being able to laugh at his own mistake and call himself a 'bloody fool' in front of the squadron. A clown who is a 'bloody fool' and not afraid to admit it to his fellow men is a great improvement on the usual run of the mill.

That particular clown has since become a damn good soldier, impressing a lot of people with his sheer guts and determination. If there are any qualified to write a book on what makes things 'tick' in the SAS, then he must surely be one of the few.

During that trip to Oman there was some problem over the Baraimi Oasis, which is on the border of Northern Oman, and had been a disputed territory for many years. Saudi Arabia had some idea of taking over the Omani territory and possibly the Trucial States territory, thereby claiming the whole of Baraimi Oasis which was, and probably still is, shared by all three countries. I never knew all the 'ins and outs' of the situation but someone called us in to help out.

A large contingent of the Saudi Army had arrived at Baraimi to back up their claim, so some of us, I think about two troops, were asked to make like a large military force in the desert about two miles east of Baraimi.

We had about eight trucks and less than thirty men but we went to work with a will, drove like hell all over the place making huge clouds of dust when we arrived, then keeping up the dust cloud until dark. We then got all the tommy-cookers we could spare and made dozens of little camp fires all along a low ridge so they could be seen by the opposition.

Next day the Saudi unit had gone, so we went off and got on with our training. Whether or not we had any effect on the situation I never heard.

Some of our people went off to get experience of desert patrolling on camels, something I had no ambitions with. I like animals, but for some reason I could never get on well with camels. Luckily I didn't get 'volunteered' for the camel patrols and instead was sent with two trucks to check on a salt mine in the desert, about two hundred miles south of our base. Having no idea what a salt mine looked like, or consisted of, we used our imagination and, of course, got it all wrong.

Arriving at the correct latitude and longitude we could see nothing in the way of mining activity, so did a lot of searching around in a vast expanse of hot, flat desert. There were two or three small rocky hills in the area, a few miles apart, so two of us climbed the largest one (about 300 feet) with the idea of getting a good look around with our binoculars for the elusive salt mine.

Reaching the top of the hill we found it was hollow, like a volcano, and there was the salt mine. It was at the bottom of the 'volcano'. The miners were three old men and a camel. They were mining rock salt, and not very much at a time. Every few days they sent out a load of salt on the camel, which brought back their supplies of food and water on its return. They were a long way from any habitation and I couldn't help thinking it would be rough on them if the camel broke down on one of its trips.

There was a crack in the side of the hill, through which the camel could just squeeze when loaded. The desert wind hid the occasional tracks made in the sand, so making it one of the best-hidden salt mines in the world. No wonder we had problems finding it.

On one of our trips to the Persian Gulf area someone bogged up the aircraft booking and didn't have enough seats in the aircraft to fly home the whole squadron. It was just before Christmas, and there were hopes of getting Christmas at home.

The squadron commander decided we would draw lots for which troop stayed at Bahrein. So the four troop commanders (I must have been a sergeant by then) drew straws and, as usual, I lost. The troop was disgusted but that didn't help, so off went the squadron – with a lot of cracks about saving us some Easter eggs – leaving us to find our way home any way we could.

I went to the RAF types who know all the answers about what flies to where. They got us fixed up with a lift that night, on the 'milk run' Comet. The only snag was it was via Aden, Khartoum and Malta – the long way home – and would take two days. When we arrived in Aden, the aircrew realised we couldn't land at Khartoum in uniform, so we either got civvy clothes or took our chances on another aircraft from Aden. We had about half an hour to solve the problem.

We were all stood near the passenger terminal building, stony broke and taxing our tiny minds for a solution when it came walking right up to us. An aircraft from UK had just landed, bringing dozens of white-faced young lads for their first tour of overseas duty. And they were all in civvy clothes! I don't know what happened but suddenly we were back on the Comet in rather tattered civvies.

The best of that story was us getting home days before the rest of the squadron. Their aircraft developed a problem, and they spent four days in El Adam, or somewhere beautiful.

The regiment was into the business of exploring all possible types of military operations and free-fall parachuting was beginning to catch on. My friend Keith, the shotgun artist, was killed on Salisbury Plain when the regiment took the British high altitude free-fall record. He didn't pull his rip-cord. No one seems to know why. In memory of Keith a clock was purchased to stand in our UK base. The clock tower is inscribed with the names of men killed while with the regiment on training and operations. When things looked a bit dodgy sometimes, we used to joke about beating the clock. Considering the training and operations over the years, there are not that many names on the clock. Still too many though. Free-fall parachuting was something I had no ambitions with. Mother Earth was still too fond of me and rushed me back too quick.

I had a slight brush with the watery stuff when I was sent to Devizes to have a go at the Devizes to Westminster canoe race. I was a dismal failure. The others had built up to paddling the twenty-five miles from Devizes to Newbury before I arrived, so I had to paddle that twenty-five miles the first time I ever stepped into a canoe. We did it three days on the trot, then started on the stretch of canal from Newbury to Reading. I did the stretch twice, I think, before the old injuries put a stop to it. I had thought canoeing might be a good thing to strengthen my weak arm and shoulder, but I think I went too far too soon. I stayed with the canoe team, driving the safety vehicle, until they finished the race, beating all previous records. One of my friends, who took the record for his class, lost a stone (14 lb) in weight in the twenty-four hours it took to win.

One of the worst experiences I can remember, involving water, was something we did in Hereford – to impress a visiting general. It was mid-winter, we had just returned to UK from somewhere hot (climate-wise). It was decided a demonstration river crossing would be a good thing for the general to watch. On getting 'lumbered' to be one of the four-man patrol, I could think of a lot of other things the general would be interested in, but there it was – we were stuck with it.

A practice session the day before the general's visit went quite well, in spite of the freezing conditions, but overnight the weather changed for the worse. What might be called 'a cold snap' set in. We did the crossing somewhere upstream of the old Wye Bridge at Hereford, with all our operational kit and weapons of course. It was

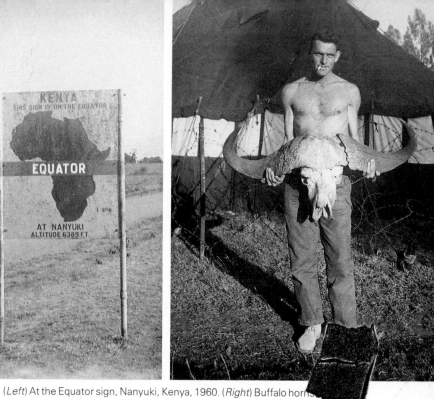

(*Left*) At the Equator sign, Nanyuki, Kenya, 1960. (*Right*) Buffalo horns.

(*Left*) Jungle sentry, (*Right*) Brewtime after a Kenya patrol.

First CQB range in a bomb crater on the slopes of Mount Kenya.

Weapon cleaning.

an early morning job. There was a bit of mist, and when I got my first sight of the river I nearly died of shock. It was well up, as it usually is in winter, there was hoar frost everywhere and ice on the river, going out about ten feet from both banks.

Alex was first to go. I really felt for him as he smashed the ice and dropped into the water. Then it was my turn. Believe me, it was bloody cold. I never thought I'd reach the far bank. My whole body seemed to seize up with the intense cold. Brass monkeys would never have made it intact! It was 'touch and go' whether we would! But everyone crossed safely and moved off from the far bank as an organised patrol, under the eyes of the 'brass'.

Once out of sight, however, we were given a goodly shot of hot 'toddy', wrapped in blankets and rushed back to camp for a quick change. A hot shower never felt so good.

Sometime in 1961, 22 SAS decided to have each troop in a squadron specialise in a particular type of warfare. Personnel were shuffled according to their abilities. 16 Troop, which I had been with since joining SAS, became 'D' Squadron's 'Free Fall' Troop. 17 Troop were made 'Boat' Troop, 18 Troop 'Rover' Troop and 19 Troop became the 'Mountain' Troop. Almost every man in 16 Troop was transferred to 18 Troop. We went to work on all types of vehicle operations. Desert navigation and all types of cross-country driving in Europe and North Africa. We all trained on mortars and machine-guns, and mastered the art of bringing jet fighters and bombers to attack targets.

The Free Fall Troop seemed to do very little except free fall, at which they became pretty good. The Boat Troop worked with the Marines quite a bit getting to know the ropes with all things 'watery': beach reconnaissance, submarines, diving, etc. Mountain Troop went climbing mad and climbed everything in sight. They also specialised in Arctic warfare, ski-ing and all those problems.

Nevertheless we all had to keep in touch with our jungle skills, and rarely went long between Bergen humping of one kind or another. There was always a damn great mountain to climb somewhere.

Between 1959 and 1962 several instructors' courses came my way. I became an instructor in 'Heavy Drop', the parachuting of vehicles and equipment, and 'Airportability', the loading and unloading of vehicles on different types of aircraft. I also qualified as an instructor in 'Astro-Navigation', 'First Aid', 'Nuclear, Bacteriological and Chemical Warfare', 'Air Photo Reading' and 'Desert Navigation'. The only course I didn't get on with was

'Nuclear and Blacktreacle'. I did that one just after getting a bad concussion (parachuting) and couldn't concentrate or remember anything. I scraped through, but only just.

We all did a lot of other training and courses on a wide variety of subjects. Parachuting reared its ugly head on several occasions, but somehow I survived, never injured enough to stop me from sensible training or operations. The 'heavies' in the squadron were always interested in ways of slowing their descent by parachute. There was a theory that a really heavy load would contribute to a soft landing. When jumping with equipment, we dropped it to dangle on a line fourteen feet below us after leaving the aircraft. The theory was, if the equipment was really heavy it would cause a faster descent until it hit the ground. Then there would be a good braking effect on the parachute due to the extra air pressure, before our feet touched.

There was so much argument over the pros and cons of the theory, I decided to try it. We were jumping onto Hereford racecourse. My kit weighed something in excess of two hundred pounds. I could hardly lift the damn thing when it came to standing up ready for the jump. One of my friends, 'Big Doc', was behind me in the stick to help with the exit from the aircraft, as there was no way I could make a good exit with that lot, and I certainly didn't want extra complications.

The exit went well, with a massive push, well timed by Doc. Then I whistled down like a bomb, wishing all the way down that I wasn't so thick! So the theory was correct on the first part. A definitely fast descent. The rest of it wasn't so good. I wasn't hurt, but that bloody load towed me into the ground like a train. There must have been some brake effect or I'd have been injured, but it was the only time in my life I said, 'Jesus Christ!' before I hit the ground.

The great theorists, some of who had landed previously and watched my effort with great interest, now argued it needed a longer line to give the brake effect more time to work. Others claimed the answer was to jettison the pack at about forty feet.

My answer was, 'OK, but next time – you bloody try it!'

On New Year's Day 1962, four of us flew out to Bermuda to train a local militia unit, 'The Bermuda Militia Artillery'. They were no longer an artillery unit and were trained as infantry. There were two militia units in Bermuda. The BMA was all black personnel and the 'Bermuda Rifles' was all white personnel. Why they were segregated we couldn't figure, but they were both happy enough with the arrangement. We found the BMA was a damn good crowd to work with. They had a typical British Army sense of humour and the training went well.

One small incident stands out in my memories of Bermuda. I was using ten of the men to give a demonstration of 'fire and movement' to one of the companies. The Bren gunner was about two metres tall (6 ft 6 ins), had arms like my legs, muscles on his eyelashes and made the light machine-gun look like a toy in his hands.

All went well at first, then the 'Rifle Group' were firing and the 'Bren Group' weren't moving. Before I could stop myself, I shouted, 'Come on, you black bastard – move your ass!!' The monster came tearing up from his fire position, waving the machine-gun in one hand, a big grin on his face, shouting, 'OK, you white bastard – I'm a-coming!'

After that it went like clockwork, but I felt about two inches high – and wished I was less. The thing is I would have shouted the same words if he had been white, red or blue. There were times when the whole bloody Army called anyone 'black bastards' in those days. There was no malice in it, and certainly no thought of racialism. Luckily the company was in good humour as usual and took it all as a joke.

We were each given a small moped with which to get around the sights and scenes of Bermuda. Being the only 'biker' among us, it did my pride no good at all to be the only one to fall off. Apart from feeling a bloody fool there was little damage. A gashed knee and a few holes in a good suit.

During the last few days we were there Bermuda had its annual shooting competition, a sort of miniature 'Bisley', when all their rifle clubs and armed forces teams entered for various cups and prizes. The competition was open to any forces based on or visiting Bermuda. Just about everyone who could be there in fact. There were teams from the US Air Force, Navy, Marines and Rangers. The Royal Navy, the Royal Canadian Navy and possibly other visiting or Bermuda-based forces.

Our friends in the Bermuda Militia Artillery insisted we enter in the 'Falling Plates' competition, saying, 'OK, you four – pick a four-man team for the "plates".'

Being put on the spot, at the last minute, we were not too sure of our abilities with their old ·303 rifles – which we didn't have time to zero properly. But there was no way out so, in for a penny, in for a pound, we did our best.

Our erstwhile trainees did better than they had ever done before, reaching the semi-final, where they were eliminated by a team from the US Rangers. This left us to face the Rangers in the final, an unenviable prospect, so we decided to play it our way.

The competition is quite simple. Twelve plates to be knocked down by each team. Each man has ten rounds (bullets) to fire. The ammunition is placed 200 metres from the targets, then the teams move back to 500 metres from the targets and, at the signal to start, rush forward to the ammunition, load their rifles and commence shooting. The winners being the team which downs all their plates with the least ammunition, in a time limit of two minutes from the start at 500 metres.

Two of us were from 'D' Squadron and two from 'A' Squadron. Throughout our stay we from 'D' Squadron had taken some stick about our unflappable laid-back approach to all things military. The BMA troops had enjoyed the difference but found some things difficult to understand.

Several hundred people were watching this final with great interest, including nearly every man-jack of the BMA. From the 500-metre point we were looking through an avenue of people to where our ammunition lay. At the signal to go the Rangers and our 'A' Squadron types took off like hares. We two commenced a steady walk. The crowd went mad. In a couple of places along the way, much to my amusement, I heard the words, 'Come on, you black bastard – move your ass!'

We arrived at the firing point with our breathing unaffected. I think I knocked down two of the plates before my friend had demolished the rest. He is a damn good shot and the credit for our win is all his, although 'A' Squadron had done their share. But we were in the business of training people and it was a good demonstration of the merits of 'unflappability', there are many ways to skin a cat, etc.

We were exceptionally well treated in Bermuda, and made a number of good friends. After five or six weeks we flew back to UK, spent one night in Hereford, then flew out to Malaya where the squadron were doing some jungle-bashing. I spent six weeks in Malaya, two of which I was again instructing. This time four of us were sent into the jungle with a crowd of Military Police from Australia, New Zealand and UK to introduce them to the art of jungle warfare. One of the Aussies managed to shoot himself through the leg; otherwise that was another uneventful session.

The Malay Police Field Force provided me with the best couple of days on the trip. Two of us had to deliver some radio spares and a few odds and ends to a troop deep in the jungle. We travelled most of the way by boat. Two boats, in fact, supplied and crewed by Police Field Force personnel. At first we were on a fairly big river and the speed was welcome. It looked like being a pleasant trip. The boats were made of wood, long and slim with a twin set of 40 hp Johnson outboard motors giving ample power.

Then things began to warm up. The river became narrower, there were rapids and rocks, swirling water and spray everywhere. The police folk obviously knew their job and were familiar with every ripple on the river. They must have been, as the pace hardly slackened. We were travelling upstream and I, for one, found it harder and harder to appear relaxed and nonchalant in the face of what appeared to be imminent damp death. I sneaked a glance back at my friend in the other boat. A white face and sickly grin did nothing for morale.

At some stage, when I could chance letting go of my hold on the bouncing, twisting boat, I tied my rifle to my left wrist with a piece of para cord. By that time I was working out my route back to civilisation – from wherever the inevitable happened – overland of course! But it never happened. We went under trees, over trees, scraped the sides and bottom of the boat on jagged rocks – which seemed to come at us in an endless procession of near destruction.

In a couple of places at least we had to go through shallows when avoiding obstacles in the deeper water. The crew aimed the boat at the selected spot, went flat out, then lifted the engines at the last minute so we slid through a few inches of water for several yards into deep water again. After we turned into a smaller river the speed slackened. In several places we had to jump out and push the boat through shallows.

The trip up river took nearly a whole day. We two Brits were damn glad to get on our flat feet and hoof to the RV point when the boats could go no further. Two days later we rejoined the boats for the trip back to base.

Coming upstream had been scary. Downstream was bloody terrifying. I won't even guess the height of some of the waterfalls we flew over, but when you fly over the edge and know you are going to land in froth – because that's all you can see – it tempts breakfast to the tonsils.

I consoled myself with the fact we'd made it upstream OK –

when I'd thought there were heavy odds against it – and tried to enjoy the 'flight'. The downstream run, back to base, was completed in three hours less than the upstream run. Nuff said!

In the last few weeks of the squadron's training in Malaya, three things happened which were unusual. It must have been 'Animal Madness Month'. In one instance a patrol was charged several times by a rhino, only succeeding in 'breaking contact' when they fired several rounds over its head.

Within a few days of that, an elephant stomped a troop base camp into the deck and tree'd a certain friend of mine for several hours. I wasn't there but witnesses swore there was no way anyone could have climbed that tree under normal circumstances. It must have been a big tree or jumbo would have shaken him out of it. Trees don't usually have branches lower than about forty feet in the jungle.

The third 'animal happening' didn't concern our people; it happened to a Gurkha sentry. He was attacked by an elephant, so shot at it. According to the report we received the elephant took the sentry's rifle, smashed it against a tree, then threw it away, walking over the Gurkha as it did so. The Gurkha had only a broken finger, which had been through the trigger guard of the rifle when it was snatched. He was otherwise unhurt.

It seemed strange that there were these 'contacts' with large animals all in the space of a couple of weeks, when the regiment had operated in Malaya for years without such happenings. There must have been a few brushes with the big ones during those years but I only ever heard of one. A corporal in 'D' Squadron bent his shotgun barrel over a bear's head when they met unexpectedly over a fallen tree. The bear ran away – holding its head with both paws.

Before leaving Malaya we spent an afternoon in KL, so I decided to go and have my favourite 'nosh' at my favourite eating house, the Rex, on Batu Road. I had a drink at the bar then sat down at a table. Recognising the same head waiter when he approached my table, I just said, 'The usual please.' He didn't bat an eyelid. Five minutes later I had my usual in front of me. I hadn't been in the Rex for over three years but they hadn't missed a thing: it was all there – T-bone steak, double roast pork, double mushrooms, tomatoes, two fried eggs, four sausages and chips. Those people are true professionals at their job, without a doubt.

After the training in Malaya we returned to UK. I went on several more jobs until somewhere in mid-1962 I was posted to 23

SAS, a Territorial Army unit with Headquarters in Birmingham. My time with 23 SAS was rather mundane after the mad rush of 22 SAS. I found the part-time soldiers trained hard when their clown department didn't get in the way. Most of their training was organised by Paddy Nugent, who did an excellent job of keeping up SAS standards. Sometimes it was a difficult uphill battle. On some occasions I would probably have given up trying, but Paddy's quick wit and clear headedness, plus long experience of dealing with 'super-clowns' always seemed to save the situation at the last minute.

As an example of Paddy's 'unflappability' there came a time when an officer of 23 SAS, under heavy pressure to raise the number of men passing the Selection Course, decreed that instead of the Selection Course, the next batch of recruits would only fire a normal Army range course to qualify for SAS. I threw my usual 'wobbler' which got me nowhere. Paddy just gave a knowing wink and said, 'Don't panic, Joe, we've got a couple of months yet. A lot of water will go under the bridge.'

Water went under the bridge all right but every move to put things right stumbled into failure. Although Paddy and I thundered back and forth to Rhayader area and all points nasty every weekend, pushing the recruits through their normal pre-selection training, the hard fact hung in front of my nose. There was to be no Selection Course at the end of it!

Time passed. The date arrived. The recruits assembled and were kitted up as normal for Selection Course. I had great faith in Paddy but as the trucks roared out of Birmingham, heading for the rifle ranges near Brecon, I was wondering how the hell we were going to live this one down.

We arrived at the ranges and found another unit already in residence. There was a lot of 'waffling' telephone calls and angry officers, but we found we had not been booked on the ranges. They were fully booked for the next two weeks.

Paddy came to the rescue. 'OK, there's no problem. I can get accommodation in Dering Lines (Brecon). We'll just have to go walkies for a couple of weeks.' And so we did. It was obvious to me that the accommodation in Dering Lines, plus land clearance for all the Selection Course routes, plus a lot of other things like rations, etc., had all been organised long before. Paddy gave a big wink. 'I must have forgotten to remind the Adjutant to book the ranges. Never thought to check on it.'

Selection Courses for 23 SAS went on as usual after that. They were very hard, and the pass rate was the same as for 22 SAS, 10 per cent. There were always pressures to get more men through the selection process, by lowering the standards, but thanks to 'the Nuge' and a few others, as far as I know 23 SAS has remained a well-selected SAS unit.

At some stage during my two-year stint with 23 SAS, some comedian with a vast sense of humour had me sent on a Parachute Jump Instructors' course. Of all people to get stuck with such a thing. I hated bloody parachuting and everyone knew it. The 'PX' parachute saved me; it was on its final trials before being issued to replace the old 'X Type'. Being a bigger chute it gave a slower rate of descent, so I survived the sixteen or seventeen jumps necessary to complete the course.

The course was run by No 1 Parachute School, RAF Abingdon. When writing my report at the end of the course the RAF boss of the Parachute School put one of the most apt footnotes I've ever seen. It was a very good report, and I had passed, but, as a little footnote at the bottom, he wrote, 'Not suited to parachuting – either in size or inclination.'

As a measure of the very low profile favoured by the SAS in those days, there were a few words I'll never forget, from a farmer's wife in the Cotswolds. A big 'escape and evasion' exercise was being laid on in the north Cotswolds, and letters went sent to all farmers and land-owners requesting permission for troops to cross their land. Some of us were sent out to collect the written permission and check for any problems.

Arriving at one farm I was greeted with a cheery 'good morning' by the good lady, who looked duly impressed by my smart appearance. (SAS beret and badge, camouflage smock with black belt, olive green trousers, shining back anklets and boots.) I wished her good morning, then said, 'I'm from 23 Special Air Service Regiment; we sent you a letter a couple of weeks ago requesting permission to cross your land.'

She looked rather puzzled, then it dawned. 'Oh', she said, 'you've come to spray the crops.'

There were many interesting and comical experiences during that two years, far too many to record as usual, but one in particular is too good to miss. 23 SAS often do exercises for a few days in Europe, sometimes parachuting into some country during the dark hours, sometimes landing the normal way and being put in by road or helicopter.

We had parachuted into Denmark and were on our way home on Sunday afternoon after a fairly strenuous few days. Our transport was two ancient Beverlys, one of which developed a 'hiccup' in one engine. Both aircraft landed somewhere in a hayfield. I don't know what country; must have been Denmark, Germany or Holland. One of the flight engineers borrowed a ladder from a nearby haystack, climbed up to the offending engine and routed out a lot of odds and ends, like nuts and bolts and things.

The aircrews decided the aircraft was OK to go again, but as it was a bit suspect it was decided all the men who had to be back at work on Monday should go in the other aircraft, and all the Regular Army personnel and self-employed types go in the dodgy one.

We got everyone shifted around according to their work problems and both aircraft took off again. About ten minutes later the same engine (port inner) started performing again, and gradually got worse. I was going around the people in the freight bay, getting their names, etc., for the flight manifest because of the passenger change.

There were two young lads sitting together looking rather nervous, as well they might considering the noise from the ailing engine. I had just got the name and number from the first one when there was a decent-sized explosion from 'port inner' and sheets of flame were passing the window they were facing. I couldn't resist it, I continued calmly with the next question, 'Next of kin?' They both looked at me in horror.

The pilot asked on the intercom if we had any parachutes on board. We had a few decidedly 'second hand' ones in a hamper, which no one was about to use, so we said, 'No.' He decided to head for the Dutch coast but warned he might have to ditch in the sea. We all got to ditching stations. Then the pilot decided he would make the coast. He had thrown it about a bit, presumably in an effort to put out the fire. From where I was sitting it had obviously failed!

The engine was screaming fit to bust, so I presume the crew couldn't shut it down. We reached the coast, with flames everywhere on the port side. The pilot decided our best bet was to make for Schipol, Amsterdam International Airport. So we flew on for a while, with great faith in the RAF, if nothing much else going for us. As we landed at Schipol the airport emergency services were with us before we touched down. Matching their speed to that of the aircraft they smothered good old 'port inner' with foam.

We opened a door, put the little ladder in place, gathered our belongings and wandered off in an orderly fashion. The Dutch were

amazed and tried to organise a panicky run. They said there could
be an explosion any minute. One of the TA types said, 'I don't think
so, you've all done a marvellous job. Just keep it like that till I've
had a smoke.'

The engine was still smoking, hissing and glowing through its
ever increasing layers of foam, but it did no more than that and
eventually subsided, as all good engines do.

In 1963 I tried to return to 22 SAS as the Borneo problem had
begun and the regiment was involved in real operations again. I had
all my arguments ready when I went before the CO of 23 SAS, but
I'm not much good at Army politics. The CO was a past master.
He shot down all my arguments (to his satisfaction if not mine) and
I came out of his office a firm, if reluctant, member of 23 SAS.

From then on I just kicked my heels and waited for the few
months to pass. I was due to return to the fold in mid 1964 so
patience was the order of the day. Easier said than done when your
friends are being killed and you can't even get off your backside.

CHAPTER SEVEN

Clowns and Clangers

Early in 1964, while still with 23 SAS, I had been sent back to Hereford for a few weeks to help staff the overloaded Selection Courses which were made necessary by the reforming of 'B' Squadron. 'B' Squadron being reformed was great news to all of us as this meant the regiment would be more able to cover all its commitments – without burning out the troops in a continual yoyo of operations.

For a time, just before returning to 22 SAS, I had a worry that I might find myself being posted to 'B' Squadron. Nothing terrible in that really, but, although many of my friends were now in 'B', I felt a strong identity with 'D' Squadron, and had no wish to change.

In the event there were no problems. I returned to 18 Troop in mid 1964, felt immediately back at home and became submerged in a deluge of training. The training was fast and furious. Our feet hardly touched the ground before we were off on another caper. Any time we spent in Hereford we utilised for range work, mostly on the 25 metre range near the camp, sometimes at the Ross-on-Wye rifle range, occasionally on the field firing ranges at Sennybridge, in South Wales.

Every week, while in base, I took 18 Troop to the Black Mountains for a bit of bergen humping. The only way to keep fit to carry a bergen, is carry a bergen. Gymnastics and jogging are great for gymnasts and joggers, but I had seen too many PT instructors from the rest of the Army, loaded up with muscle and gymnastic ability, go 'squelch' in the first few days of a Selection Course. My theory was they had never been really knackered before in their lives, whereas being smashed out of our minds with fatigue was the norm for we lesser mortals.

On our trips to the Black Mountains we carried in our packs only the essentials for survival, topping up the weight to fifty or sixty pounds with rocks picked up at the drop-off point. The advantage of this was that if anyone had a slight injury he could dump the rocks and be left with a relatively light load, to make his way to the pick-up point or one of the emergency RVs.

We always dropped off in pairs from a truck on the west side of the mountains, and made for either one troop RV or, occasionally, separate RVs along the road east of the mountains. The inevitable wet, cold ride back to Hereford was much shorter from east of the mountains.

A man's physical and mental ability to pull his weight, do his job, remain operational was largely his own responsibility. That is where the self-discipline comes in. The troop were never supervised with loading their packs for training walks. For all I knew I could have been the only one carrying any rocks, but it was in everyone's interest to make the most of opportunities to keep their physical and mental abilities at a peak. In fact I knew some of them were carrying far more weight than I.

I always carried binoculars on my trips to the mountains, and if it happened to be clear enough to see I kept an eye on the progress of other pairs anywhere I got the chance. The reasons were safety. A man is easily injured carrying heavy weights over rough country – even when he is an expert! Other members of the troop also carried binoculars for the same reason. Binoculars can save a lot of time and leg work when searching for anyone missing in the mountains. They can also let you see at a glance whether a man is carrying any weight or just an empty pack.

A couple of times men arrived at the RV with empty packs. They didn't try to hide the fact, and had their reasons. As far as the rest of us were concerned they had done the sensible thing.

During my SAS soldiering years I had my fair share of good and bad officers. All the squadron commanders I served under were very good soldiers; men who could cope with responsibilities and situations far beyond the normal for their rank in the Army. All were good, some were brilliant. Field commanders who seemed to have a natural touch for knowing the capabilities of the men under their command, so that we could achieve the 'impossible', but 'miracles' were never actually demanded (only tried for, sometimes!). Troop commanders on the other hand were a different kettle of fish. Mostly they were too young and inexperienced to be expected to cope with handling an SAS troop on operations.

The good ones tried not to get in the way, learnt fast from their experience and finished their two or three years with SAS very much advanced in their knowledge of field work and just about able to cope with their position.

There were some, like Rory Walker, who were brilliant, and great to work with. They were the type who could give and take, listen to the more experienced men around them and make the right decisions when it came to the crunch. But there were others.

Once, on a hoof over the Black Mountains, I had the misfortune to be accompanied by one of the 'others'. As was normal practice in the troop, we dropped off in pairs along a road west of the mountains, making for an RV on the east side, so that the wet, cold ride back to Hereford was not too long. We only carried in our packs the essentials for survival in the mountains, topping up the weight to 50 or 60 pounds with rocks picked up near the drop point.

I was paired with 'his nibs'. We duly loaded our packs and set off. About two thirds of the way up the first climb he was way ahead of me, going well. Before the top he started shouting for me to hurry. At the top of the first climb he ordered me to dump my rocks, saying I was obviously too old for it and couldn't keep up the pace. I refused, so he got angry and told me he had dumped his rocks way back – so I should do the same or we would not be first into the RV, and, as an officer, he must be first!

I couldn't believe my ears. Was this an SAS officer? I asked him what would he throw away first on operations, his rations or his ammunition? He rushed on ahead, cursing me for my age, my lack of fitness and just generally for existing. I plodded on as one does plod on with a bit of weight to carry, ignoring the patter.

At noon, finding myself in a sheltered spot with a good mountain stream nearby, I stopped to make a brew of tea to wash down the cookhouse sandwiches. The clown nearly had a fit. He rushed around here and there, cursing loud and long. I told him to go on ahead to the RV if he wanted, but he wouldn't. It occurred to me the bum couldn't trust himself to find the RV. But surely he had passed a Selection Course?

Luckily that type was a rarity which never lasted long in the regiment, but I did have another problem once, which was worse.

We were training overseas, and had a clown along who just had to do everything wrong. A lot of problems were caused, some annoying, others downright dangerous. Eventually I blew my top, a stupid thing to do, but then, I think everyone has his boiling point. Show me a senior SAS soldier who has not blown his top over clown problems – and I'll show you a saint.

The training was nearing its end. 'Old Joe' (much younger than me) had a poisoned foot which eventually had to be lanced. He had struggled along on two hard night marches in some considerable pain, but after the lancing job he couldn't force his boot on, so was virtually off the road.

We were going off on light order patrols for the day, leaving our packs at our last stop, near a village. Joe had been ordered to take his patrol out but no one had been detailed to stay behind to look after the packs, so I told Joe to stay put, one of the troopers could take his patrol, there was no problem.

It was a very hard day's work in my case, and I returned rather smashed just before sundown, to be met by Joe who was very upset. The clown we had along had returned just before me, realised Joe had not taken his patrol, and tore into Joe, calling him a 'skiver', waste of rations, and a lot of other things.

My natural reaction to this news was as natural as anyone's. I said, quite loudly, 'The bloody idiot!' The clown stepped from behind a rock, yelling about being called a 'bloody idiot', ranting and raving in great order. When he eventually subsided it was my turn. I gave him a quick but precise rundown on his ancestral history, then brought him right up to date. For the first time ever he was speechless. Then he looked around for witnesses. Where there had been most of a troop there was now an empty space. Silence. Nothing. Telling him to 'go away' in my best Trog's English I got on with the important task of making a brew.

A few days later the clown tried to frame me, and even had me under open arrest at one stage. Needless to say he was not the type for SAS and didn't last long either. On another occasion, in the middle of an operation, we were sent a new troop commander. I don't know his background, but I expect we were victims of the system whereby 'little snots' (young second lieutenants) on passing Selection and further training were promoted to captain and made troop commanders – when they had nary a clue.

Unlike the troggery who, to join SAS, throw away rank, pay, promotion prospects and cushy jobs, to get away from bullshit and be real soldiers, the officers were automatically promoted to captain, as the SAS had no lower commissioned rank. This did their future prospects a power of good, often being a good boost up the promotion ladder. Perhaps, in the 'machinery' of getting good squadron commanders, it was all very necessary, but it meant a pig's life on ops when a troop got stuck with a 'little snot'.

This particular child tried to impress us with his great superior knowledge of all things military. He was a great success as a bloody idiot. One of his greatest cock-ups in the man management department made him (and us) the laughing stock of the whole squadron. At the time we were a very experienced troop and were operating smoothly in the situation. The clown gathered us together and complained we were making too much noise when moving at night, then gave us a quick lecture on 'Individual Movement In The Field' – followed by demonstrations of the 'monkey run', 'leopard crawl' and 'ghost walk' (very basic methods of night movement taught to every soldier during his first eight weeks in the Army, mostly only of any use in European type terrain – which we were most definitely not in at the time!). At first, as he had only joined us about three days previously, we thought he had a great sense of humour and was trying to relieve what he thought was boredom. Then we realised he wasn't enjoying his demonstrations as much as we were. Especially when, red faced and totally pissed off, he wanted us to practise the 'techniques' so he could check us for faults!

Most of us had at least ten years' military service behind us, a lot of it on operations. Several had been infantry instructors, and for this wet-behind-the-ears prat with all of eighteen months' service – nuff said!

A few years ago I noticed the poor old Marines had the same problem. They ran an officer-recruiting advert in various newspapers and magazines. It had a group photograph of a reasonably hard-looking crowd of 'Royals'. The words under the photo read something like, 'Are you aged 18 to 25? Have you so many "A" Levels, "O" Levels, etc.? Could you lead these men?'

Anyone who answered that advert on its face value was a prime candidate for the 'funny farm', and certainly could not have come within the hat size range of the Marines or any other service.

The officer, even on SAS operations, always has the advantage afforded by the chain of command. He gets the orders for his troop, then passes on what he thinks is necessary. This can often be a problem when he's a flaming idiot to start with. I am often assured things have changed considerably since I left the Army but, having noticed very little change in officer problems since (according to history) the Charge of the Light Brigade, up to the time I left the service, perhaps I can be forgiven a little scepticism.

In November 1964 'D' Squadron went to the Aden Protectorate for a training stint. We hoofed around a lot of desert and mountains over quite a large area, west and north-west of Aden. A lot of operational techniques were tested. Some worked – some didn't. We did a few 'new-fangled' things involving aircraft, and a lot of hard, hard flogging. We spent five weeks in Aden, then returned to UK, where we went into a bout of intensive training, punctuated by Christmas and New Year, preparing for our next trick.

After a bit of leave and re-organising we were off to the Far East. A war is a war, but the war in Borneo had to be called a 'confrontation'. Presumably because we didn't flatten Jakarta (the Indonesian capital), and they didn't attack Malaya or Singapore with aircraft. The 'confrontation' was more or less confined to one area, Northern Borneo. Mostly only land forces were used to any extent in an aggressive role by either side.

In 1963 Malaya, Sarawak and Sabah, all ex-British territories, had joined together to form the Federation of Malaysia. Sarawak and Sabah, together being about the same size as mainland Britain, but almost entirely covered by dense jungle, have a roughly 700-mile border with Indonesia and are on the north coast of Borneo, which is the world's third largest island. The vast bulk of the island is Indonesian territory, called Kalimantan.

President Sukarno of Indonesia had ambitions of making a federation with Malaya and the northern Borneo territories, to add their undoubted riches and roughly eight million people to his already vast empire of thousands of islands with a population of about one hundred million.

The Indonesian army was large, well-equipped and well-experienced in jungle warfare. Sukarno was getting a little unpopular in some quarters of his own land, being a virtual dictator, so, when the Indonesian Communists became entangled in a small revolt in the northern Borneo territories, and tried to exploit the situation – Sukarno decided this was his great chance. Units of the Indonesian Army were deployed in late 1963 and our forces in Sarawak and Sabah found themselves coming up against more and more regular Indonesian Army units instead of the original Communist raiders and infiltrators.

Owing to the rugged terrain of Borneo, the border was generally a very isolated area, far from any lines of communication, making it very difficult for either side to deploy large forces across it. All movement was on foot as no vehicle could get anywhere near the border. On the other hand, because of the all enveloping dense jungle, no movement could be seen from the air. So the Borneo confrontation was very much a man to man war. Rifles and

(*Right*) Because of possible 'animal problems' leading scouts carried Bren LMGs in Kenya.

(*Below*) Building a luxury basha, Kenya 1960.

Charlie at work in the Northern Oman desert.

Bogged Down.

Mined.

bayonets at very close quarters. Sudden, savage encounters, with victory or defeat often obscured initially by the tangled mass of dense undergrowth. Leading scouts walked on a razor's edge, only the fastest gun had any future.

At the start of the trouble SAS personnel had been deployed in ones, twos, threes and fours along most of the 700-mile front to make friends and allies of the jungle tribes. The tribesmen have always been very pro-British, and, although their liking for head-hunting was often emphasized by grisly relics hanging in their longhouse, the SAS trogs cheerfully accepted these little quirks of behaviour and soon became almost part of their local tribe. The eyes and ears of the jungle tribesmen augmented those of their SAS guests, who passed on information of enemy movement by radio.

British and Malaysian forces deployed in Borneo had no chance of holding a normal front line to defend Malaysian territory, so, as Indonesian 'incursions' were detected, forces were moved to intercept them. Sometimes the Indonesian attackers were followed for days by SAS personnel, in order to find out where they were going so that a right and proper reception could be prepared.

SAS personnel, like all other forces under Allied command in northern Borneo, were strictly forbidden to cross the border into Indonesian territory. However, by the end of 1964, everyone agreed this was giving the enemy too much scope to mount his operations. In consequence SAS patrols were allowed to cross the border, on purely intelligence-gathering missions, to a depth of five kilometres.

The restrictions on our cross border movements, and behaviour on the other side, were gradually lifted as the war – I mean confrontation – progressed. Malaysian forces were almost all based in Malaya to defend against a possible Indonesian invasion. They were in fact used to good effect when the Indonesians made an airborne landing in south-west Malaya.

The brunt of the fighting in Borneo fell upon the infantry battalions, notably the Gurkhas, whose jungle expertise kept one or other of their units at the forefront throughout the war. But it was eventually a Commonwealth effort, with New Zealand and Australian troops fighting alongside British, Gurkhas and Malaysians. All Commonwealth forces seem to work very well together not only the front-line troops but also the vital supporting units. Although we were already outnumbered in Borneo, the skill and determination of those men in the forward areas prevented the enemy from becoming too big for his boots and the confrontation consequently turning into an extremely bloody war.

In January 1965 'D' Squadron again landed in Borneo. It was the squadron's third tour in that theatre, my first. We took over from the newly formed 'B' Squadron. Things had changed since 'D' Squadron had left Borneo in June 1964. The regiment was now committed to 'cross border' operations into Indonesia, in order to gain advance information of Indonesian attacks, and do a bit of tickling to slow down any build up, etc.

We spent a short time polishing our jungle techniques and Immediate Action drills, then got down to work at last.

My first operation was a fiasco as far as I was concerned, although we brought back a lot of information which Brigade HQ found very interesting. Three patrols went 'in' together, with one patrol acting as 'step-up'. Two patrols being tasked onto targets further on. We went into a border LZ by 'chopper'. The operation was scheduled to last fourteen days. 'Old Joe's' patrol was doing step-up; Alex's patrol and mine were going further. Joe's patrol could do some recce work if the 'climate felt right', otherwise he stayed put until we returned, then we would return as a three patrol group through the border.

We went south and west for about six or seven thousand metres, by which time we had found rivers where there were none on the maps and at least one big river flowing in the opposite direction to its course shown on the maps. It was mountainous country but no hills were shown on the maps. They were correct in one detail though, there was jungle.

The jungle in Borneo was very similar to the Malayan jungle in that it was normally very dense tropical rain forest. There were however a lot of things which made it feel different. Perhaps it was mostly the contrast in local geography between those areas I worked in the two countries. There were very rugged areas in Malaya but, compared with most of the jungle areas in which I worked in Borneo, the Malayan jungle was rolling hills. In Borneo there were more cliffs, ravines, very narrow ridges and spurs. There were very few places in Malaya where a distant view could be seen. In Borneo it was quite common to be able to see for miles across the tree tops.

In the leafy, 'rubbishy' twilight of deep jungle fairly fast quiet movement was possible in most places due to animal tracks and old or little used hunting tracks. Away from any type of track, movement was considerably slowed and usually unavoidably noisy.

When I say 'hunting' or 'animal' tracks, I'm referring to tracks which the untrained eye could never follow. The acquired knack for following such tracks, like looking through the trees instead of at them, takes some people a long time to learn. To me, such things were natural due to my childhood in the woods. The training I had received and my previous jungle experience sharpened my abilities in deep jungle so that I felt immediately 'at home', confident, on top of the situation.

To the untrained eye, the all round view in deep jungle can be compared to that seen from the middle of an average room with two or three windows, at dusk. Except that the view through the windows would rarely be more than thirty metres. Walls of greenery blank out the remainder as solidly as the walls of your room. On the other hand the trained eye will see usually at least twice as far all around but rarely more than forty metres anywhere. Most of the time even well-trained, experienced eyes can see no further than twenty-five to thirty metres. There are places where it is quite easy to see forty odd metres in all directions. There are other places where it is impossible to see more than three or four metres in any direction. The absolute tangle of the jungle impedes all movement, but training and experience can always find a way through. There is no such thing as 'impenetrable jungle'. The occasions when one is forced to use a knife or parang to make progress are extremely rare. Only once during the Borneo operations was I ever forced to use my knife to cut tangling vines, even then it was due more to anger, frustration and lack of patience.

One of the greatest problems of operational movement in jungle is the junk lying on the ground. Noisy, crackling dead twigs and branches often lie upon the ground like a carpet. Overlapping and intertwined. Dead leaves of all sizes and shapes rustle, crack and pop at the slightest touch. So it is of prime importance to take great care where you land your size twelves. There is almost always somewhere quiet to step. Another acquired knack – made all the more difficult by the ever present requirement to see your enemy before he sees you.

About six pairs of eyes would be very handy at times. Hanging vines and small saplings must be avoided like the plague. Just a gentle pull or knock at ground level can wave high branches like warning flags to signal your approach. Those hazards are mostly five or six metres apart at best in average jungle. Huge fallen trees and branches can usually be climbed over, or crawled under.

Sometimes it is necessary to make quite a detour to find a way past them. They occur much more often than the uninitiated might imagine, probably averaging one in every hundred metres.

Above about four metres high there is usually a considerable thinning of the vegetation. Mostly tree trunks, the tops of young trees at various heights and the great rope-like vines trailing down from the jungle canopy which again is very dense upwards from about 120 feet.

Borneo lacked two of my pet hates, most common in Malaya in the areas I worked. I saw no attap. There were also very few leeches, or at least I saw nowhere near as many as in similar areas of Malaya.

We climbed a long spur onto a high ridge and, finding a small stream, made it our step-up RV. All was as it should be. No sign of enemy forces, nothing except the normal sounds, smells and sights of the jungle. We did an area recce for a day before leaving the step-up RV, so as to check the area for enemy signs and know enough to make the RV easy to find on our return. An hour away from the RV I realised I had lost my watch, which had been hung on a cord round my neck.

We were about five hours on that recce and I was moving back towards the RV, thinking I must be pretty close to it, when I saw fresh tracks a few feet ahead. The patrol stopped and I went forward to investigate. There was no doubt about it being our own tracks. The first thing I saw was my watch among the leaves.

The next day we moved off towards our targets. My target was a place called Kapoet, a small village believed to be an Indonesian Army base, possibly a Special Forces camp. My task was to get a look at the place, and the troops in it, collecting all possible information about them.

The patrol had only reached a point a couple of thousand metres further than our area recce of the previous day when further progress to the west was stopped by a sheer cliff. We were confronted by a sheer drop of roughly eight hundred feet. We searched the cliff top for about a thousand metres in each direction but there was no possible way down.

The next day two of us went on a light order patrol along the cliff top to the south, leaving the other two to look after the packs. We had covered about 2 km when I heard a sound up ahead. We both decked and waited. The sound was approaching. It began to sound like something big crashing through the trees towards us.

Then I knew it was something big coming towards us. But what? It was certainly much too big to be human.

Elephants are rare in Borneo, but even they didn't usually crash about like that, unless they were terrified! Of what? Then I could see the tops of quite large trees swaying, about a hundred metres ahead. I began to feel a bit nervous. Knowing the jungle, I knew it would take a tank to cause the kind of movement. There was no wind, and in any case the movement wasn't wind induced. Every sense was straining to the limit to understand what was this monster bearing down upon us. I glanced back. Twenty yards behind me my wing man's eyes were like 'chapel hat pegs'.

Then all was solved. Two huge ginger apes, one chasing the other, were swinging through the tree tops. They came right over us, looking big and ugly but travelling very fast, swinging from branch to branch, tree to tree. The jungle canopy at that altitude was only about sixty or seventy feet above the ground, not as thick as that in the valleys, so we had a really good look at the apes, which I later found out to be Orang-utans.

For several days we tried to get down the cliff. Searching a cliff top in dense jungle is much easier said than done. No animal tracks went more than about fifty feet down, but we had to explore each one. We could see the rooftops of our target, a few thousand yards west, but there was no way we could get at it without a long, time-consuming detour. We were limited in our explorations to the western half of the plateau as we had no wish to bump into one of the other patrols somewhere unexpected.

Time ran out. We had achieved a big fat zero and returned to the step-up RV. Joe's patrol had been to check a jungle village, made contact with a jungle tribe and had a great success while waiting for us to return. Alex had achieved more than I had in terms of distance but very little else. He too had been frustrated by cliffs, but had eventually found a route down to the south-east.

Before going in on that operation our packs had been weighed. We had been limited to fifty pounds for the fourteen days. The squadron commander, a damn good soldier well liked by everyone, made the 'fifty pound rule' with the very best of motives. Basically I agreed it was a good idea – but not in my case. A big engine tends to have a big fuel consumption, and I was no exception. Before the operation was over I was absolutely starving.

Luckily for me, Alex was trying to pack up smoking. A fifty pound pack gave him ample rations. So, when we all arrived at the step-up RV I carefully got up-wind of Alex, lit a cigarette and let the smoke drift past his nose. After which it didn't take a diplomat to organise a bit of swapping so that Alex smoked and I ate. That was the last time I tried to operate from a fifty-pound bergen. There were ways and means through the regulations, much easier than being half starved.

Returning to our base at Kuching I felt I had achieved very little, but at least our patrol was now well switched on to jungle operations. We faced future tasks knowing we could work well together. There being no suitable accommodation available in Kuching we were using the Palm Grove Hotel as sleeping quarters. It was in the centre of town and a good place for relaxing. We averaged four or five days between ops. The first day after returning was mostly taken up with a detailed de-briefing by the SAS Operations staff, and a session in the Brigade Intelligence Centre, where we passed on any information they required.

Brigade had a really good air photo interpreter, a Staff-Sergeant Watson, who helped me considerably with his superior knowledge of air photography. How he did it I'll never know, but from his air photos he could tell me the height of corn growing in a field to an accuracy of a few inches. And the photos were taken from a height in excess of 10,000 feet. I suppose that was the difference between an air photo reader and an air photo interpreter. Such information was vital when selecting a spot from which to watch the enemy, especially in a country where field crops could vary in height from two or three inches to two or three metres.

Watson also knew the rate of growth of any given crop and added on the appropriate inches according to the date of the photo. He made the planning of operations a lot easier than it might have been.

A day or two relaxing sometimes followed the debriefing, then would come the briefing for the next op. Every possible known fact about the areas, the enemy, the local people, the terrain and nearest friendly forces. Long studying of any maps of the target areas. Hours bent over a stereoscope studying every millimetre of air photographs. Practice of all IA drills with live ammunition. Test firing weapons, then cleaning polishing and oiling them very carefully. We all carried self-loading rifles in my patrol.

The SAS were not the only residents of the Palm Grove. There were various other service personnel billeted there, among them some Royal Navy types who were with minesweepers operating around the Borneo coast. On a couple of occasions I noticed a very drunk rough looking individual in civvy clothes consorting with the Navy types. He was of stumpy build, always in uproarious spirits. I wondered where he fitted into the scheme of things. Somehow I knew he wasn't Navy. Didn't much like the look of him either.

One operation was another crack at Kapoet and its environs. For various reasons I had a 'scratch patrol'; two of the patrol were men I didn't know. Again we went in with Alex and Joe, but this time dispensed with the step-up method, going our separate ways from an LZ right on the border. Kapoet is on the north bank of a fairly large river. On the north side of the river it was surrounded by cultivated land. Several different crops varying in height from a few inches to a few metres. On the south bank of the river there was a cultivated area stretching from opposite the village to the edge of the jungle, and to the east. It was about 400 metres square. West of that cultivation was young secondary jungle from right opposite the village to the primary jungle, about 400 metres south. Primary jungle is that which has never been cleared, at least for a hundred years, if ever. Secondary jungle is that which has grown again where once it had been cleared.

The difference is very apparent on the ground and also on air photographs. The reason for the difference is that most jungle trees grow at the same rate, so, when they get a fresh start and all grow together they are all roughly the same size and usually grow thicker together on the ground. There are no giants among them to keep out the sunlight and no spaces left by dead or fallen trees. The trees become dense and uniform – very unlike primary jungle which, by comparision, is often a pleasure to walk through.

Putting myself in the Indonesian commander's position I would have expected trouble to come from the north, the direction of the border. I would not expect an enemy force to cross the river and approach from the south, where they would have to cross the river again to reach the village.

My safest approach to the target was therefore from the south, where we would have the cover of secondary jungle right to the river bank. That would put us within fifty metres of several buildings on the opposite side of the river. Closer approach from the south however would only be possible during the hours of darkness. This would depend on the state of the river, which at Kapoet is narrow and deep. No bridge showed on the air photos, but, as the jungle completely overhung the river in places there was a good chance of a rope bridge somewhere. Staff-Sergeant Watson confirmed my opinion that the village could be seen from the primary jungle to the south-east, as the crops in that area were only eighteen to twenty-two inches high – or would be by the time I got there – and the ground rose gently up to the jungle's edge.

There were snags, of course. The river could rise and change completely in less than an hour, stopping us from crossing to the south side, or cutting us off for days once we were there. It was that sort of river. There could be, and very likely were, snags with that all too easy patch of secondary jungle. If, as our people thought, Kapoet was a Special Forces base it would most likely be guarded by more than a few mines and booby traps. Special Forces, if they were any good (and they were said to be very good), would certainly take precautions with that neck of the woods so close to their base.

My task was as before, to carry out a recce which would make Kapoet a target for future offensive operations, or cross it off the list for a while. Top priority, as always, was the safety of the patrol. Casualties must be avoided. I was forbidden to initiate any offensive action on this operation on the information was deemed top priority.

The four of us got our heads together over all the facts and figures we had collated. We estimated time and distance, danger areas, ways and means of overcoming this problem or that. We made a very flexible plan and argued the pros and cons. So, in we went. The approach march was unremarkable. We saw no sign of the opposition and few signs of the jungle people. Reaching the target area we did an area recce of the jungle up to the edge of the cultivations, spending a lot of time moving slowly and listening a lot. No signs or sounds rewarded us.

On about the fifth or sixth day of the operation we had done a recce north looking for tracks, which took two or three hours. I then decided to cache the bergens and move towards the village through the cultivations to find how close we could get on the north side. We didn't get far. We hit a patch of open 'grass' which looked like a lawn. There was higher ground ahead and I started across, only to find there was a foot of black sloppy mud under the 'grass'. Seeing no quick way around it I went on through – leaving a huge track. Then found a well-used track, wide enough to drive a truck on, running along the higher ground. There was no way anyone on the track could miss seeing my tracks through the mud.

We pulled back to the edge of the jungle. I made a quick decision. We would compress the whole recce into what was left of that day – about five or six hours of daylight. A 'shit or bust' move through the rest of our rough plan, ignoring the north side approach, going straight round to the south side for a 'look-see'. Trusting in our jungle expertise and, if it came to it, our Immediate Action drills to get us away with it.

At that point there was a tremor of doubt from one of the patrol but I ignored it. We headed for the river, fast and ready for anything. The usual river track was big, and on the north side. As with all other tracks we had found – no boot prints. Finding a good crossing point, we used our own patrol crossing method. This entailed watching the opposite bank for a couple of minutes, then, with two to give me covering fire if required, and one watching their backs, I moved out to the centre of the river. At this point on this particular river it was about 70 metres wide and just over knee deep at the deepest.

Reaching the halfway point I turned and checked the river bank I'd left, as far as I could see in either direction. If all was clear (and I didn't get shot), I moved on to the far side and checked a few yards around in the jungle. If that all felt OK I returned to the river bank and signalled the next man to cross, covering the far bank while he did so. He would cross near me, then go a few yards into the jungle and cover my back while I waved the next one over, and so on.

I noticed a big fish trap in the river a few yards downstream. It was not in use. We had crossed the river about 800 metres east and upstream of Kapoet, so, once into dense jungle, we moved quickly in a westerly direction to hit the edge of the open cultivation south-east of the village. After about twenty minutes I could see the open ground through the trees, so changed direction slightly south so as to follow the jungle edge to higher ground, from where I knew I could get a good look at the target. Reaching a high point we moved carefully to the edge of the trees and there, as promised by the air photos, was Kapoet.

Half an hour was spent in that position, using binoculars to examine anything and everything which might tell us of the enemy presence. The range was about 500 metres. Nothing stirred. There was no sign of anything. The joint was dead.

Rain began to fall as we moved on to the west. This rain was good news as it would cover the sound of faster movement. We made good time and reached the point where the young secondary jungle joined the primary. Now was the time for extreme caution. This was now the nasty bit. Every bit of ground was examined for signs of booby traps and mines, also every tree was checked before we passed. The patrol was on 'hair trigger', moving very slowly. There was no sign of recent human presence anywhere, and in a place so close to a village that was bad news. The further we went through that mess of trees the more sure I became that something was wrong. Then we were through. The river track was a few feet in front of me. Beyond was the deep cutting made by the river, about thirty feet deep with almost sheer sides. Thatched roofs showed on the far bank. Leaving the patrol on stand-by I moved parallel with the track for a few yards, checking for bootprints. There was none. The track had been well used. Nothing much had moved on it for at least two or three weeks, probably a lot more.

There was a screen of young trees and bushes between the track and the river, the patrol came forward to deploy along the edge of the track so I could better do a binocular recce of the village.

Then our troubles began. The man who had been getting more and more nervous suddenly cracked. Under other circumstances I would have hit him, but if I hit too soft or too hard we would have a bigger problem. We had enough problems already. There was a job to be done, and we were going to do it – shit or bust. Leaving the patrol in a situation of one holding down one, while the other kept watch, I moved off to do the recce. Their orders were to bug-out the way we had come (which was the only way out) if there was any shooting before I returned.

Now the rain became a menace. I would not hear anyone approaching, and that is not clever when you have your eyes glued to binoculars – or just looking in the wrong direction. I had to keep moving further along the track to see into buildings and around buildings on the other side of the river. The place looked deserted. No soldiers, no people, no animals or chickens, no clothing hanging to dry, no smoke, no steam. Nothing. I got right on the edge of the river but could see no bridge of any kind. Strange. Why no bridge? There wasn't even any sign of a bridge having been there in the past. No track ending at the river bank. Nothing.

I began to worry about the patrol, and as the binoculars were continually steaming up in the now heavily pouring rain, I put them away. I looked hard at the river and its banks. If we crossed, and I was wrong about the place, there would be little chance of getting back across to safety.

Being narrow at this point the river was deep and fast flowing. I didn't much fancy my chances of crossing safely. Odd jagged rocks breaking the swirling surface were decisive. No bloody way. The thoughts of fighting a 'war' with that at my back was decidedly off-putting.

So what more could we do to make sure there was no enemy base here? I searched further west along the river, found nothing west of the village so returned to the patrol. I felt I could have spent more time looking in the right direction if I had been accompanied on the trip along the river, but it was impossible under the circumstances. Things had changed little, except he was no longer being physically restrained.

Taking the bull by the horns we moved east along the river track to the edge of the cultivated area. Looking across the open ground I noticed an earth bank running from nearby to the edge of the jungle, right across the middle of the open area.

The bank was about five feet high, man made, but was old and may have been to do with drainage. I checked it out and decided we would use it, partly to get away back into the jungle and partly to make a final check on the village.

At its nearest point the earth bank was about 100 metres from and in full view of the village. If there were troops in the village they would be unlikely to resist shooting at an enemy soldier walking along that bank.

The light was very bad and the rain was falling like curtain rods. The weapons of troops engaged in jungle warfare are rarely well zeroed, as long distance shooting doesn't happen, and the rigours of jungle movement are bad for weapon sights. Also I have very little faith in anyone's ability to hit me.

I put the plan to the patrol, two of which agreed and one of which went into shock. Then he refused to move. There was no way he could be coaxed to his feet, he sat and shivered, looking like terrified death. I thought back over the years to Lieutenant Peal of the Glosters, and his instant cure for this type of shock, put the muzzle of my rifle hard under the man's chin, clicked the 'safety' off loudly, told him he had three seconds, counted 'one, two' and he was on his feet. He knew as well as I did, I would have shot him.

I walked along the bank to the edge of the jungle, while the patrol kept their heads down and moved, well spread, level with me on the 'lea side'. No shots, no problem, nothing. It was about 300 metres, maybe 400 metres, across open ground in full view of the village all the way to the tree line, where we were about 400 metres from the village,

We watched for a few minutes, but there was no reaction. The village remained dead. Nothing moved anywhere. We had about an hour before dark, so moved off quickly through the jungle to try to reach our bergen cache before the light failed.

I took a route which looped to keep well clear of our route coming in and hit the river after about twenty-five minutes. We crossed as before and I congratulated myself on my navigation as I could see the fish trap about 100 metres away.

Just as the last man reached the jungle I saw movement some distance along the river track, to the east. Going into an immediate ambush position we watched as two jungle tribesmen came towards us. They were unarmed except for long parangs (machetes). The older man had his on his shoulder. As I stepped into the track a few feet in front of them I kept a sharp eye on that parang. The tribesmen looked a little nervous, but no more than expected, we had no time for the niceties of life and I thought the best move was to question them on the whereabouts of enemy forces right away, while they were a little off balance.

My problem was language. My patrol linguist was in shock but I called him forward anyway, hoping he could get some information. He stood staring at the two men, then blurted out, 'Apa matchum?' They stared back at him, as well they might. He repeated his question about four times before I sent him packing. I knew enough Malay to know his question was 'How's it going?' or words to that effect.

I gave the men the big grin, a 'thumbs up' and waved them on their way. Before they were out of sight we were walking eastwards on the track, to put any would-be followers temporarily in the wrong direction. Then we skipped off the track at an appropriate spot, leaving no obvious tracks.

Before we left the river I noticed it was rising fast and felt good to have crossed it in time. The rain roared down like it was trying to bore holes in us. Knowing exactly where I was, I took off at a fast pace to find the bergen cache.

Then things began to go wrong. The ground didn't go like it should. The jungle thinned and we were in a densely overgrown 'ladang', part of the cultivations surrounding Kapoet on the north side. It was impossible to see more than a few feet in any direction. I rushed on, smashing my way literally through a wall of greenery so thick that in places I had to throw all my weight forward and lay on it to make an impression. In places there were strong tangling vines which forced me to use my knife.

Eventually I stopped, exhausted, and sat down in the mud to re-assess the situation. The patrol gathered round and we had a quick 'Chinese parliament'. Everyone was baffled. Navigation-wise everything was wrong. We had a smoke. All of us thought back along our route. I tried to concentrate on the ground we had crossed after leaving the bergens, before reaching the river. The others did the same. The only fact we could pin down was the fish trap in the river. That had been the point common to the route in and the route out, apart from the river itself.

I knew from my hours of studying and memorising the air photos there was no isolated cultivation surrounded by jungle. There was no chance Watson and I could have mistaken this ladang for jungle, even though its growth was ten or twelve feet high.

The only thing which could have thrown me was that bloody fish trap. It wasn't the one we'd seen on the way in. Had it not been there I would have carried out the usual navigation procedures to establish our position before leaving the river. I studied the map and compass, working out the possibilities and impossibilities until I had something to go on, then off we went again, due east.

As darkness fell we reached the friendly arms of the jungle. Now I knew where I was to within a couple of hundred metres. The relief was great, but the bergen cache was at least 1,000 metres away through jungle which was bad enough in daylight, no chance at night. Except for the obvious exception, morale was high. I had no worries about the patrol right now, but I did think a lot about what shape we would be in tomorrow. I was pretty well whacked, as I deserved to be, but sleep was difficult in the ice-cold pouring rain. We had about eleven hours of darkness to look forward to, with no shelter except what we could rig with leaves in darkness. That wasn't much.

I deserved the lesson, the rest of the patrol didn't – but they didn't curse me too loud or too long. You can't win them all, but what a time to pick for bum navigation.

If there was a special forces base anywhere near we could expect a follow-up the next morning. On this type of operation, until we made contact with the enemy, or gave away our presence in an area, we were very much the 'hunters'. But, due to the enemy's great numerical superiority, once they knew we were there we became very much the 'hunted'. They would quickly deploy considerable manpower with one thing in mind – our destruction or capture.

For our part, I'm sure almost all of us did a mental change from 'hunter' to 'hunted' at the appropriate moment. Nearly always, on our return to the border (when we would 'head for the pass' as we called it), we would definitely feel hunted. It was fairly certain the enemy would have discovered our tracks somewhere during the couple of weeks we had wandered among them.

I had plenty to think about through the long cold night. We had two brews of hot coffee during the night but ate nothing of our emergency rations. They were for emergencies, not bog-ups!

As soon as enough light filtered through the tree-tops we headed for the bergen cache, and found it with little problem. My troubles, however, were not over. Being a person of habit, especially when those habits concerned staying alive (and were strongly recommended by the operational directives of the regiment), I took one man to check the area for some distance around before settling down to eat, drink and be signalling. How I did it I don't know, but I got lost on that stupid little area recce, and couldn't find the bergens again. All kinds of excuses spring to mind but that's all they can be – excuses. And weak ones at that! It took us over an hour, and several animal calls to locate our bergen cache. My navigation was about as good as a drunk in a maze.

Reaching the bergens at last, then moving to a new site, I told the patrol there would be no movement that day, a decision made during the night. We slapped an ambush on our track and played the waiting game. Anyone wanting to play bloody fools could come and get us. We were not going out to play until we were fit.

Next morning we were fit, and commenced the march back to our LZ on the border. All went well until we reached the LZ. We had been told by radio that morning there were 'no friendly forces in the area', except the other two patrols who would be lifted out at the same time.

The patrol checked out the LZ area, then moved in to check the LZ itself. We were the first patrol to arrive, so posted ambush sentries and rigged the radio to report our arrival to base.

The signaller was working on his set at the west edge of the LZ, near a couple of native huts. As I couldn't leave the 'problem' on his own, he and the other man were in ambush on our back track. I had just been to check another track and was halfway back across the LZ right in the open, when a pair of little brown men in uniform, carrying pump guns, came walking around the corner of the nearest hut. They were about thirty metres from me and taken by more surprise than I was. I would have shot them, but just in time I realised the white bands around their jungle hats meant they were supposed to be on my side.

As this was happening I heard a slight sound to my right. Turning

I saw the head and shoulders of Joe's leading scout coming up over the hill about 40 metres away. The two little brown men saw him at the same time, and were in some consternation, as well they might be. I quickly called to the leading scout and smiled at the little brown men, letting my rifle hang down loosely in one hand. The tension eased, guns were lowered. A platoon of Scots Guards came wandering along the track behind their two little brown scouts.

The consternation of the wee men over Joe's leading scout was understandable. He was Fijian and, like many of our people, wore a sweat band – Geronimo fashion – rather than the usual jungle hat. I hate to think what would have happened if any one of the people there had been trigger happy, or if I had not been where I was – an obvious Brit. There would have been a war between us and the Scots Guards most likely, before anyone could recognise anyone else. The jungle is no place for slow reactions or the niceties of 'Who goes there?'

Alex's patrol arrived a few minutes later. We were all lifted out within the hour. Arriving back at base we bitched heavily about the signal stating 'no friendly forces in the area', which all three patrols had received that morning. I felt a great relief when we handed in our weapons after that operation. Relief that I no longer had a heavily armed potential nut case – who probably hated my guts – walking behind me.

The 'problem' assured me he would leave the regiment as soon as possible as he would play on a medical problem which would get him out of the Army. He left as promised.

A lot more than is written here has some bearing on the 'problem'. I should mention he had been on operations previously where his patrol was in an extremely bad situation, entangled with enemy forces for several days.

It takes all sorts to make a world, an army, a regiment. There are some sorts an army and a regiment would be better off without, but a world? That's beyond my ken. The nervous strain of SAS-type jungle operations is well known to any who have participated in such activities. Throw in a few bad experiences at the wrong time and how many more would crack?

Talking of the 'all sorts' to make whatever, this chapter reads like a catalogue of cock-ups – mostly mine!

CHAPTER EIGHT

Borneo

My regular patrol was a man short and I thought it likely my next job would have to be done with a three-man patrol. This didn't bother me but I told my two remaining patrol members to think hard about our operating procedures and contact drills, as we might have to do a bit of revision. Most of 18 Troop had different procedures and contact drills to those as ordered by the squadron and regiment. We had a lot of hard, long experience in the troop and pooled our brainpower in all things operational.

Every time we went on the jungle range, between ops, we had to practise the contact drills as laid down by the squadron, but by various means I made sure my patrol practised our own contact drills as well. It was our lives depended on them.

Then Paddy, my signaller, was rushed into hospital for an appendix operation. That left two of us. Pete and me. Right at that time the squadron was really pushed. An Australian infantry battalion was taking over from the Gurkhas on a notoriously bad stretch of the border. An Indonesian attack was expected at the worst moment, before the Aussies had time to get to know the ground. To give the Aussies some warning and help break up the expected attack, the squadron was to be deployed over the border a few thousand metres, as a screen along the battalion front.

A spare signaller was found to take Paddy's place, and an old friend, Bert, came as my medic. The unstoppable Bert, whom I had first met in Korea, then at Brecon, had been a member of 'D' Squadron for a long time. We had done a few jobs together before. It always amazed me to realise Bert had been in the Anzio landings during World War II. Now here he was again, twenty-odd years later, still soldiering on – and doing a damn good job of it – in one of the most demanding types of military operations. What a player! What a bloke!

We were genned up for the job, then spent some time working on our contact drills and operational procedures. There was little problem with maps and air photos as we only had to reach our designated position, then lie in wait.

(*Right*) In Bermuda, 1962.

(*Below*) Training in Santubong, Borneo.

Training in Santubong.

The patrol was flown to the forward positions, then escorted by a Gurkha platoon to about a thousand metres short of the border. The border at that point was a small, sluggish river, flowing through sparse jungle, scrub and ladangs. The patrol approached the border cautiously, for Indonesian patrols were known to be very active beyond the river. Slipping into the cool, murky water I eased slowly across. The water came up to my armpits at the middle point but there was hardly any current. I did the usual check around on the far side, then, finding no sign of problems, returned to the river bank and signalled the next man to cross.

Bert was last man, and not much over five feet tall. He reached the middle of the river. I 'curled up'. There was just a hat, two hands and a rifle showing above the water. Bert reached the bank, ejected a mouthful of water (no fish!), whispered, 'You – long bastard!' Then he slithered out of the water and into the undergrowth.

For various reasons we had to make a radio call to base as soon as possible after crossing the border on that particular job, so about 100 metres from the river I stopped and gave the signaller the go-ahead to send the appropriate codewords. The radio sets in use at that time had no voice capability, all signals were in morse code. A wire aerial also had to be strung in the trees in the right direction.

Bert went about twenty-five metres one way from the signaller. Pete went about the same distance in the opposite direction to watch and listen for any problems. There was nothing hard and fast about their positions. Trained men instinctively find the right place at the right time. (As I was about to find out!) I had strung the aerial and went back to the signaller to check it was working OK. He was sending our call sign, then listening for an answer. I heard the morse screaming in the headphones, and glanced at Bert. He was standing with one foot on a log, his rifle across his knee. I knew something was wrong. Bert was motionless, frozen – but coiled.

Then, under some branches about fifteen feet in front of me I saw feet moving. An Indonesian patrol was passing us, going towards the river. I glanced down at the signaller who had just turned down the volume of the radio.

Our glances met and he knew. He froze. Sitting with his back to a tree, not big enough to hide him, the headphones over his ears, unable to move he stared at the rifle lying at his side while the sweat poured down his face. He could see nothing, so knew the problem was behind him.

Very slowly I turned my head to look for Pete. He was not where he should have been. I couldn't see him. Shit! Where the hell was he? He wouldn't have gone for a shit without telling me. Was he aware of the enemy, or were they about to bump into him? The signaller was now watching me, standing about three feet in front of him. I knew he was waiting for the first signs of trouble, to go for his rifle. Bert was still frozen.

I hadn't been able to count the feet passing, but the only ones I had seen had been bare feet, no Army boots. I knew it wouldn't be local tribesmen, for they had more sense than to wander about in an area shattered by shell fire, where men hunted each other in the jungle and tall grass. The Indonesians, like us, employed local tribesmen as scouts and trackers, to move ahead of their troops or with them, as the case may be.

We waited a long time, motionless, until all was quiet. Then Bert was looking at me. I looked at the signaller, nodded towards his rifle. Thankfully he took off the headphones and slowly picked up the rifle. I signalled Bert to stay put, turned to go and look for Pete. He was stood right behind me. I said, 'What the hell are you doing?' He said, 'Well, you always told me – if there's going to be any shit flying – get behind something thick!'

What can you say? In fact he had good reason to be where he was, but couldn't resist the funny stuff.

We moved off quickly and sent our signal from another place. But the worry was with us that the opposition might find the unavoidable marks where we had crossed the river. Good trackers wouldn't have much problem tracking us from there. The usual precautions were taken but the terrain was such that tracks were inevitable in places.

Arriving in our appointed patch, a swamp, which luckily was dried up at that time of year, we found a good spot from which to carry out our task. There was one problem: water. We didn't want to make tracks looking for a stream. We had seen no water since leaving the border river, but water we must have – if we were going to stay there for two weeks.

Bert got to work on the problem, digging a hole in a likely spot. After about twenty minutes there was enough black, oily-looking water in the hole to make a brew of tea. Bert then went to work on straining and sterilising the liquid to remove the 'impurities' – obvious and otherwise.

Pete became interested in the techniques of using socks, towels and sand to strain the water. One thing led to another. Before I knew it, Pete was being taught all the 'ins and outs' of the medic pack. We were on shift two at a time, and every spare minute between shifts Bert and Pete were in a huddle. The Indonesians saw fit to steer well clear of us, so, at the end of two weeks, Pete had received a concentrated Medical Course. On Bert's recommendation he did the patrol medic job in my patrol from then on.

The time came to return to friendly territory, by now held by the Australians. When we met the Aussies they were quite surprised. Their people had written us off due to two of their patrols taking a fix on a short sharp battle, and coming up with our location as the hot spot. We had heard several skirmishes, and some artillery shelling at times, but assured the Aussies nothing had happened in our patch.

After partaking of some really good Aussie hospitality, especially in the food line, we were given a lift in a chopper back to Kuching. Base were glad to see us as they had been a bit worried by the Aussie reports of a contact being heard in our patch, even though our radio reports had been on time. They couldn't understand our not reporting enemy activity in our area. There had been a suspicion the signaller may have been captured and forced to send negative reports. It was all a bit up-market from reality for us, so we handed in our rather humdrum report and departed to drown our sorrows.

Later, the squadron commander said to Bert and myself he'd had no worries we'd get ourselves captured again. I wasn't sure if this was a separate joke or a continuation of the one he'd pulled before we went in, when he said, 'Hey, you ex-Glosters, make sure you've got no white handkerchiefs in your pockets on this one!'

The spare signaller who took Paddy's place on that operation was, as well as being a very good signaller, very prone to letting his hair get rather long. It was thick and blond, very noticeable when beyond the bounds of military good sense. As he had been in my patrol the 'powers that be' leaned on me to get his hair under control. I told him to at least go for an estimate soonest, just as a hint, but next day the heavy thatch was still there.

The way we were living at the time there were no secrets. The hair problem became a prime target for the comedians, and they made the most of it. The first I knew about it, Pete told me in a whisper, 'You were a barber in civvy street – one of the best!' A few minutes later the target was being wound up on how he could save himself a trip into town and the price of a haircut if he could talk me into giving him an expert trim.

I did my bit by playing hard to get, claiming I'd joined the Army to get away from barber shops, so I didn't want to know. It worked like clockwork. Within minutes I found myself standing over the mop with scissors and comb at the ready. Lots of snapping of the scissors and flexing of wrists, then got stuck into it.

The 'idiot handle' (as it's known in my trade) was soon lying around in tufts all over the place. I made such a mess he had to go straight into town to get it tidied up, or at least down – almost to the wood! How the comedians and the rest of the crowd keep quiet during the cutting was a miracle, but they made up for it afterwards.

I reported to HQ to pick up the details and briefing for my next op. Having got the general details I was called by the squadron commander. He had a chat to me about my next job. We discussed the pros and cons for a few minutes, then he glanced past me towards the door, and said, 'Ah, yes, Lofty, here's your replacement.' I turned to the doorway and nearly asked him if he was joking. Standing in the doorway, looking like he always did, was that stumpy, ever uproarious, always inebriated character I'd seen a few times in the Palm Grove.

I shook hands in a daze, but noticed the twinkling blue eyes were now stone cold sober. There was hope. Little did I realise at the time I was looking at the final part of the jigsaw that made a team complete. This was Kevin, a Yorkshire lad, who (I soon found out from the Ops Room) had gone on three operations but only spent four nights in the jungle, having been chased out twice by the Indonesians and shelled out once by our own artillery. He had a knee injury which was still suspect, but was keen to get into the jungle again.

That's all I needed, a dose of bad news – and a suspect knee thrown in for good measure. I knew we were pushed for men, but why pick on me? A three-man patrol looked a far better proposition.

Later that day I introduced Kevin to the tried and trusted members of the patrol. Pete, who may have been a barrow boy in London (rumour had it), couldn't treat anything or anyone seriously, made a joke out of everything and everyone. A born comedian. And Paddy, from southern Ireland. Scruffy as hell unless he wanted to look smart. One of the best signallers in the SAS. Treated his radio set like the crown jewels and everything else like shit – except his rifle! I always swore he only looked after his rifle so he could look after that bloody radio. Another comic, whose occasional seriousness was ridiculed into laughter by Pete. Out of the jungle they forever clowned and got into trouble. On operations they would have a go at anything. Their coolness and guts could only be admired. But I was the only one to see them on ops, when it counted. Alex summed it up one day. He said, 'Lofty, I wouldn't go in the jungle with any one of your comedians – let alone all three!'

The first operation Kevin came on I put him where he would have to be if he stayed with the patrol, at the back, 'Tailend Charlie', a position which has its special responsibilities on that type of operation, calling for an 'over the shoulder' alertness. We had hammered him with our own brand of operational procedures and contact drills. He took to it like a duck to water. (An unfortunate turn of phrase in Kevin's case!)

Although Paddy had lost his appendix in a hurry less than three weeks before, he insisted he was fit enough to be back in the jungle. I warned him, if he gave me any trouble he would get the 'three seconds to move' treatment – but with the rifle barrel in a more painful place, out of sight! He in turn claimed he couldn't trust us to go wandering in the woods without him. So, after checking with the medical types, I gladly accepted Paddy and his undoubted expertise back into the patrol.

Again we were to look for the enemy special forces base. I looked forward to another fourteen days of very 'dodgy' movement, looking for trip wires, booby traps, mines and the like. As Kevin said, we couldn't possibly go on getting away with it, never getting chased out – especially with him along!

The patrol had not covered 2,000 metres – we had just reached the bottom of the border ridge, in what was considered a 'hot' area – when I came to a small stream, about six or seven feet wide. I jumped the stream easily, as the far bank was a bit lower than the near one, then moved on along the bottom of a cliff. The patrol were all in place behind me as I rounded a corner of the rock face, so I kept going. After about thirty metres I stopped. Pete had not come round the corner. I waited. He didn't appear so I cursed and started back.

As I rounded the corner I could hear a splashing sound. A few yards away Pete was in a state of collapse, tears of laughter streaming down his face. I walked past him, not seeing the funny side, to find Paddy sat on the ground, choking with suppressed laughter. The splashing was louder. Then I saw it.

Kevin – being stumpy – had got right to the edge of the higher

bank of the stream for his jump. The soil had given way and his feet
had gone through into some tree roots. He had fallen forward, face
down in the stream and the roots had a perfect lock on his feet. He
was doing press-ups to breathe as his arms weren't long enough to
keep his head above water.

I had to kick their backsides to go and get him out. I think a bit
longer and he would have drowned. The whole scene was like the
Keystone Cops. Kevin was savage as hell when Paddy got him out,
but within a few minutes was curled up with laughter at their
descriptions of his predicament. There was nothing wrong with his
sense of humour. But I wondered about the suspect knee. Kevin
declared himself fit, and off we went again. The knee was obviously
no problem.

From that time on I realised that if we were all killed on
operations it would be most likely we would all die laughing. The
worse things got the harder those three threw themselves into it.
Morale was never a problem. The only problem I had was
suppressing the high spirits when the situation demanded.

Communication between patrol members was all in signs and
very low whispers, but that didn't stop those three from grinning.

On one of our early operations in Borneo I did manage to stop
Paddy from grinning. As mentioned earlier, he was rather careless
and scruffy with his kit – apart from the radio, its equipment and
his rifle. Most of the kit in our bergen rucksacks was packed in
waterproof bags, so a bit of damp getting in the pack didn't do much
harm. In Paddy's case, however, he usually managed to have to
search for some item before we had been in more than a day or two.
When Paddy searched his pack he would often pull out waterproof
bags, etc., and empty their contents back into the bergen. We called
the result 'Bergen Pie'. To compound this problem, Paddy also had
a bad habit of forgetting to close and fasten the pack when we were
at night stops. I was about fed-up with kicking his backside over it,
and decided he would have to learn the hard way.

The night came when Paddy had made a really good 'Bergen
Pie'. I noticed the pack was left wide open, but refrained from
warning him. It poured with rain in the night, half filling Paddy's
bergen. His cigarettes, which had been tipped out of their
waterproof bag were a sloppy mess. I watched Paddy trying to
salvage some of the cigarettes, knowing there was no hope.

The next day, having smoked all his remaining dry cigarettes,
Paddy tried to scrounge some of mine. I refused his pleas for the

next twelve days of the operation, only giving him a cigarette when he used the radio, and after our evening meal. Paddy's bergen packing and general care of his kit improved no end from then on.

As far as the enemy was concerned our operations continued to be mostly uneventful. We were forever going off into 'nasty' places, only to find we were too late, or the information which sent us there was wrong. I began to suspect the Indonesians didn't have any special forces. It was all a bluff to make sure my patrol stayed in for fourteen days every time.

Searching for special forces is not my idea of a relaxing sport. No matter how good or bad the special forces are they always seem to have plenty of fancy kit, especially in the demolition, mining, trapping and booby-trapping departments. Always being interested in staying reasonably alive, I made it my business to find out what the Indonesian special forces were likely to have in the way of defence equipment. They had just about everything anyone could think of. Having been trained (and were likely still being trained) by the US special forces, they were liable to have just about anything.

In Viet Nam the Americans were putting to use just about every diabolical trick known to man, and were inventing new gimmicks all the time. We had no doubt the Indonesians would have access to a lot of 'very difficult to beat' fancy goods from the American armoury, so we could expect their jungle bases to be protected very effectively.

It was pretty sure they would have Claymore mines available, either the manufactured off-the-shelf job or equally nasty home-made copies. The Claymore is a sort of directional explosive, fair shares for all ball-bearing spreader, with quite a good range, able to be set off electrically by a sentry or by the intruder touching a trip wire.

I don't know why, but the one thing which worried me most, of which we knew they had plenty, was a very simple little contraption containing one bullet. It could be placed in a small hole in the ground, and, when stepped on, fired its bullet upwards. Very simple to position and virtually impossible to see – when covered by one leaf – in a sea of leaves! According to some reports, which I saw no reason to disbelieve, the enemy special forces were experts in the art of arranging surprises with the aid of local materials. The kind of thing which finishes up with people like me being skewered on a big lump of sharpened bamboo. Or maybe several 'big lumps!' All very well if you know where the base is in the first place, but we never did – except in the case of Kapoet, where there wasn't one! It was always three or four square miles of dense jungle, somewhere nasty to get at and 'they're in there somewhere'. Of course, that few square miles of jungle was always surrounded by a few million more square miles of jungle, all looking the same, so where do you start, having found it?

You start by looking for tracks. Circle the suspect area to find any tracks which may head for the base, bearing in mind your information could be a couple of miles wrong and you could wander into the defence perimeter of the place before you find any track. Having found a track, you read it for signs, then, depending on what you find, you either watch the track for a day or so – depending on time available – or you start following the track towards the mostly likely direction of the base. But never use the track! It will be the focus of all the diabolical tricks aforementioned, and be almost certainly watched.

You push off, back the way you have come, a couple of hundred yards, then work on your map, what you have seen of the ground, etc., to decide where the track is most likely to go. A 'Chinese Parliament' is favourite at this stage – four trained heads being always better than one.

Then you loop around where you think the track will run. Maybe two or three hundred yards, maybe a thousand yards from where you found it. Two things of prime importance must then be borne in mind. First, you may reach the enemy defence perimeter before you find the track again. Second, an enemy patrol will make no noise at all on the track as you come blundering through the bushes. All very sweat-making.

By the time three months had passed I would think we were the only patrol who had not been chased out of the jungle. The others seemed to be getting all the fun. The terrain we covered was typical of the whole area. Jungle-covered mountains, with sheer cliffs and deep ravines in places. The going was always hard.

At one LZ right on the border, we made friends with the local tribe, giving some of their members medical help. Their 'longhouse' was close to the LZ and, as it was in a 'dodgy' area, we made an agreement that if all was clear (no enemy around), the children would come out into the LZ and wave to us when they heard the helicopter. This worked well and made life a lot less nerve-racking on two or three occasions. The helicopter pilots appreciated the arrangement too. They always looked relieved when I told them to only approach for landing if the children gave the 'all clear'.

There were other LZs, of course, which were extremely 'sweat-making'. I always felt very vulnerable just before we touched down. Sometimes the 'chopper' hovered just above the ground and we jumped out, in case of mines.

All the jungle people I met on our side of the border were very friendly towards us. They always had been very pro-British and some had fought with distinction against the Japanese during World War II, when Borneo had been under Japanese occupation.

Thoughts of the occasional lapses into their old games of head-hunting and using their blowpipes to zap poisoned darts at people, were pushed from our minds when we got to know them. Nevertheless we were well pleased no Brits had got the jungle tribes' backs up over the years.

Our medics had a field day almost every time we met any jungle folk, with pills for this and stitches for that. Their response to medical treatment had to be seen to be believed. One man I remember in particular had a very nasty five-inch gash in his leg. When we first saw him, on our way in to cross the border, the gash was wide open, about three or four days old and in a terrible mess. The wound was cleaned and stitched. The man was given some antibiotic tablets with verbal instructions on when to take them. When we returned, fourteen days later, the man met us with a big grin and no sign of a limp. The gash in his leg had completely healed and looked about six weeks old. Our medicines, etc., probably had maximum effect because those people had never had modern treatment before.

They were good people to be with, not 'grabbers' like some I know in other parts of the world, and took a gift or any help as an act of friendship – not a god-given right. There was a lot of trust between the jungle tribes and the SAS. Many good friendships had been made in earlier days when time was not so short. We could shake the hand and believe the smiling eyes, ignore the well-used blowpipe in the other hand – and that which probably hung decoratively in the longhouse (often, I've heard say, around a proudly possessed portrait of Her Majesty, Queen Elizabeth II).

Owing to the nature of our work we saw a certain amount of wild-life. Some interesting and some dangerous. As far as I know, only the snakes were dangerous. Even they would move away as quickly as possible rather than cause any bother. On one occasion I almost stepped on a cobra. It was behind a log I was stepping over, curled up in a small patch of sunlight. My foot stopped in mid-air about a foot above it, then, when I put my foot on the log it awoke and took off, fast.

Another snake, about seven or eight feet long really made me jump. I was climbing a steep bank out of a shallow stream, pulling myself up over some tree roots, when it came out of the roots right in front of my face. It went over my shoulder, hitting my arm and shoulder as it went. It was dark brown, but I have no idea what type (E-type perhaps – judging by its acceleration!).

There were a few scorpions about. One I saw, just in time, was as big as my hand, black with a tinge of green, at least eight inches long from nose to tail. I missed a rare sight once when I left the patrol to do a recce on my own. They watched a python attack a large squirrel-type animal. Can't remember the outcome, but they described how the two tumbled from a low tree and rolled along the ground almost at their feet.

Our biggest problem in the wildlife department were 'pig' flies. The little ones in UK are called 'Old Maids' or 'Horse flies'. The ones in Borneo were all sizes, mostly big. They would creep up on carpet slippers then stamp with red-hot boots. Paddy once lost his temper and slashed at a pig fly with his knife. He only succeeded in cutting our roof nearly in half, much to my disgust.

Another danger in most areas were pig traps, set by local hunters, These consisted of a very sharp bamboo spear attached to a springy sapling. They were triggered by a hidden trip 'wire'. A few of our people had been terribly injured by these devices during the campaign in Malaya. They could, of course, be set at a height to trap men. The ones I saw in Borneo, however, were definitely set for pigs, being at about knee height or a little higher. Luckily for me I detected the traps before springing them, except one which had killed a pig before we arrived on the scene.

On our way back to Kuching, after another uneventful slog, Pete produced from his pack a roll of white material, used for weapon cleaning. He induced us all to tie a piece around our left upper arm. Away from the noise of the chopper, he then explained.

Amid curious, suspicious glances we turned up at the Operations Centre, and, as luck would have it, the squadron commander was the first to crack. 'What the hell are you all wearing white armbands for?' Quick as a flash Pete ripped off his armband. 'Sorry, sir, we forgot to take them off. That's how we've been getting away with it all this time – we've been going in as umpires!'

Pete's patter was not always good for morale, as in one case I well remember. We had been on a very strenuous and tricky problem, were on our way back towards the border, having carried out our task without too much cold sweat, and were stopped for the night. Pete was eating his curry and rice in complete silence, which was unusual. Suddenly he turned to me and said, 'Lofty, what the hell are you doing here?' I just stared at him, there was no knowing what might come next. He went on, 'Do you realise, a sergeant in the Ordnance Corps, whose greatest risk is dropping his wallet on his toe, is getting more pay than you are?' Having noticed these strange quirks of Army pay a long time ago I said nothing. He rubbed it in. 'The bastard's getting Trade Pay and will be all set for a good job when he gets demobbed. What good is this lot to you? You can't do this in Civvy Street, you know!' I didn't lose any sleep over it, but some people might have, in our position.

Kevin's friends in the Navy offered to take the patrol on a trip in their minesweeper. It seemed a good idea, as we could leave one day and be back the next by changing ships as one took over patrol from the other. Before checking with our people we decided to have a look at the minesweeper, and meet some of the crew. Arriving where the ships were berthed we were impressed by their 'battleship grey' smartness. They were small, as ships go, but seemed quite large to us. With their few guns they looked quite effective. We were welcomed aboard and, as is inevitable, taken to the small wardroom for a drink.

Enjoying my drink I gazed around and noticed slim wooden pegs sticking out of all the walls in a very haphazard pattern. Not wanting to appear ignorant, I contained my curiosity for as long as I could, hoping all would become clear, without questions. Just before we left, I could wait no longer, and asked about the strange wooden pegs. The Navy types glanced around at the twenty or so pegs around the small room, and one said, 'Oh, we haven't got around to proper repairs yet, they are the bullet holes from our last trip.'

We thought they were joking. A closer inspection of the ship proved they weren't. Soldiers don't think of naval problems much, and the fact that – because of magnetic mines – minesweepers have to be made of wood. To us the ships looked bullet proof in their smart grey paint. It came as a rude awakening to realise these merry matelots were riding around in a bloody sieve. Needless to say, we chickens found strong operational reasons for not taking up the Navy's generous offer of a trip. Our type needs its feet firmly on the ground before taking on spiteful people with guns.

A lack of communication, or mistakes in communications, led to some near scrapes for us on several occasions. One of these was quite lucky, as it happened. The LZs along the border were always dicy places, sometimes downright dangerous. After one particular job we came out at a point on the border some distance from our entry point, to an LZ we had not visited before. Having found the LZ we signalled base we were ready to be lifted out.

There was a long wait while base told us to maintain 'listening watch' on the radio. After about ten minutes they sent a message telling us to move at once to a forward infantry position. A 'sandbag fortress', about 4,000 metres north of the border, and about 5,000 metres from where we were. The infantry were expecting us, we were to move openly with our hats off, to prevent mistakes (if we met infantry patrols) and be easily recognised as Brits.

Accordingly we moved to a track marked on the map, which turned out to be a once well-trodden path through the jungle, leading almost directly to the fortress. We arrived at the position to find it almost deserted. The infantry officer looked at us in amazement. 'Where the hell have you come from?' were his first words, then, 'Who the hell are you?' I told him we had come from the border. (We were not allowed to mention going over the border in those days.) He asked me if I had seen any of his ambushes. I told him we hadn't. So he asked which way we had come. When I told him he looked shocked. 'No one uses that track,' he said. 'It's a death trap. We ambush it, the Indo's ambush it, and in any case everyone has mined it! I didn't put an ambush on it today because it's a waste of time – nobody uses it any more!'

I told him he was in good company – we hadn't seen any of his opposite numbers' ambushes. 'And while you're thinking about it, you'd better check on your mines, they're not working today either!'

It turned out, as we'd come to half expect from previous experience, the infantry knew nothing about us being in their area. Returning to base we did the usual bitching, which got us nowhere. One of my crew drew some sour looks when he mentioned it was safer going over the border than coming back. 'Perhaps we should ask the Indonesians next time – they seem to know all the safe crossing places!'

Asking why the chopper couldn't make it to our border LZ, we were told it was considered too dangerous, there was too much enemy activity in the area at the time. I got the impression we were to blame for that. One of my voices in the background muttered, 'Another fine mess you got us into!'

Going in on another job, we went by chopper to a forward infantry position which was, I believe, manned by a Guards unit. We arrived just before lunch and were due to be lifted to a border LZ later that day. A very smart, 'regimental' gentleman 'buttonholed' me and said, 'Would you please come with me, sergeant.'

Wondering what was required, I left my crew, who were heading for the cookhouse, and followed the 'gent' to what turned out to be the 'sergeants' mess', where a huge and beautiful meal was already laid out for me. Never having been one to turn my back on the better things in life – especially when it would offend a most generous host – and having been told the boys would be well looked after, I set to with a will and demolished some very excellent cooking.

Rejoining the patrol when the chopper arrived I got some 'old fashioned' looks, but nothing much was said. That night, when we made camp and went through the usual signals and meal preparation routine I noticed a few things different, and there was a strange 'feel' to the patrol. Then I noticed a bit of paper stuck in a split stick in front of my poncho. I picked it up, and on the other side it said, 'sergeants' mess'. Paddy said, 'If we're not good enough to eat with out there, we're not good enough to eat with in here, so cook your own bloody scoff?' It was a send-up which lasted a few days and caused a lot of silent laughter among us.

In operational theatres the SAS always had an 'all ranks' mess. Everyone from the Brigadier Commanding SAS Group, or the Commanding Officer of 22 SAS, down to the newest young trooper in the regiment took it as normal to sit down together for meals in the same mess – the same table if it happened to be the one vacant. Perhaps it was after that job, when the 'sergeants' mess' send-up was still in the air, we arrived back at Kuching by chopper and landed at Brigade HQ. Well, not quite at Brigade HQ but really just outside, next to a little bar we knew quite well. We had a quick drink to sort of clear our throats, then I went off to ring our people for some 'wheels' to get us and our gear back to SAS base. It took me some time to get through and organise transport. By the time I returned to the little bar the other three were looking suspiciously the worse for the time I had taken. By the time I'd had another drink the wheels arrived and it was then I found they had put all their drinks on my 'book'! The bill was horrific, I could hardly believe so much could be shifted by so few in so short a time, until I saw them struggling to get in the back of a Land-Rover like it was Mount Everest!

During that trip to Borneo we were joined on operations by a half squadron of New Zealand SAS who fitted in with us like very few non-Brit troops can. Their sense of humour and general approach to life were very compatible with ours. Like us, they enjoyed the challenge of operations, pitting their wits and skill against a determined enemy.

Of all the various 'foreign' troops with which I came into contact the Kiwis were most like our own people. But of course we didn't think of them as 'foreign'. I don't think any of us thought of any Commonwealth troops as foreign, so it was always a good start to getting on with things we had to do together.

CHAPTER NINE

The Koemba Job

'D' Squadron's tour of duty in Borneo was nearing its end. We were due to be relieved by 'A' Squadron, and would return to UK for a short break before going on our next job. There was however time for the squadron to have one last try at a job which had already been tried six or seven times by patrols from 'B' and 'D' Squadrons. It was a mental thorn in the mind of our squadron commander. Brigade HQ were warm under the collar about it. We all knew that no job could be termed 'impossible'. In fact it looked dead easy. The main problem was the opposition also knew it looked dead easy, and, as previous patrols had found out, were dead set on making it dead hard!

Everyone on our side of the border wanted to know if the Indonesians were using the River Koemba to build up their troops and supply them. If they were, to what extent? And what could we do about it? Everyone on the other side of the border had seemed, so far, to be very much against the idea.

We didn't even know if the river could be reached along most of its length near the border because of vast swamps in the jungle. The swamps made most of the area operationally impassable. The other bits were well patrolled and more easily watched by the opposition. Reading the reports of previous patrols I got the impression if the swamps didn't get you the Indos would.

For some inexplicable reason the squadron commander got it into his head that my iittle band of comedians would crack it. (Or was this his final attempt to rid the scene of too much operational hilarity?) I seem to remember asking him if he really believed that about the white armbands.

Before briefing me for the job the squadron commander asked me if I felt completely fit and 'up to scratch'. I assured him I had no problems. Then he asked me about Pete, and told me to give Pete the option of dropping out of the patrol for this last job. When I asked the reason, he told me Pete and myself had been continually on operations, mostly difficult ones, for too long – according to 'medical advice' – so it was only fair to give Pete the chance of a rest.

I didn't fancy changing the team, but gave Pete the option anyway. Just as I expected, Pete blew his top. His reply was unprintable, very much to the point – and just what I wanted.

I was given all the 'gen' to study. Then the big question. Did I think we could crack it? I thought we could give it a damn good try, and said as much.

The other patrols who had made the attempt had all been sent to specific areas of the river with boundaries which they could not cross for operational reasons, such as other patrols in adjoining areas, artillery target areas, etc. My first request was for freedom of choice for the route in, and freedom of movement anywhere within reason. This was granted.

I went down to Brigade HQ and my good friend Staff-Sergeant Watson. We went over those maps and air photos with about everything. All the information we could glean from other patrol reports we related to the maps and photos until I formed an idea of the only possible route which would be worth trying.

There was a spur of higher ground running south from the border towards the river. The spur vanished from both maps and air photos a long way from the river, but, following the line of that pointing finger, there was a corresponding bend in the river. It was little enough to go on, but it was all we had. A detailed study of that particular bit of jungle revealed almost nothing. The only 'holes' in the trees on the air photos revealed water. Even Watson couldn't estimate the depth of water through little holes in the trees. I remember there were only two holes anyway, in an area of several square miles. There was an Indonesian military set-up, a small garrison base, less than 1,000 metres from where I thought I might reach the river. It was on the north bank of the river, the near side, and was probably the base from which their patrols covered the area to the border.

It was obviously on high ground, clear of flooding from the river, so, at a push, I could get close to the base and use 'their' high ground. The main task was to get all the information we could. The secondary task was to disrupt any military river traffic we found. To help with our secondary task I requested a Bren light machine-gun to be carried by myself, for added firepower. Being the biggest patrol member, well able to use a Bren like a rifle, I thought it was a good idea.

LZ. Waiting.

LZ. Loading.

LZ. Lift-off.

Paddy and Kevin in SAS Pink Panther, Libya.

Rovers in the North African desert.

The squadron commander, however, thought the extra weight and more cumbersome weapon just might tip the balance the wrong way and interfere with our primary task. The Bren was not granted. He did suggest I take an AR16 (Armalite) but at that time we only had two in the unit. One was being carried on operations already, and the other – you would never guess – had been taken to Labuan, a safe base area hundreds of miles from Kuching, by a gentleman who, in that situation, didn't need a weapon at all! Having a fancy gun to parade around would do his ego a power of good, but very little to help the unit effort in the field.

I counted it a small price to pay for peace and quiet, so, although a few alternatives were available, I opted to take my tried and trusted SLR. At least it had the punch we wanted, if not the rate of fire.

The patrol worked out on the jungle training areas, firing and checking our weapons as well as all our contact drills and operational procedures. By the time we set forth we were well pleased with every detail. Confident in ourselves, in each other, and in our ability to do the job. We knew we were going to reach that river – come hell or high water!

Our departure was marred by something we could do nothing about. Our weapons had been checked, cleaned and oiled to perfection, our lives were likely to depend on them. They were then handed in to the squadron armoury for the night and brought with the vehicle which picked us up to take us to the airfield in the morning. It was several miles from Squadron HQ to where we were then billeted, then a few more miles away from SHQ to the airfield. When the vehicle arrived we piled in and immediately grabbed our beloved rifles. There was a yell at once from Pete: 'Where's my rifle? – I don't want this bloody thing!'

Somehow the wrong rifle had arrived and Pete didn't want to know it. There was no time to go back for the right weapon so we had to take it. I told Pete it must be OK. We would try to test fire it at Lundu, to where we were flying by fixed wing aircraft, a Twin Pioneer. In the event there was no time, as we went straight from the 'Twin Pin' to a chopper which couldn't wait because of a tight schedule. Arriving at a very dicy LZ right on the border in a 'hot' area, there was no chance of test firing the weapon. Pete went into the jungle a very unhappy man that day.

None of us was too happy with the situation. We worked together like a well-oiled machine, there was no room for a suspect part. Pete had stripped the weapon on the aircraft, checked every bit. Tested everything that could be tested short of firing it. But he distrusted the damn thing, losing no chance of letting the rest of us know his feelings.

The first night in the jungle we all checked the suspect weapon. I for one pronounced it perfect, advising Pete to ignore the possibilities, we had enough problems already. Pete said he felt better about it, but I knew him too well.

Information from another patrol's report (Old Joe's) told where the best route lay for most of the distance, so I kept well away from it. We might need it on the way back. There are many problems with jungle movement under operational conditions. One is tracks. No matter how good you are, you are bound to leave tracks in most places. So on the first day or two we moved on a steady bearing towards a point west of where we were really heading. After that we made for a point east of our real heading. After that we hit swamps and our choices finished. We were limited to where was possible.

On the second day, I heard a slight sound up ahead. Leaving the patrol I went forward and found an Indonesian unit of probably platoon strength right in our path. We pulled back a little, made a detour to the east of them and pushed on. The enemy platoon were stationary. Some were cutting small branches, making the noise which gave them away. So we had no idea which way they were heading or what they were doing. It was too early in the day for them to be making a night stop camp. There was no track anywhere we could see which they might be ambushing. But as we didn't find their tracks we knew they must have come from west of our route, so it was possible, or probable, they would cross our tracks when they resumed moving. Not good news. We did what we could with our track problem. Kevin keeping an extra sharp look and listen to the rear.

The edge of the swamp was just a matter of splashing in and out of areas of shallow water onto areas of low firm ground. Further in, the water became gradually deeper, the ground above water level became less firm, then just mud. A jungle swamp is not a nice place. Under the black water tree roots tangle and jam unwary feet. Deep holes are not usually common, but they exist. The jungle is still there above and below the water, in all its tangled glory, but now decorated with hanging moss and drapes of jungle rubbish up to the high water mark. In this case several feet (up to 9 or 10 feet) above the present water level. Fallen trees and branches are still obstacles to progress, but often no longer visible.

Sometimes a thick green scum covers the surface of the swamp over large areas. This particular swamp had an extra hazard. Huge leaves, mostly four or five feet long and two or three feet wide, which had fallen from a type of tree which was apparently very common in that area. The leaves crackled like a tin roof when walked upon, and still kicked up a row when moved to one side on the water.

By the time I had been waist deep for about half an hour at a stretch, trying in vain to move silently southward, I had this recurring vision of a grinning enemy watching me approach noisily to the muzzle of his heavy machine-gun. The water crept above my waist and I stopped. The decision, silently made a long way back, was that no way was I going to fight a war more than waist deep in that lot.

Turning onto a westerly bearing we moved until we found dry ground. There we took a break, having spent about ninety minutes in the water. Leaving Paddy and Kevin to look after the packs, Pete and I went south again, looking for a way through.

We were probing the east side of where the spur should be – if it still existed – and would continue pushing south towards the river as far as we could on each probe, moving west after each failure. At one point I came to a fallen tree, about a foot thick, lying in the water. It was just under the surface, the water was nearly waist deep. As I reached the tree and prepared to climb over it the water swirled on the other side and I glimpsed a large patch of light brown 'scales' going down under the tree towards my legs. I was nearly airborne by the time I realised it was only a turtle or tortoise.

After about an hour, we were stopped in waist deep water while I checked the map, compass and memory for anything which tallied with the terrain we had crossed.

Pete was probably as smashed as I was. It was bloody hard work. I glanced back at him, he was about 20 metres back, right where he should be. Seeing my glance he whispered something. I couldn't hear the words so signalled him closer. Closing up to about ten metres, he whispered, 'I hope we're the Goodies!'

In a daze of problems I stared at him. 'What?' He repeated the same sentence. Losing patience fast I said, 'What do you mean?'

Pete closed up a couple more metres, his face and eyes serious, 'Well,' he said, 'if we're the Baddies, we'll just as likely finish up with our hats floating on top of this lot!' Then he let the grin slip, and I had difficulty in keeping the laughter silent. After that I felt more relaxed, and inwardly blessed that comedian for his sense of humour.

For two or three days we pushed and probed, then we cracked it. We had been so close on occasions, we had heard the heavy diesel engines on the river, within 100 metres of us. When we got through we were all moving together as a patrol. I could hardly believe my eyes. There were the muddy swirling waters of the elusive Koemba. Part of the shock was seeing it about seventy metres away, down a steep slope through a rubber plantation. I checked the area, then brought the patrol forward so they could see what had stopped us, and deploy to cover me while I checked all around. The rubber plantation was not in use, although cups still hung on the trees. Tappers' tracks were old and overgrown. There was a track along the top of the bank from where I first saw the river but that too was disused.

As I moved forward to check down to the river, the whole plan became clear. I signalled the patrol to follow as soon as I knew it was safe. They came down through the rubber taking care not to leave tracks. The place was made to measure. There was an old ditch, about three feet deep and ten feet wide, just short of the river bank. A few bushes hid the ditch from all sides. We moved in.

In front of us now was a good view of the river, right on a sharp bend. The bend would slow and turn river traffic so we could get a good view. The ambush possibilities were beautiful. Our only problem was tracks. We thought back over our last bit of dry land after the swamp, and decided it was worth taking the chance. To go back and look would only create more problems so we decided to stay put.

At first, it puzzled me why the rubber plantation didn't show on the air photos. Then, when I looked around, I could understand it. The rubber trees were planted haphazardly, not in rows. There were odd jungle trees growing among them down at the river edge and along the lower slopes. The higher ground put the rubber trees up to the height of the jungle near the edge of the plantation, giving an overall flattish canopy right across.

Assessing our position, we decided our weak spot was the high ground from which we had first seen the river. But the only time we would be exposed to view from that side was when in our actual ambush firing positions. On normal watch there was no problem.

The whole situation tickled our sense of humour. Morale was sky high. What kind of fool would hide under a few bushes in a rubber plantation, within a few hundred metres of an enemy base – when there was a whole damn jungle everywhere else? It looked ridiculous as a hiding place. Enemy patrols would concentrate on the jungle, they wouldn't give our bushes a second glance, even if they came anywhere near.

Night came, we cooked a good curry and slept on it. 'Top exponents' of jungle warfare, and young lads wanting to learn the art – each group trying to impress the other – should read no further. Very likely on real pain of death. From apoplexy in the one case and from trying to do the wrong thing in the wrong place in the other.

To the good, tough, resolute fighting men of the British Army who had suffered ambush positions of complete silence, no smoking, no hot drinks, no cooked food (no farting?) for days on end, sometimes a week or two, maybe more, the hard truth (never told before) which follows, may be too much to bear. Or believe. I could cloud the whole scene in bullshit, without mentioning realities, but so far I have stuck faithfully to the truth of my memory and see no reason to change.

We all knew the rules laid down by the regiment, concerning ambushes, observation posts, movement in enemy-held areas and a whole bible of operational situations. I make no excuses. I had my reasons. I know I have been unorthodox, but on purpose, with a logical reason.

Our position would be good until the shit hit the fan. We had passed the 'cut off' tracks, freshly cut in nice straight lines. We had seen sign of enemy patrols and almost bumped one. We were not far from an enemy base, and knew we had to go nearer to it when we bugged out – if we were to make a fast escape from the potential trap we were in.

I wanted fitness and morale at its peak for the 'bug-out', which we all knew would come. I wanted a cock-a-hoop patrol which would take on the world with a grin. So I got one.

We smoked. Even Pete, the non-smoker, had the occasional cigarette. We had a brew of coffee or tea about every two hours. We had a good meal of curry and rice every evening. Relaxation, as far as is possible under those conditions, was the order of the day. We got most of the information required in the first twenty-four hours. Although we had to stay put as long as possible to gain as much information as possible we were not too bothered about picking a fight to finish the job any time anyone wanted to try us. We felt very secure in our own confidence.

The first thing we saw on the river nearly finished us. Kevin was 'fishing' for water. He had his water bottle on a cord, dangling it in the river, which was about seven or eight feet below the sheer bank in front of us, when a canoe carrying two men came silently upstream from the west. They came just past the position then turned to face us. I watched them closely. They could have been locals, but I didn't think so.

One was working his paddle hard and staring at the bank just to the left of me. The water bottle cord was away to the right, thank God. The other man was staring into the muddy water and working with a 'stick', which turned out to have a hook on the end when he pulled up a fish trap. Situation explained.

I continued to watch them closely as they moved upstream and lifted other traps. There was no sign they had seen anything of us, so we let them go. Being a suspicious lot, the patrol had all been looking the other way, in case the fishermen were being used as a distraction.

Several diesel launches had passed us during the second day. Heavily laden going upstream, empty on their way back. Then an open boat with an outboard motor appeared. There were three men in it, all wearing blue shorts. They looked too big, too 'military' in appearance to be locals, but I wasn't sure.

They beached the boat about twenty-five metres upstream from us, then went to work on baling out the boat and refuelling the engine. The patrol was in an all round defence posture. I watched the men closely. I can't remember seeing any weapons, but there could have been some among the kit in the boat.

I thought of taking them prisoner. They could probably give our people all the information they wanted if we could get them back over the border. Three or four things were against taking them prisoner. First, I wasn't sure they were military. Second, it would be difficult enough to reach the border even without a prisoner. Thirdly, they might have had no knowledge of use to us, whether or not they were military. Fourth, I had explicit instructions not to initiate any type of offensive action until my primary role was completed, and I received authority from base. So they finished their work and went on their way, never knowing how lucky they were.

The days passed. We informed base of everything which moved on the river. On one occasion a raft came down the river with three or four men on it, all singing. One was doing the lead singer's job quite well, he had a good voice. I glanced back at the patrol. They all had their arms waving in the air like they were conducting an orchestra. Morale was high.

The time came when I calculated we had done enough. Time was running out, so I sent a signal requesting permission to carry out our secondary task. Being of an extremely distrusting nature, I didn't trust the opposition not to have the necessary radio equipment to get a fix on our position when we used our radio to send messages. As a result, all our messages were as short as possible, with Paddy and I spending a lot of time finding the shortest possible way to code each message.

It was 1965. The James Bond films were at their height. Checking for a short way through the codes, we found the shortest. The message read 'Request "00" Licence'. Everyone at base would be expecting the request. I thought it was unmistakable. Everyone at base understood exactly what was required – except the clown who was in charge of the Operations Centre at the time. With everyone else in the place telling him it was obvious, he sent back a signal saying, 'Message not understood'. The difference in time sending the next shortest alternative coded message was about twenty seconds instead of the original four or five seconds.

There is no way around stupidity in high places, when you're out on a limb. I only wished the squadron commander had been in the Ops Centre at the time, but he wasn't. We sent the request the hard way, and hoped (as we always did when working to base from close to enemy positions) that no enemy signals type was getting his pop music interfered with by our morse code. Having penetrated the thick skull with a long hammering message, we received permission to proceed with stage two of the operation.

Now it was a matter of finding the right target at the right time. I wanted the biggest possible military boat moving upstream in the late afternoon. The rest of the patrol wanted any floating object as soon as possible and get to hell out of there.

We agreed to a deadline of one hour before dusk. If we had not found a target by then we would wait until the next day.

Our big problem was not the ambush, but the getting clear away after it. The enemy base just down the river would be sure to hear the attack and could well be in a position to send troops along the deployment tracks to the north of us, thereby cutting off our escape. If they reacted quickly they could reach the crucial point before us, as they had less distance to go and good tracks to move on. There was not a lot of room between the swamp and the open rubber plantation, both of which we must avoid. If the enemy could get troops to the north end of that strip of jungle we would have big problems.

I estimated we could get past the deployment tracks in about half an hour if we moved fast. Once out of the bottleneck our chances would be good – if we could keep moving fast.

I also estimated the enemy would deploy without their packs, being so close to their base, so would have two chances late in the day: either to return to base before dark, or to spent the night cold and miserable in the jungle. Either way we would have the advantage the next morning – if we had cleared that bottleneck. The enemy patrols further north might, or might not, still be there. Luck would likely be the major factor in their case, so there was little we could do about them. There was also the chance we may get into problems and be glad of darkness to cover our escape. The jungle is not impassable at night in that situation.

A straight beeline for our extraction LZ (the same one we entered by) would not be wise, with those patrols to the north, so I planned to put an easterly 'crank' in our route, partly to avoid interception further north (which could be organised by enemy troops following our tracks, and sending the position and bearing to those ahead of us), partly to take advantage of the 'good going' mentioned in Joe's patrol report. The patrol had haggled through all the pros and cons. We were all satisfied we had taken care of all foreseeable possibilities (plus a few others). We all knew what to do once the ambush was over.

So we waited. Noon passed and the optimum time was approaching. Two or three launches passed. They were too small or going the wrong way. Those going downstream were obviously going faster and would quickly be carried out of sight. There was a sharp bend in the river right in front of us. The downstream traffic came straight towards us, then turned and soon vanished to our right. The upstream traffic came slowly from our right, into the bend, then slowly away from us, to disappear on another bend about a hundred metres away.

Our plan was to destroy a boat. We were not too interested in inflicting casualties. There had to be casualties to prevent return fire but the main firepower would be directed at the stern of the boat, just above the water line, hoping to destroy the propeller drive and hole the bottom of the boat, also destroy the engine.

To do this, the three other members of the patrol would

concentrate all their firepower on the stern, while I would take out any possible retaliation. I would also watch for other problems. The patrol would be lying in their fire positions, I would stand slightly to one side, level with their feet to be able to see all around. Firing would commence as each reached his position and found the target. All shots would be well aimed, there was no rush. We would each fire twenty rounds into the target.

Mid afternoon came, and with it the rain. At first a gentle pattering, but distant thunder promised a heavier dose was on the way. My thoughts turned to the swamps. Heavy rain would spread the swamp area considerably, very likely making our exit much more difficult by narrowing that bottleneck. That's if we were still there next morning.

The roar of the rain muffled the sound of the launch as it approached upstream. I was on almost continual watch, as the decision to attack had to be mine. Peering through the intervening greenery and the rain I saw a new sight on the river, a gleaming white launch with glinting brass-work. This was no ordinary run of the mill river craft. It had to be something special. I could feel the tension of the patrol behind me, waiting for the signal. The launch was nearly upon us and my right hand was held out ready to turn the thumb up, or down. Then I saw the woman. She was standing on the bridge of the launch, between two men in uniform. One in Navy whites, the other an Army officer.

The target was perfect, just what we wanted. The launch was a good 45 foot long, a nice boat, very naval or military in appearance, its Indonesian flag, and various pennants flying proudly.

Neither I nor any man with whom I served in the British Army had ever intentionally made war upon women and children. I saw no reason to change. The thumb went down. I watched the people on the boat flash past, thirty or forty feet in front of me. They were laughing, enjoying a joke, the woman's black hair contrasting with her white dress, oblivious of sudden death just a few metres away.

As the launch disappeared from view I heard someone mutter, 'What's he bloody waiting for? The frigging *Ark Royal*?'

The patrol had only been able to see the back of the launch as it turned and went away from us. When I told them there was a woman on the bridge, so very likely others as well as children on board, they were in full agreement with the decision not to attack.

Again we waited. The tempo of the rain increased. Thunder rolled and crashed all around. Lightning flickered and flashed in the dim light of the storm. Conditions were perfect, perhaps too perfect. I wondered if river traffic might call a halt until the storm passed.

I can't remember whether I first heard or saw the next launch. We were almost at the deadline for that day. I was beginning to think of tomorrow's luck when suddenly it was there. It was coming steadily upstream, a big one, at least forty feet long. Canvas drapes were rolled down at the sides, because of the rain, so I couldn't see the cargo. As it passed me I saw men in jungle green sitting as you often see troops in the back of Army lorries. The thumb went up, and the patrol hit their firing positions. I sprang to my fire position and took out the two men visible at the back of the boat, then put five shots into the cargo compartment to keep that happy.

The patrol was firing steadily, hitting the flat stern of the boat, centre of the water line. Pete was having trouble with that bloody rifle. I watched him go through the drills, trying to clear the problem, then I put another five shots into the boat to keep them busy, and turned to have a good look along the high ground behind us. Nothing showed, so I again turned my attention to the boat. Pete was still having problems, having to cock the rifle after each shot.

The boat slowed and lost way, smoke began to billow from the darkness under the canvas roof. I spaced six rounds across the middle of the target area, then changed the magazine. Only Pete was firing so I yelled 'Stop!' and that was it, we were on our way. Paddy and Kevin grabbed their packs and ran to the high ground, while we covered them. Then it was Pete and I who ran. But halfway up the bank I remembered my brand new water bag, of a type very hard to come by, so, begrudging its use by the opposition, I ran back to get it, followed by Pete who thought I had seen something up ahead and was bugging-out in the wrong direction. He looked fit to bust as he watched me empty the water bag and stuff it in my shirt.

Then we were away. My last sight of the boat, it was dead in the water, beginning to turn as it drifted back, almost obscured by thick smoke. Something man-size toppled like a log into the water from amidships. The boat had a list to starboard and the orange glow of fire was visible under the shadowy roof.

About a hundred metres into the jungle we stopped to check everything was OK. Everything was – except Pete's rifle. He was savage as hell. We were all savage as hell come to that. It was bad enough having our firepower depleted in the river ambush, but it could be lethal for us if we had a head-on contact with the enemy while moving fast. Especially for me. I relied completely and with confidence on Pete to get me out of trouble if we hit anything. His fast reactions and ability with a weapon were crucial.

We agreed on adjustments to our contact drills which ensured we could do our best, come the crunch, and headed out fast. With any luck the uproar of the storm had covered the sound of the ambush, but it wasn't something we wanted to bet our necks on. The chances the enemy would be waiting for us were about 50–50 (much better than the 10–1 odds against us without the storm).

The advantages and disadvantages of slow or fast movement in different types of jungle have to be weighed against the requirement of the moment, the likely enemy situation and the type of jungle encountered. A considerable amount of know-how and experience is required to get the right balance, in the right places and at the right time. An enemy lying in wait has everything going for him – except when! He's ready to blow you in half but never knows when you will appear, if ever.

Trying to move up silently on someone who is switched on and expecting you is one thing to avoid in jungle. It is almost impossible. Smashing through the sticks like a rampaging bull elephant gives ample warning of your approach, ensuring a hot reception.

We were now going to move as fast as possible, because we had to, but that didn't mean we were throwing caution to the winds, or making things easy for the opposition. To do it right, every member of the patrol has to be very good at this job to give the leading scout that hairbreadth of time afforded by surprise.

The leading scout has the job of finding the way through, as quietly as possible, while still navigating to maintain overall movement in the right direction. At the same time he has to be ready to react like lightning. The only way I could do it was to fix in my mind, 'The bastards are there – go get 'em!' To think that they will appear as surely as the hidden targets on the jungle range – and go for them. Confidence in your own abilities, training, experience and extremely fast reactions under pressure can help a lot. But you still know that if Lady Luck is not smiling upon you – the rest is rubbish.

Every patrol member must be just as switched on as the leading scout. Their extra problems are that their friends are probably between them and the enemy. They must be ready to bring instant fire to bear in the right places while being careful not to hit their own men.

They must keep their eyes open to left and right for any sign of problems, and make sure the man behind is still where he should be. They must keep in sight of the man in front but be far enough back not to be caught in the same burst of automatic fire, mine, or booby trap. In a contact with the enemy they must react instantly, guided by the actions of the man in front of them, or what happens to him. Complete, unwavering trust in each other is essential to any patrol on operations.

Lady Luck had smiled upon us in the ambush, with a thunderstorm at the right moment. She now continued to smile to the accompaniment of pouring rain which would cover the sounds of our movement. Nevertheless, fickle lady as she is, the rain could be switched off and a platoon of enemy could be waiting right in our path. She continued to smile.

The patrol had almost reached the point of greatest danger, the deployment track at the north end of the bottleneck, where our route lay nearest to the enemy base. I was moving swiftly up a short sharp slope when a movement ahead stopped me.

It was a snake, on the flat ground at the top of the slope. We saw each other at the same time, meeting head on, both in a hurry. The rifle was lined up on it before I knew what it was that moved. It stopped at the same time as I did, and reared up like I'd never seen before.

I had never seen one before, but I knew only too well I was facing a king cobra, at a range of about six or seven feet. It reared up to a height of at least four or five feet. As it was on slightly higher ground it looked enormous. We were eyeball to eyeball. The rifle had followed it up and was aimed at the centre of the hood, which swayed slightly but was almost still. I remained perfectly still, with my brain in overdrive. I dare not shoot except as a last resort. A shot would not only give us away to the enemy, but would put the patrol into its head-on contact drill. In other words create a small war on a snake, with a lot of ammunition being expended and possibly quite a delay to further progress in the right direction.

How far can the damn things reach when they strike? Is there any warning they are about to do so? How I wished I'd learnt more about snakes. We stood there, both poised to strike, not knowing each other's abilities, and, hopefully, neither wanting to start anything.

It seemed an age we froze like that, but was probably less than ten seconds, then, as quickly as it had risen, it dropped down and rushed away behind a log. Beautiful, sensible snake. I looked back at Pete, signalled 'snake', pointed to the log and moved on past it. The snake had vanished.

We rushed on, reached and dashed across the deployment tracks, then began to breathe easier. No sign of the opposition.

The rain, which had given us such good cover, both for the ambush and for the mad dash through the bottleneck, had slackened off by the time we took a five-minute break.

I checked back along the patrol. Reaching Kevin, he asked me what the sudden stop had been for. I told him, 'A snake'. For some reason Paddy hadn't told him at the time. Kevin looked past me at Paddy and whispered, 'You Irish bastard – I could have been bloody scoffed!' Kevin was not at all fond of snakes, unless they were curried.

Pushing on fast until almost last light we were well pleased with our progress by the time we looped and lay among some fallen trees, ambushing our back track. Then we heard the mortar firing from the enemy base. We listened with bated breath for the shells to land. They were a long way from us, and someone said, 'Thank Christ for that, they think we've gone further east.' I hated to spoil that peace of mind but had to say it. 'Why do you think they're not shelling this area?' There was a silence, then someone muttered, 'Shit!'

After dark we cooked a good meal, then settled down for the night. We didn't all take off our boots and belts. It was a free choice, I took off mine and crawled thankfully into my sleeping bag.

Before first light in the morning we were ready to go, waiting for the first glimmer of light to give us enough to move. We had each drunk a cup of coffee, were ready for the day and anything it might bring.

Paddy was the only one with any weight on his back, as he was carrying the radio and would not let anyone else share the load. 'None of you bums could use it properly anyway,' was always his final argument.

Once we got under way again I kept check on Paddy as he had had some sort of 'bug' before the operation and wasn't as fit as he might have been.

We put in a distance to the east-north-east soon after starting the day's march, which quickly put us away from our original bearing and into Joe's 'good primary jungle', where we were able to move faster and quieter. Once or twice animals or birds gave me a start and stopped us dead in our tracks, but of the opposition there was no sign. Their tracks showed in a couple of places, but the freshest ones were days old.

Our next problem was finding and checking the LZ, a task which cannot be done in a hurry without risk of springing an ambush.

Base told us by radio there were no friendly forces in the area. I remember hoping they had it right this time, as we were travelling fast on a 'hair trigger'. I had already come within an ace of shooting a small deer, a bird and – would you believe – a falling leaf. At less than 1,000 metres from the LZ we stopped to give base our ETA (estimated time of arrival). I noticed Paddy was getting to look rough. He had almost stopped sweating, a bad sign under those conditions. He said he kept feeling dizzy, when Kevin accused him of 'walking like a drunk!'

I had to re-think the angles. We may yet have a 'war' on our hands. A sick man was something we could very well do without.

There was another problem. None of the previous patrols to return through that particular LZ had been able to find it easily.

There was absolutely nothing between the river and the border which showed on the maps, except the spur, which was almost impossible to find on the ground due to the 'lumpy' nature of the whole area. We had nothing on which to check our position since leaving the river. With a very likely enemy 'follow-up' party, possibly (by my estimation) within an hour's march behind us, there was no time for errors. They could have been a matter of minutes behind us, and with that thought in mind Kevin was way back on our back track, watching and listening, ready to slow them down a bit. I made a quick decision. A few minutes now could be well worth it later. We sent a signal requesting a helicopter to come and hover over the LZ for fifteen seconds so we could get a definite fix on our approach. The request was granted almost at once and we were quickly on our way.

When I estimated we were about 500 metres from the LZ a chopper came over, but instead of hovering over the LZ it circled around as if searching for us. I saw the chopper through a gap in the trees and could see the crewman leaning well out, looking down. I knew they were looking for us so took out my homing device and switched it on. The chopper came straight over us and the winch cable was lowered. It was too short to reach us, so went back up, then came down again with an extension on the end. This time it reached, so I told Pete to go first as he had the useless rifle. With the extension on, the winch couldn't be fully wound in, so Pete was dragged up through the trees and away, swinging and spinning under the chopper. His eyes were like chapel hat pegs.

The chopper went off a short distance then returned; it was Paddy's turn. But the winch-man leaned out and threw down an empty beer can with a note tied to it. The note said, 'Move 100 metres east.' This we did (and in so doing crossed our outward bound tracks on the way). The chopper had found a place it could get low enough to winch us up properly.

Paddy went first, then Kevin. I went last and expected the chopper to rush off. It didn't. The crewman looked at me and pointed down. He shouted, but the noise was too great to understand him. Then I realised he had lowered the winch again.

Suddenly all became clear. I was sat in the chopper with the homing device still switched on. The crew thought there was another man still to come. I sheepishly pulled out the offending instrument and switched it off, signalled the crewman there were no more to come, then we got out of there fast.

The LZ was about 300 metres away – full of a platoon of the Argyll and Sutherland Highlanders. I was glad to see so many friendly faces, but all I could think was, 'Shit!! they did it again!' We picked up Pete and were rushed straight to Lundu, where a Twin Pioneer was waiting to get us back to Kuching. A few more minutes and it would have been too dark for the aircraft to take off or land or something. So we only just made it in time to save ourselves a night at Lundu.

Years later I was told the Indonesian officer, whose life was spared by the presence of a lady, was Colonel Moerdani, of the Indonesian Parachute Regiment, who was then commanding the RPKAD, an élite para commando unit in the area. He later led the 'peace mission' which went to Kuala Lumpur and finally wound-up the hostilities in Borneo. Some years after that, Moerdani came to London as a general, and somehow Pete and Kevin got to meet him. Their opinion is he's quite a 'good lad'. Worth saving!

The patrol task to the Koemba was typical of the operations carried out by all of 'D' Squadron's patrols on that trip to Borneo. Each patrol's work was made easier, often possible, by work done before by other patrols. Information fed back to our Operations Centre by previous patrols certainly made my job possible. We all looked upon our work as squadron, if not regiment, effort.

There was no brainwashing, or political rubbish involved in making men drive themselves to the point of collapse, risk horrific injuries and a lingering, screaming death in a war thousands of miles from home. We were defending a friendly nation from the military might of its neighbour. We had no doubt about who was invading whom. The Commonwealth infantry units, who took the brunt of the war, were in a thin defensive line, in no way were they in a position to go on the offensive. There is no place like the front line to find out what is going on in a war.

The operations we carried out undoubtedly saved many lives on both sides. In my case, that one ambush, on what had been a secure supply line, caused the opposition to pull back troops from the front to guard it. Those troops still had to be supplied and a supply line can only cope with so much. The fact is, there were no more Indonesian attacks across the border in that area after we hit the supply line. It could no longer support enough troops at the sharp end. It had been proved vulnerable.

My patrol's efforts were an average minuscule part of the regiment's contribution in Borneo. We knew before we went in, whether we tried or not, whether we lived or died, the squadron, the regiment, the Army would go on – regardless. Commonwealth forces would achieve their aims in Borneo. So why bother?

In my case, the challenge. I considered myself an expert at my job, an expert with a big 'L' plate. No one knows it all about anything much, least of all about my trade. I always knew I would never learn it all but I had to keep learning, keep trying. Operations were to me like a great chess game, with the highest stakes. There was no greater thrill in life than to pit my wits and whatever expertise against a good opposition. Not so much to kill him as to outwit him. The more difficult the job, the greater the odds against me – the better I liked it.

There is no way I can speak for any other member of the regiment when trying to pin down what makes a man drive himself to the limits of danger, endurance or whatever. But, if there is one common factor, I would say it is that which is destroyed by putting drill and bullshit above real military training. Pride of arms.

CHAPTER TEN

Aden Protectorate

'D' Squadron returned to UK soon after the Koemba job. After a week or two on leave we were back into the mad rush of training and exercises here and there. All those skills which are not kept sharp by spending four months on jungle operations had to be aired and sharpened. There were also various little jobs to be done around the world to keep everyone happy and in touch.

Two courses of instruction came my way about that time. I was trained as an 'interrogator' at an Army Intelligence School. As it turned out, I never had the opportunity to try out their theories for real, but was called upon from time to time afterwards to interrogate 'prisoners' on Army exercises.

On the same course there was a man from 'A' Squadron whom I only knew 'by sight'. We were roughly the same size and had similar appetites. We got to know each other during that course, but few people realised we'd met, when, sometime later people were going to put a lot of money on which of us could eat the most steaks in a well-known Hereford steak house. It was one of those inter-squadron rivalry capers, but it fizzled at the last minute. Perhaps they realised we had the situation weighed up and were going to eat to a draw – so we could do it again.

The other course I did at that time was more interesting and of much more use. I was trained as a forward air controller. This gave me the ability to call on ground attack fighter aircraft and guide them to targets on the ground. Very interesting. It leaves model aircraft looking a little flat when you can do it with the real thing. There is a special thrill to watching jet fighters attack a target on the ground, especially when you know your words over the radio are guiding them.

In September 1965, 18 Troop went to North Africa for a few weeks. We took our Land-Rovers and again got stuck into desert driving and navigation. Every man in the troop became reasonable to good at astro-navigation, using theodolites, star charts and all the other kit necessary. Most of the troop had done quite a bit of desert

work before, the two or three who hadn't were in good company to
learn quickly, and did so. There was a certain amount of time
wasted by the usual clown trouble, but that was to be expected.

It was on that trip I found something I'd never seen before, much
to the merriment of some and the horror of others. We were in an
area of fairly big sand dunes. The dunes were in long lines like
waves. They were about 800 metres apart, separated by flat areas
of 'good going'. The dunes were about two or three hundred feet
high in some places, at least one hundred and fifty feet high at their
lowest. We would rush at them at about 50 or 60 miles per hour to
have enough speed to reach the top. The top was always soft sand
which would stop the vehicle if the driver didn't get the gears right
and keep his boot down. Once stopped there was often a lot of hard
work to get moving again.

On the far side the vehicle would fall, often two hundred feet to
the desert floor, in a great avalanche of sand. This called for slight
acceleration and good control to keep the vehicle pointing in the
right direction. Paddy had never done this type of desert driving
before so I started teaching him. The first two or three dunes he
came to he braked when he reached the top. We had a lot of sweat
and cursing to dig the truck out and move it on. Then he got the
hang of it. We went over two or three more in fine order.

The next one was the one I'd never seen the like of before. I didn't
go back up there to check, but I'd swear it had a concrete top! We
went up fast, Paddy got the gear right and had his boot right down
as we levelled out. The vehicle didn't slow. We accelerated out into
space on the far side. About eighty feet down, the tail hit the dune
and the nose crashed down. Kevin came over the top of us from the
back and did a hand-stand on the bonnet. Paddy had the sense to
accelerate hard to keep control, which stopped Kevin going on over
the front, and allowed me to pull him back in.

We drove on out, onto the flat, then, just as Kevin had got back
to his seat, we hit some soft sand and Paddy braked. This time the
Rover stopped dead and Kevin went over us again to land in a heap
a few metres in front. There's probably, even now, a patch of blue
air somewhere in the Libyan sand sea. Never before or since have
I found that type of sand dune with a hard top.

On another occasion, we had been a long way south and were
heading back towards our base at El Adem. In the shimmering heat
haze ahead we could see a black blob. Then we noticed a couple
more off to the left and right.

A few minutes later we reached the one we had seen first. It was a signboard, with its back to us. On the other side, the front of the sign, we found in big black letters the words '*Achtung – Minen!*' (Attention – Mines!). Whether or not it was real we couldn't be sure. It certainly looked old enough and we knew there had been vast minefields in the area during World War II. The debris of war still littered the desert in many places.

The last couple of weeks of our stay in Libya were taken up by a big military exercise. There were more British tanks in Libya than at any time since World War II. Our job was to find the main armoured columns, report their position, numbers, types, etc., then bring in fighter ground attack aircraft to make mock attacks. This we did with great success. On every attack we called, the RAF claimed a successful strike.

We were not the only people engaged in bringing in air strikes, but according to information received later we were the only ones achieving any success. The reason, I believe, was our navigation. We knew exactly where we were all the time, day and night. So when we found a target we knew exactly where it was and could bring the aircraft to the right spot – on the right bearing. The RAF squadron involved, flying Hawker Hunter jet fighters, were impressed enough to send a nice 'Thank-you' letter to our base in Hereford after the exercise.

We didn't realise at the time, it was the beginning of a good partnership between us and the Hunter squadrons. Early in 1966 the squadron flew out to Aden. Hostilities in that area had been warming up for some time. 'A' Squadron had taken casualties there and although the opposition was rubbish, as is normal in that part of the world, there were a lot of them.

The port of Aden had been nothing much until it became a British colony before World War II. The colony was in fact only a small area with the sea port being the only item of any importance within its borders. Aden was well placed as a strategic base and link on the long British lines of communication to our commitments in the Far East. Its importance was enhanced by the British withdrawal from bases in Egypt. A fairly large city grew around the port and it became a strong trading centre. Situated at the south-west tip of the Arabian Peninsula, the port saw some of the trade passing between Arabia and Africa, as well as the more obvious sea route between the Red Sea and Indian Ocean, which passed its front door.

The Aden Protectorate, on the other hand, was a wild, mostly

desolate area stretching east from Aden almost six hundred miles
to the border of Oman. It bulged north into the 'Empty Quarter',
where its border with Saudi Arabia became rather vague. Its
population was very sparse and consisted of various Arab tribes
who jealously guarded their tribal areas against all comers, mostly
other tribes, as no one else had any use for such inhospitable
land.

A fairly flat coastal plain surrounded the sea port, but north of
that were barren, savage mountains which went north to the border
with Yemen, and beyond. In an attempt to bring stability to the area
a Federation was formed, linking the colony with the various tribal
sheikdoms between Aden and the Yemen border. As usual, the
various politicians over the years made a grand mess of things,
leaving an easy target for subversion and armed rebellion.

Yemen, to the north, had its own typical 'Left Wing Military
Coup' (Commie takeover) in 1962 and obtained the aid of the
Egyptian army and air force to quell any opposition and keep the
population in line. Egypt was at that time holding hands with the
USSR, so the obvious next step was to instigate trouble in Aden,
then called the South Arabian Federation.

Our people made it easy for 'outsiders' to instigate trouble 'up
country' from Aden by causing trouble with the tribes over what was
really no more than an old custom. For probably hundreds of years
the tribes whose land the Aden to Dhala road ran through had
collected 'tolls' from anyone (originally camel trains) who passed
through. Dhala is a town up near the Yemen border and, as it grew,
more and more people had to pay a small sum to the tribes. It was
really a 'protection racket' but was of very little consequence
compared with the wars made to try to stop it – and the eventual
handing over of Aden to the Commies.

We, the British, through short-sighted political stupidity made it
very easy for agitators to stir up trouble in the whole of the Aden
area, so of course the commies stepped in. Their long term aims
were to establish a Soviet base in Aden, from which to dominate
North-East Africa. As can be seen from the wars ever since in
Somalia, Ethiopia, etc., as the communist tentacles spread. As the
politicians bog it up, so the Army has to suffer. We were due to pull
out of Aden in the not too distant future so, from the Trogs' point
of view, it was all a waste of rations. Aden had never been a popular
posting for the British Army; so as far as we are concerned the
Russians are welcome to their colony, now known as South Yemen.

The media in UK made much of the Army's predicament in the Aden Protectorate, with stories concerning the terrible 'Red Wolves of Radfan' etc. In reality the problem was in catching up with the so-called 'Red Wolves'. Apart from sniper activities – using rifles, machine-guns, rocket launchers and even mortars on occasion, from the safety of darkness or their mountains – they just didn't happen.

'A' Squadron casualties, two killed and some wounded, had all happened when a nine-man patrol in the 'Red Wolves' area had been caught on the hop by one man falling sick. The patrol had finished up surrounded by about fifty (maybe a hundred) 'Red Wolves' for several hours of daylight, and had fought their way out, to return most of the way back to base on their flat feet. Put the other way around it would have been ridiculous. Nine 'Red Wolves' surrounded by fifty Brits would have been 'no contest'.

When 'D' Squadron arrived we were based in a small Engineers' camp at a place called El Milah on the Aden to Dhala road. The road at that point, as on most of its length, was what we called a 'graded' road. It had been levelled by the Engineers using huge grading machines and bulldozers. So it was essentially a dirt road, easy to mine but also easy to repair.

The village itself was quite small, probably less than a hundred small, mud and rock-built houses, and a small fort – belonging to the local militia, nothing to do with the Army. The military camp was a very temporary affair, twenty or thirty tents, a vehicle park, a helicopter pad, all surrounded by a reasonable barbed wire entanglement perimeter fence. It was well away from the village, being six or seven hundred metres east of the village and road.

The surrounding area was reasonably flat, mostly gravel and sand, but the jagged rock of hills and mountains rose steeply a couple of hundred metres east of the camp and across the valley, about five hundred metres west of the road.

It was a very hot place. Very little wind seemed to touch the camp. The heat haze blotted out the floor of the valley most of the day, but there always seemed to be a few 'dust devils', twisting this way and that, somewhere within sight.

The tent occupied by my troop had a small trench in it, near the entrance. The trench was only a couple of feet deep, quite narrow, but it had been partly covered over by sandbags resting on several steel barbed wire pickets. No one in the troop appeared to take any notice of the trench. It was next to my camp bed. On our first night in El Milah, about midnight, having been in a deep sleep, I suddenly found myself wide awake with the sound of a mortar in my ears. The echoes were going the rounds of the local rockery. Where there should have been the sounds of breathing in the tent there was an uncanny silence. Absolute silence.

Then the unmistakable sound of an incoming mortar shell. The tent erupted with the sound of camp beds overturning, and I found myself jammed in the entrance to the narrow trench. Jammed because there were two of us. The coward from across the tent had the same idea as me – and must have moved like lightning to arrive at the same time.

The shell exploded nearby and we two were laughing fit to bust, each with our head and shoulders in the narrow, open part of the trench, and our backsides raised to the heavens. Like a couple of ostriches. We stayed there while a few more shells landed, cursing one another for sheer cowardice and finding all the bum reasons we could why the trench should belong to which of us!

I don't think any shells landed within the perimeter of the camp that time. There were no casualties anyway. 18 Troop were a well-experienced troop. Many of us had been in the North Oman campaign and in various other capers around the Middle East. I remember we were the 'oldest' troop in the squadron at the time, possibly the oldest in the regiment, our average age being thirty-two. And that in spite of having a couple of youngsters of twenty years old among us. The troop didn't give a damn for the so-called opposition and looked upon operations in that area as another training exercise with the added fun of real targets – if we could catch them.

We were doing about five days on each operation, limited by how much water we could carry. Lying-up during daylight, watching for bands of armed rebels in the mountains, then spending all night in ambush on a likely track. It was a terrible routine. Sleep was practically impossible during the day due to the intense, baking heat and hordes of flies. Then at night, lying in the cool ambush position, sleep tried to overcome us, just when we had to remain alert.

On one of our first jobs we were 'inserted' halfway by road. Every night three or four armoured vehicles rushed down the road, checking for mines, and checking the culverts under the road for explosives. We and another troop were taken on these vehicles then dropped off when they stopped to check a culvert. The other troop was to take the lead as we pushed off into the mountains. Later in the night we were to split, go our own separate ways to our designated areas.

The leading men moved out. I was at the tail end of the column. We hadn't gone twenty yards when the column came to a stop. After a few minutes we moved off again, then, after about 200 metres, we stopped again for about five minutes. There were a few mutters from the men in front of me, it's no fun standing around with something in excess of a hundred pounds of kit on your back. Again we moved off, and again we stopped. The mutterings in 18 Troop were turning to a growl. I went forward, and arriving at the front end asked what was going on.

The man at the front explained. His troop commander and a troop NCO were going forward to check all was safe before moving the column forward. When I realised who the two were, I could see the funny side. They were the two 'Mr Magoos' of the SAS. How they had ever joined I've no idea. Both wore spectacles but still couldn't see past their noses with any clarity. Their eyesight was legendary in the squadron. The funny side of things, however, was going to do nothing to help my troop. I realised there wasn't one man in the other troop with desert/mountain experience. In other words – they hadn't got a clue. Which only goes to show how bog-ups can be made – even in the best run families.

Movement in that type of country, if you want to cover any reasonable distance, has to be mostly in the wadis (valleys). These are dry river beds and can vary in width from a few metres to a few miles. They are generally flat with gravel, sand, solid rock or areas of small loose rocks covering a haphazard pattern right across, and the whole length. Some wadis are thick with 'camel thorn' trees and various low 'bushy' vegetation. Others are almost bare. Most have large areas of completely open ground, where it is impossible to walk without being seen. Perhaps for half a mile or more.

The edge of a wadi can vary considerably but is usually either hills of gravel and rock, solid rock cliffs or jumbles of great rock slabs. Sometimes, obviously, a mixture of everything.

Between the wadis the hills and mountains rise steeply to jagged, often razor-edge summits. It is always difficult to move along the hilltops – even in daylight. At night it is almost impossible. The only routes through the mountains are the wadis and the occasional tracks or paths linking them.

Operational movements in hostile areas of that type of country are therefore hazardous due to the possibilties of ambush. From the high ground, in daylight an enemy can see you approaching at a great distance, giving him plenty of time to organise a hot reception. At night, things are different. Ambushes are difficult to organise because the enemy doesn't know which wadi you will use – or even if you will come at all. Nevertheless, there are an abundance of prime ambush sites in any wadi, so moving through them at night can be dangerous.

The technique used by my troop when pushing through that type of country at night was basically the same as that used in the jungle. Our greatest assets were our long experience and know-how, backed up by very fast reactions and the trained ability to shoot by instinct rather than aim.

The leading scout had to be much further ahead than in jungle work, unless the night was particularly black. Our biggest problem was the possible weight of fire which could be brought down on anyone in the 'killing zone' of an ambush.

The enemy was well equipped with light machine-guns and rocket launchers, and it was likely almost every one in the ambush party would be able to see and aim at the leading scout. The only chance for the leading scout, if he didn't discover the enemy before they fired, was for the men behind him to react very fast and take the weight of fire off him by hitting the ambush party hard and heavy.

As with the jungle, there is no answer to a well-laid ambush, once caught in it, but very few ambushes are perfect, – especially at night. Enemy ambush tactics in Aden were a completely unknown quantity to us, as no SAS group had ever been caught in one.

Our main tactic for night movement was travel fast and ready for anything. That way you had the chance of coming upon the enemy too quick for him to be at his best.

So we wanted away from that 'Death March' approach as soon as possible. Suggestions that 18 Troop take over the lead position, or at least put a scout group ahead, were turned down flat.

There was nothing we could do to help the other troop but I had to get 18 Troop onto an operational footing as soon as possible. Checking the map, I found we could get away from this stupid situation at the price of a small detour, so we did, arriving at our appointed place just before first light. Any more delay and we wouldn't have made it. The other troop was caught on low ground the next morning, compromised (seen by the opposition) soon after first light, and had to be lifted out by helicopter soon after. They had made less than halfway to their destination.

In the end, they got the best job. Another troop saw a group of rebels at a distance and our erstwhile companions were put in by chopper to intercept them. They were put in too close to the opposition and had their troop sergeant badly wounded before they could get organised, but put up a good show nevertheless. 18 Troop and another troop were lifted into the area to help out.

The lack of good officers then began to show. When 18 Troop landed, we were about 800 metres from any action. Well away from everything, on low, exposed ground. Useless. I requested, on the radio, permission to close the enemy. To my astonishment I was told to keep the troop where it was.

My troop officer, being one of the youngest members of the troop and never having been shot at in his life, lacked experience of such situations. He was a good lad, tried hard, would listen to advice – even act on it sometimes – and I liked him as a man. His main attribute was he had managed to evade the Big Needle (the one used to extract all common sense from officers) but the patter he was getting in the officers' mess must have conflicted with what he heard at troop level, as he was very dubious of our attitude to the opposition.

The squadron commander was obviously too busy to bother with a troop which had been landed too far away and, knowing his men, would leave them to sort things out for themselves. The troop officer had not been with us long enough to 'read between the lines' and couldn't really be expected to, as this was his first action, so I told him I would take some men onto the higher ground, overlooking the troop position, as a safeguard.

The opposition had a tendency, in those situations, to converge on any skirmish from all around the surrounding countryside and attempt to pick off any 'strays' or easy targets, in an attempt to take the heat off their own people, also to be able to claim participation in any battle which just might go their way.

'Face' is a great thing in that part of the world; any opposition in the area who didn't join in, when it was possible, would 'lose face'. The troop was in a prime position to save someone's face, certainly not their own.

There were five of us including Hughie, an American special forces sergeant we had lugged around since returning from Borneo. He was quite a good lad, with a dry Southern sense of humour.

Having reached ground high enough to give a view of the area, I realised all was overlooked by a peak about 700 metres away – at the end of the ridge we had climbed. So, while heavy firing continued from where the first troop had landed, we scampered along the ridge to take the peak before the opposition got the same idea – if they hadn't already!

About 200 metres from the peak we sorted out for the approach. I went forward to check for any problems. Seeing none, I signalled the others to close. Pete and Big Ron were coming up through a gap in the rocks when a burst of machine-gun fire sprayed around them. They were fine examples of the confidence and experience of the troop. They took no notice, just kept coming. Big Ron's white teeth flashed in a grin on his sunburnt face, then he shouted, 'I thought you said it was safe up there!'

I couldn't see where the machine-gun was, and he didn't fire again while we took the peak. It is quite likely he was part of an enemy group who had the same idea as us. If so, we had only just beaten them to it. This was fortunate for the troop which was heavily engaged, as from our position above them they were easily seen, as were the enemy.

Having taken the high ground I tried to whistle up the rest of the troop. Our little clown would have none of it. 'The squadron commander says we stay here – so here we stay!' My remark on the radio that the squadron commander didn't even know where the troop was didn't make any difference. Then the troop must have had a couple of spent rounds go overhead and all I could get out of our troop officer was, 'I'm twenty-one today, and being shot at for the first time in my life!' How the rest of the troop, chafing at the bit, would take that gem of news I could only imagine.

So we were stuck. With only five of us holding the high ground we could hardly put in a decent attack on the opposition's flank. We had a good view of the skirmish but, as the enemy were about 350 metres away and below us, they were too far for effective fire.

Pete managed to chew a couple of them a bit with the machine-gun. One maybe dead, another wounded for sure. But once they realised where we were they made difficult targets, so all firing on our part ceased. Those of us with rifles never fired a shot. We never reckoned to fire at them at ranges in excess of 200 metres under normal operational conditions.

A chopper brought in a mortar crew. Ranging shells were fired, landing not far from where we could see the opposition. I tried to correct the fire, but although I had the best observation point and the squadron commander knew where we were, the shortsighted troop commander of the heavily engaged troop below us knew better. So I kept quiet – until I realised he was trying to range on us! We watched the opposition disengage and move back to new positions. There were not that many of them. The men in my group were wanting to go down there and sort them out.

It was tempting, but we didn't know if there were other enemy close by who would take the hill if we got off it, putting us right in trouble. So I elected to stay put, be a spectator to what looked like developing into a classic bog-up. It was all very frustrating. Especially as we knew the squadron had taken at least one casualty, and, as the chopper taking him out had passed low over us as we moved along the ridge – so we could see blood all over the windows – it looked like a bad one.

Our people were being held back everywhere. Troop sergeants were asking permission to close the enemy from at least two other sides, and being told to stay put. I turned to Hughie, and asked, 'Do you get officers like this in your Army, Hughie?' He considered the situation a few seconds. 'Well,' he drawled, 'I reckon we got 'em all right, but we don't seem to get 'em all in one bunch, like this!'

An enemy sniper was putting a shot every half minute at some of our people away to the right of us. We couldn't see where he was located. The great piles of jumbled rocks echoed every shot so that it rolled on, bounding from rock to cliff for several seconds. We decided to try to draw the sniper's fire so we could locate him easier. So everyone looked and listened in the right direction while I stood right on the peak of the hill to tempt a shot. Hughie was lying on a ledge a few feet down the forward slope just in front of me. I think the wrong sniper fired. The shot hit the ground just below my feet and just in front of Hughie's nose. It had definitely come from a lot closer than it should have, showering us with dirt and gravel.

Deciding he was too close to be given another prime target, we kept our profile a bit lower. No one had been able to pin down his range, except we all agreed it was close. He didn't fire again, and we never did find him.

We were not allowed to close the opposition, and were eventually withdrawn at dusk, having killed a few of them, but not enough in my opinion to compensate for our one badly wounded casualty, and two choppers full of bullet holes. The most galling thought was that the survivors would claim a victory – having tangled with the Brits and survived to see them 'run away' at dusk.

I expect the decision to hold us back was more political than military, as usual. The whole scene was typical of the situation in Aden at the time. We were committed to pulling out of Aden in the not too distant future. It seemed pointless to put us into operational situations just to build up enemy morale by making us look useless.

Quite regularly our base camp was sniped at or mortared. We

could have easily clobbered the culprits if only a few of us had been allowed out to play at night. But no, we had to sit and take it. On one occasion at the open air cinema show, during a 'western' movie, we had to put up with real bullets coming through the screen. It was rather a lot to ask.

Every morning, a little lad in the Engineer unit drove down to a well the Engineers had sunk, to check all was OK with the pump. The well had been drilled to supply water to the village, it also supplied the temporary camp which was our base.

One morning the brave people shot the young lad, presumably because he was a Brit, alone and easily got at. That summed up their guts perfectly. As far as I know, nothing was done about it.

What we were doing in Aden remained a mystery to all of us. Ours not to reason why.

On one operation, moving at night, I had a fall down a cliff which injured my back and both feet. It was comical really. We were climbing a steepish spur of many-coloured rock. I mistook sand about fifteen feet below for a sandy rock, and tried to step up onto it. Luckily the sand was soft where I landed, on my feet after a beautiful somersault, but the hundred pounds of kit on my back didn't help.

At the time I made light of the injuries, feeling a bloody fool, and carried on for the two or three days left of the operation. Then marched the fifteen miles from El Milah to Habilayn, a big military base further north. Why we had to move base on our flat feet, at night, I can't remember, but I do know that by the time I reached Habilayn my back and feet were unbearable. I was forced to report to the Doc, who put me on my back for a week, to rest.

While I was laid up I had the terrible experience of watching from the tent as my troop rushed to helicopters to go and deal with a problem in the Dhala area. I had never taken a back seat before. The suspense was bad, until they returned, all laughing their fool heads off.

The last thing I said to them as they left was, 'Bring him back alive!' They knew I meant our child troop officer. They nearly didn't. He obviously thought he would put on a good show for the troop, and insisted on edging along a narrow ledge to put a grenade into a cave, when the experienced heads all around him said there was no need – they could fix it quicker with a rocket. He didn't make it to the cave. He slipped from the ledge and plunged out of sight into the ravine below.

The boys fixed the cave in time-honoured fashion, then peered into the depths below. Someone remarked loudly, 'The bastard's dead!' and a shaky little voice came up from the unseen, 'I'm not dead!' He had been saved by a tree growing out of the rock face, about forty or fifty feet down. So they fished him out and sent him to hospital with some rather large gashes to be fixed. Poor lad. Another case of boyish enthusiasm not keeping pace with hard experience.

We got a lot of snide remarks from jealous people in the squadron who had bigger problems and couldn't unload them. We laughed all the way to the mountains. About the same time there was a small happening in the Habilayn base which was comical, but very bad for the 'SAS image'.

Our senior Magoo, a captain, was outside the wire fence watching one of our mortar crews get some practice. Someone shouted to him to report to the ops room, where his presence was required urgently. He came at a steady gallop, and the crowd of people from other units who were lining the fence quickly parted, thinking the big hard SAS captain was going to jump the six or seven foot high wire fence. Of course, Magoo saw the gap but not the wire – and ran straight into it. Luckily for him he wasn't hurt, just bounced back onto his backside.

SAS stocks must have been pretty low on the respectability market after that little episode. The mutterings at troop level are best left to the imagination.

It was in Aden that our previous work with the RAF ground attack people paid off. By good fortune, the Hunter squadron we had worked with so well in Libya was now based in Aden, and a good working relationship was formed. It allowed the SAS squadrons more freedom of movement, knowing we could rely on men we knew to give us support if things got out of hand.

The Hunter pilots were overjoyed at being able to actually see they were hitting the right targets when we called for them. In some cases, I for one would rather have closed the enemy and given them no excuse for being beaten. Nevertheless the Hunters saved a lot of leg work and certainly did their job very well.

Considering the time spent on operations, and the exposure to enemy fire, the regiment's casualties in the Aden Protectorate were very light. A lot of the credit for that must go to the RAF and Army helicopter pilots, who were brilliant throughout. And the Hunter pilots who never let us down, and were also brilliant at their job.

At one stage the RAF, for reasons best known to themselves, made a rule that no RAF helicopter should land on an undefended LZ. As all our LZs were just places we picked off a map, where we wanted to land, we had to get around the problem by landing three or four men from a small Army helicopter just before the Air Force troop carrier landed. That way we could say the LZ was defended.

I often wondered what would happen if we hit trouble with the first men on the ground, before the RAF job had landed. Unintentionally I found out. We were then based in Aden itself. The flight up country took probably forty-five minutes or more. I was in the small Army Scout helicopter giving the pilot directions to find the spot we wanted. Unknown to me my legs 'went to sleep'. I didn't find out until I leapt from the chopper and tried to run to a firing position about thirty metres away. I hit the ground running and went about ten paces before my legs buckled. I went sprawling among the rocks.

The RAF chopper came in like shit off a shovel and the troop were into fire positions faster than usual. The Air Force pilot had seen me go down like I'd been shot, alerted the troop and came in as fast as he could, thinking we had a problem.

We never doubted the guts and skill of the pilots, but a little re-assurance from time to time can go a long way.

Before our troop officer put himself out of action he had another experience he was unlikely to forget. We were in observation positions by day and ambushing at night. A bit squeamish about the 'seamier' side of operational life, he was sharing a sangar position with one of the roughest, toughest, absolutely non-squeamish NCOs in the outfit.

The first I knew of the problem the NCO got through to me on the radio and said, 'Lofty, I've got to lay an egg.' We were in well-camouflaged observation positions, unable to move during daylight. The reason I was warned of this 'egg-laying' situation was because it was only just after midday. They didn't want to have the position in a brown fog for the duration of daylight, so wanted to know if I thought it would be safe to dispose of by throwing it into the deep shadow of a gully behind their position. I checked their plan with the binoculars, gave them the OK, then asked, 'Hard boiled or soft?' The voice on the radio came straight back, 'Not bloody boiled at all!' My heart should have gone out to our laddie, but it didn't.

A few minutes later a brown arm appeared from under the netting, a ration bag swinging, ready to throw. I had been checking the area for any signs of unwelcome company. There were none, so I said, 'OK, get rid of it.' The bag swung to and fro a couple of times then sailed back behind their position, where it caught in mid flight on one of those long springy camel thorn branches. The branch swung back and emptied the contents of the bag all over one side of the position.

The comments going to and fro on the radio are best left to the imagination. Then our lad was asking if there was any chance of getting out of there before dark. I told him, 'No chance! but thanks for taking away all our flies!' I hadn't heard him swear until then.

CHAPTER ELEVEN

Europe and Beyond

After nearly three months on operations in the Aden Protectorate we were glad to get back to UK for a break. A week or two on leave, then back to the merry-go-round of training here, there and everywhere. Much of the time the squadron was split into penny packets of maybe a troop, maybe one or two men, spread all over the UK and Europe, doing various jobs.

All seemed disconnected, and they often were disconnected jobs, but the wealth of squadron knowledge, 'know-how' and experience was forever growing in many different areas. Mostly we worked on problems related to our particular troop, but there was also a considerable amount of 'cross-training' between troops and, of course, a lot of work common to everyone's requirements.

When there was a reasonable crowd of the squadron in the Hereford base, we often did what were called map exercises. This entailed sitting in a lecture room for sometimes two or three days, working through a fictitious operation in any part of the world and solving problems as they were thrown in.

One particular map exercise was complicated by one of the fictitious patrol members having a broken leg at a crucial stage of the operation. The problem being what to do with him. There were several suggested solutions to the problem. Then the officer running the exercise picked on one of my crew and said, 'OK, Paddy, if you had a broken leg and I left you in enemy territory, with a full water bottle, five days' rations, your rifle and two rounds of ammunition, what would you do?' Paddy didn't hesitate. 'Sir, as you walked away, I'd put both rounds straight between your shoulders.'

On our last trip to Borneo the 'war' situation had changed considerably. Indonesian 'incursions' into Malaysian territory had been well contained, their supply lines and previously 'safe areas' had been severely punished, not only by SAS operations up to squadron strength but by companies of infantry.

By the time we arrived a full scale search for peace was in full

'D' Squadron, 22 SAS, Aden, 1966.

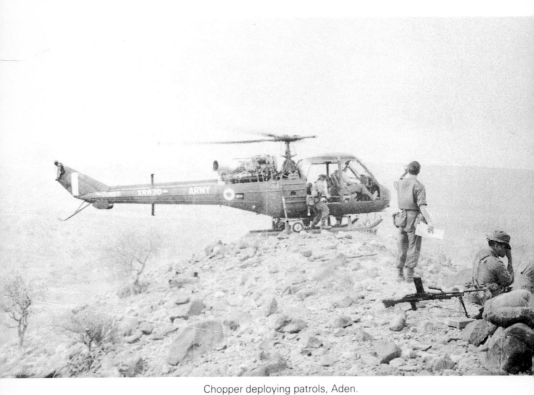

Chopper deploying patrols, Aden.

18 Troop moving out.

swing. Everyone had run out of reasons for continuing hostilities and were looking for an honourable way out. For my part I was glad enough that peace was coming to that part of the world but felt cheated somehow by not being allowed to take up where we had left off. The first month or two after arriving we patrolled the border in case of further attacks. It was the usual hard jungle slog but, with little chance of action, it fell rather flat.

The back injury I had collected in Aden gave me some trouble. There was no problem with marching all day with a pack on my back, but at night the pain prevented real sleep. After a few days' hard work with practically no sleep I began to doubt my ability as a leading scout.

On one operation when we were patrolling a particularly steep border ridge, we had to sleep one night in an area where there simply were no flat spots to sleep on. So we slept on a slope like the roof of a house – and I had a marvellous kip. I slept like a log and felt great in the morning. I had been sleeping in almost a sitting position, with my backside on a tree root to prevent me sliding downhill during the night.

For the rest of that operation I tried every night to find another steep slope to sleep on. I couldn't understand why I couldn't sleep like it again. The patrol suffered these horrific camp sites with not a little 'honking'. They didn't know why we always seemed to be in the worst possible place to sleep, and couldn't understand the situation, especially as I had previously always insisted on the best possible camp sites.

Years later, at a safe distance in time, Pete told me he had 'fixed' my evening brew to give me that good night's sleep. Then the patrol found out why they had suffered the lousy camp sites.

I would never take any pain-killers on operations, being afraid of getting caught on the hop with my senses dulled, but Pete, being patrol medic, decided a wideawake leading scout was worth taking a chance for. I'd likely have skinned him alive if I'd known at the time.

Just before leaving UK we had a couple of new lads join the troop. They were young, very fit, full of mad gallop and go, had just finished a jungle training stint and were itching to get into the real thing. One came with my patrol and I remember Pete kept rubbing it in that this 'child' was only two years old when I joined the Army. Not good for morale!

At thirty-five years old I was beginning to wonder at what age I would find all this decidedly hard physical and mental flogging too much to keep up with.

On one operation I did a light order patrol, taking the 'brat' with me and leaving the others to look after the packs. It was just another job. I didn't rush, just went on as usual, and didn't notice any problems. Years later I was told the poor brat had been smashed out of his mind by the time we joined the patrol again, complaining bitterly, 'When does that old bastard ever slow down?'

I often think of that, and several other instances involving so-called 'old men' – some much older, faster and tougher than me – when I hear of international sportsmen, footballers and the like claiming they will be over the hill at twenty-eight or thirty. They must be bloody joking. How can you compare ninety minutes of football, no matter how hard, with day after day flogging through the jungle? Combine that with a trained speed of reaction which you – and the men behind you – have to bet their lives on. Real jungle patrolling, in deep jungle, with every sense at super alert has to be one of the most exhausting ways to earn a living. Seldom are you on flat ground yet you must move quickly and quietly through an indescribable tangle, avoid touching trees which can wave a warning to an enemy, climb over or crawl under a seemingly endless mass of obstacles and still keep your rifle ready for instant use. Almost always on a steep slope (except in swamps), almost always in twilight or darker – even at midday. Try that for a game of football – and don't forget the pack.

The last few weeks of that tour we were banished from mainland Borneo. We were told it was requested by the Indonesians in return for pulling their forces back from the border during the peace negotiations. An island at the mouth of the Kuching River became our base. We arrived there in an assortment of small craft, travelling down the river from Kuching. The island was called Santubong. Our new base was named Merrydown Camp. 'Merrydown' because of the dozens of crates of Merrydown wine which somehow arrived there with the first boat. I'd never heard of the stuff before but suddenly we were almost swimming in it. Perhaps it too was banished from the mainland in the cause of peace.

On the way down river we caught a wild pig which was swimming across. It was quite a big one, fully grown and very active. George did a Tarzan job, diving into the water and wrestling the damn thing into an assault boat (with a little help from his friends). He was welcome, there was no way I would have got into the water with all those snapping, flashing teeth and tusks.

The general idea was curried pork, but we had plenty of fresh rations on the island when we arrived, so turned the pig loose on the beach. The stupid animal immediately ran into the sea and took off with a very fast piggy stroke for China. It must have been a 'swim-o-maniac'. There was no land in sight out there, so someone went out in a boat, lassoed the beast and towed it back. It was then released in the jungle behind the camp and never seen again.

The island was a few miles long and a couple wide, with a lot of jungle and cliffs rising in the centre. Merrydown Camp consisted of one derelict hut, about forty feet long and twenty wide. We used it as a storeroom and cookhouse. Sleeping quarters were anywhere you fancied – in the jungle or on the beach. I opted for the jungle, feeling more at home in the trees than on the sandy beach with the sand flies. Our daily routine became training from early morning until lunchtime. Most afternoons were free for water ski-ing, swimming, surfing or anything we could find to pass the time. We had several boats, masses of ammunition and explosives. There was a lot of demolition training, a lot of boat training, a lot of shooting and, inevitably, a lot of fishing. A few fish were caught, but we must have frightened thousands. Catching fish with explosives is easy in a river, not very productive in the open sea.

Becoming frustrated with the poor results gained with grenades and small explosive charges, the great brains of our fishing industry went along the well-worn path of all humanity. The Big One. The Secret Weapon. The Ultimate Solution.

We lesser mortals watched with interest as they prepared the answer to the fisherman's prayer. A big ammo box, appropriately packed, three separate waterproof initiation sets – each timed for twenty seconds. Nothing was left to chance. It took two men to lift it into the boat, then off they went, out to a spot about two hundred metres from the beach, where they claimed there was more fish than water.

The boat stopped, the great 'fish war' bomb was prepared, then lowered over the side. When all was just right the switches were pulled. The bomb sank from sight. The boat engine revved – then cut out. Dead!

There was a calm, organised attempt to re-start the engine. Followed by a couple of fast panicky attempts. One of the fishermen dived off the front of the boat. Some ungenerous types among us on the beach claimed he was doing a fast crawl before he hit the water. With less than ten seconds to go the engine started and the boat

stood on its tail getting out of there, picking up the swimmer –
without slowing – on its way (thanks to all that boat training).

The 'Final Solution' lifted a great lump of ocean into froth about
fifty metres behind the speeding boat. We on the beach were, by this
time, curled up with laughter. It had all been great entertainment,
better than *Tom and Jerry*, although very similar. A long search of the
area afterwards produced three or four small fish, the final touch to
a comic opera.

Living in the jungle one soon becomes accustomed to various
types of insect life. Most insects are a known quantity, either painful
to tangle with, or no problem. The one insect I was never sure of
was the centipede. I was never sure if it could bite, sting, scratch or
only mind its own business. There were no real horror stories about
centipedes. I had never seen or heard of anyone being 'hit' by one.
Nevertheless I remember a lot of advice about 'always brush them
off forwards – never backwards – as their claws will scratch and
poison if they are pushed backwards'.' I never did find out if they
were 'trouble'.

In Hong Kong I remember awaking one night on Kai-Tak ranges
with a large centipede on my stomach. I brushed it off forwards in
a panic. It did no harm but people told me I was lucky. During our
stay on Santubong I had a very large centipede on me on two
different nights. On both occasions they were lying around my
throat when I awoke. It beat me how they could get around my
throat without awakening me, then bring me wideawake once they
were in position. There are few sensations to rival awakening in the
absolute blackness of the jungle night with a nine- or ten-inch
centipede for a necklace. In both cases I sat up and brushed the
insects off with both hands. I'm sure if any claws had been available
I would have been scratched. As was normal when sleeping in the
jungle, I had a torch, a parang and a rifle within reach. Having
snapped on the torch it was touch and go whether I used the parang
or the rifle when I saw the size of those centipedes.

My ambitions with the water ski-ing scene came to a very sudden
stop when I became aware of the local shark population. One big fin
at a range of thirty metres and sheer terror kept me on the skis until
I hit the beach.

Braver souls continued to enjoy the water sports, but not me. My
training went well with my nature when decreeing, 'Only take on
a dangerous adversary at a time and place of your own choosing.'
I would take on any shark you like at the right time and in the right

place. The right time for me would be midday. The right place would be the middle of the Sahara desert.

Malaysia and Indonesia settled their differences over the conference table, so we were flown to Singapore. While languishing in a well-known transit camp on Singapore Island I had occasion to take the troop to a nearby Ordnance Supply Depot, to organise some of the regiment's stores which had arrived by sea from Kuching. We finished our task in a very short time then, as is normal when in those kind of places, had a nose around to see what was going in the way of new kit.

We found a huge pile of strange-looking new boots which, we were told, were to be burnt. I checked with a senior Ordnance type and he told me the boots had been sent out for jungle trials. Having been turned down as useless they had to be destroyed.

Almost every man in the SAS who operated in Borneo had, at his own expense, had his Army boots modified to suit jungle conditions. Now we found this vast store of boots which had been specially designed for the job. They would have needed no modifications to suit our needs. Our problem had been the issued jungle boots, which wouldn't stand up to our heavy wear and tear long enough to last one fourteen-day operation. So we had used our ordinary Army boots, which would last for several operations if necessary.

No amount of talking would get us any of those good boots so, as we had no immediate requirement for them, we left empty handed. Though there was much speculation in the troop about which clerks at which base job had tested those boots.

British Army equipment for men on field operations was, as usual, lagging behind the times. Our olive green (OG) shirt and slacks for jungle operations were good for the job. The 1944 pattern water bottle, water bottle carrier and mug were also good. Army mess tins were OK too. The compass pouch was good for the job, and that was it. Our belts fell to bits. Our magazine carriers were locally made in the Far East, and in short supply, so that the ones we had were repaired time and time again. Belt pouches were a 'hodge-podge' of allsorts. Spare water bottle carriers were a favourite type of belt pouch. Issued ammunition pouches had to be modified and strengthened to be of any use.

Almost all our personal equipment was repaired time after time with bits of parachute cord or masking tape. It was often said, if anyone could find a way of destroying para cord and masking tape, the SAS would fall to bits.

The amount of kit we had to carry on our belts went far beyond that which the belts were originally designed for. Depending on the man's job in a patrol his belt equipment would weigh between twenty and thirty pounds. The kit on our belts gave us the capability of dumping our cumbersome, heavy rucksacks, and continuing to operate for some considerable time without them. I always estimated my operational capability after dumping my rucksack as a minimum of two weeks, partly based on the knowledge that in a weakened state, with two machine-gun bullets and at least eighteen small pieces of shrapnel in me, covering roughly twenty miles per night, I had lasted ten days without food, and had not been physically weakened by it.

After that night of cold, pouring rain at Kapoet, we all carried a very lightweight waterproof sheet among our belt kit, as we knew only too well the effects of cold and lack of sleep.

Returning to UK from Singapore we once again had a couple of weeks' leave then were immersed in training, exercises and jobs all over the place.

On one particular exercise in Germany we had a better time than usual. We flew over to BAOR with our vehicles to take part in a big exercise in the Prum area. Most exercises involved a lot of footslogging as well as driving (if we had the vehicles with us), but on this particular caper we were on wheels for about two weeks. Part of the reason was to test the ability of the Rover Troop to exist as a going concern under as near war conditions as possible.

Apart from the time we spent running ahead of our vehicles at night we were with the vehicles nearly all the time. All our exercise requirements were met, and more besides. Enough to keep the brass very happy. At one stage of the exercise we were at a loose end for about twenty-four hours, so I sent messages to the other patrols to RV so we could exchange information on various things, and be better organised for the more difficult days ahead. We could only move at night, under cover of darkness, so the RV was fixed centrally, in a 'safe' area.

Having reached the RV I decided a small German *Gasthaus* (pub) in the nearest village would be a better place to congregate, so we checked it out, and moved in. The troop's six Land-Rovers were parked in the church driveway, behind the pub, with two men left to guard them. In the *Gasthaus* we found only two local customers, chatting to the landlord over their drinks at the bar. Much to our surprise, landlord and customers all greeted us in good English.

We soon found they had all been prisoners of war in UK prison camps. One had been a sailor, the other two were Army men. They all knew places and people in UK and had been back there for holidays several times since the war. There were eighteen of us, counting the two on duty with the Rovers, but those three ex-POWs in the bar would not hear of us buying a drink while we were there.

When I tried to insist on buying them a drink the landlord threatened to close shop, claiming his hospitality was being insulted. The two customers wanted to go and do guard duty, so our sentries could come in. We drew the line at that one. They understood, of course. As we pulled out, about an hour after arriving, I couldn't help thinking if those good folk received half that hospitality on their holidays in UK it would be a miracle.

Another training exercise, when the whole squadron did some training in Bavaria with the German *Jäger* battalions (Mountain Troops), we were given a very hospitable time. Having arrived in Bavaria with only our field training clothes and equipment, we were somewhat at a loss when, at the end of our stay, the German units and the Mayor of Bad Tolz invited us all to a grand dance and general drinking session. There was no way we could be smartened up for the occasion, so the German troops turned up in their field uniform too – jackboots and all. We had a memorable night in the town hall, which went down well after some good hard training in the mountains. The German troops were very much like us. They trained hard and drank hard. They all seemed to have an excellent sense of humour. A good time was had by all.

During that training, two of us spent a week in the US Army barracks at Bad Tolz, running a signals set-up for an exercise. We were well looked after by the American 10th Special Forces Group and used their 'PX' Club for our coffee breaks, etc. After a couple of days using the 'PX', we noticed that, every time we walked in, within a minute or so a Lonnie Donegan record would be going extra loud on the jukebox. It was 'The Battle of New Orleans'. We also noticed it was the same man put the record on every time. Then he would sit smiling innocently at us, clearly enjoying the situation. I decided something had to be done, so every time we used the 'PX' I went straight to the juke-box and put on 'The Battle of New Orleans'.

It didn't take long before curiosity overcame the grinning one. He came over to find out what the angle was. I told him, 'We sent a few good old boys over there all those years ago, it's nice to think they're still remembered.' I think 'Mr Grin' was thoroughly sick of Lonnie Donegan by the time we left. He'd certainly lost his grin anyway.

CHAPTER TWELVE

Frustrations in Aden

One of my last operational jobs was 'D' Squadron's last tour in the Aden Protectorate. Just as we were due to leave UK Ann was due to have our second child, so I stayed in UK for two weeks after the squadron left. The birth went as planned, and having got things organised on the home front (well, I had tried anyway!) I flew out to join the troop. When I arrived they had completed their first operation and were due to go in again that night. One of the troop corporals had been running things in my absence, as we had no clown.

It was mid-April. I had been in the cool climate of Europe for at least two months, the heat in Aden was just getting red hot. Having been flown up country we had a long, hard approach march that night to reach our designated area. I found myself sweating more than usual, needing to drink rather a lot of water. We were to stay in for at least five days. As we could only carry five days' water ration we would get a re-supply of water and food on the evening of the fifth day – if required to stay longer.

As was usual with 18 Troop, we split into two half troops to do the observation job during daylight hours, thereby observing a much greater area, also giving us the edge if one group was jumped by an enemy force. Operating in half troops was against orders from above, where they kidded themselves about the opposition. At our level we had no respect at all for the opposition and would have preferred operating in patrols of four. On this particular operation some of the troop were away on other jobs, the troop was only ten strong so there were five of us in each half troop position. At night we moved into a troop ambush position.

Late on the third day I was down to half a bottle of water, and realised I was going to be a bit pushed for liquid for the next two days. The position we were in sloped down to the south, so we got the full benefit of a blazing hot sun all day. The rocks all around reflected the heat. It was like a frying pan. By the morning of the fifth day two others had almost run out of water. I had a raging thirst and only enough water to wet my lips. Mid-afternoon came; all of us were by then almost out of water. No one had taken water from anyone else. We drank only what we carried ourselves.

A signal came to let us know we were to stay put at least one extra day, and there would not be a re-supply until the evening of the sixth day. The sixth day was rough on all of us. To make matters worse, one of the things we were keeping watch on was a well. It was about one thousand metres from our position, near a small village, and in almost constant use. It was thought likely a rebel force would use the well on their way through the area. So we watched through our binoculars. Seeing the water glint and splash just aggravated the thirst.

About one hour before dusk on the sixth day HQ sent a signal telling us the re-supply would not be coming until the seventh day, and we were to move that night to a different area.

At that point I cracked. Paddy had been listening on the radio to find out if other troops were in action or in any kind of emergency. All was quiet on the radio. No one had a problem, so I sent a message stating if we didn't get a re-supply of water within thirty minutes we would 'go and get some'.

HQ immediately responded, saying the re-supply would come right away – as originally planned. In fact we were on the start line to get our own water when we heard the distant 'boot down' snarl of the Scout helicopter. A chopper never sounded better. Water never tasted so good!

Kevin was one of those detached from the troop. He had been sent off, with a vast array of weapons (including a rocket launcher), as 'nurse maid' to a District Officer who was being shot at almost every night. Kevin carried his 'armoury' in a thing like a golf bag, and claims he travelled disguised as a 'brush salesman'. At least, that's what he was described as on his travel documents.

We had to put up with a rash of jokes from Pete, whose mind ran riot at the thought of anyone answering their front doorbell and being confronted by Kevin. I must admit, a more unlikely brush salesman would be hard to find.

We did an interesting caper with a company of Marine Commandos in a supposedly very hot area. I think it was in the Wadi Taym, your actual 'Red Wolves' country. In fact the plan was good. The Marines went in first, by helicopter, and having taken a good defensive position near a rebel village, sent platoons out in several directions a few thousand metres from the position. We were then flown into the defensive position to get a good look at the area before dark. Just before dusk we were taken out in the helicopters which were to pick up the Marines from the surrounding countryside.

The chopper carrying my troop landed in a well-hidden little wadi, full of trees and bushes. The Marines moved in from the high ground all around and were lifted out, leaving us to disappear into the 'rockery'. To enemy eyes the choppers had come and withdrawn the Marines back to the defensive position for the night. They would not expect a small party of Brits to be left behind. The rest of the plot depended on the enemy attacking the Marines in the defensive position – an almost guaranteed 'next move'. Our job was to get among the opposition any way we could and take out as many as possible any way we wanted.

There was one serious flaw with the whole scene. Some of us had 'honked' about it at the original briefing for the operation, but, to no avail. It was the village. As usual, we were not allowed near it. Nor were we, or the Marines, allowed to shoot into it, for fear of killing innocent civilians, women and children. Fair enough, but why not put the defensive position away from any village? That way there would be no risk to innocent civilians. We could have an unrestricted field of fire. The 'powers that be' knew best and we were stuck with the village – about three hundred metres from the Marine position.

Before last light we heard on the radio one of our people had been killed by sniper fire from the village. The troop involved was due to leave the defensive position after dark, and had been stood or sat in a group, being briefed on their route past the village, when the opposition put a couple of rifle shots into the group – a tempting and unmissable target. Nuff said!

Needless to say, the fire was not returned. No one could shoot into the village. The trouble with some of our educated types is they don't realise some bastards have never even heard of cricket. They had actually believed the opposition would never attack the side near the village in case our return fire hit innocent civilians. It wasn't the first or last time the British Army's codes of warfare had been used to our disadvantage – nor was it the first time these particular gutless wonders had hidden behind women's skirts.

The news of one of our friends being killed put us in good shape to take on anything – the more the merrier. After last light we moved into a position from which we could quickly get to grips with anyone in our area, and settled down to wait.

About midnight the shit hit the fan. Rockets, mortars and machine-gun fire poured onto the Marines who were quick to respond with some very heavy kit of their own. It was like the Fifth of November and the Fourth of July combined. Very beautiful to watch when it's not coming your way.

There were no enemy in our area so we moved to our northern boundary and went into ambush positions. It was obvious from the start that the main enemy fire was coming from the village, and the Marines were only able to take on those fire positions away from the village.

The Marines' fire with rockets and machine-guns was pretty good as far as I could see. It took good effect where they could put it, whereas the enemy fire was anything but accurate. Just heavy.

Every now and then a couple of the Marines' machine-gunners swept our area with quite heavy fire causing a fair bit of ducking on our part. But, of course, the Marines had no idea where we were. What we did was our problem – they had enough of their own that night. Eventually the opposition packed up and went home. No enemy came near us. None fired from our area, and we couldn't enter other areas in case of bumping our own people.

Our people, including the Marines, had no serious casualties during the night. We never heard what casualties the enemy had, but from what I saw I would think they had a few. The Marines were pretty cool with the return fire.

Everyone was lifted out by helicopter during the next morning, we having walked into the defensive position. Another flog around for nothing as far as we were concerned. Typical of the scene in Aden at the time. Some you win, some you lose, mostly it's a non-event. Things were hotting up in Aden itself. Terrorists were attacking hard military targets, such as school buses, etc.

We had men working the back streets and alleyways of the town, and they were getting the odd success. Mostly it was a lot of hard, boring work. I was never involved with that side of the operational scene and had no ambitions in that direction. It was hard enough to get a decent target up country, without trying to sort one out of the teeming masses in the town.

One of 18 Troop corporals was pretty good at poker, and won a pile of cash in his spare time. Being of generous nature he decided to buy the troop a minibus, so that when we were in Aden we could use it for shopping trips, etc. There was one problem with the minibus. The corporal got it at a bargain price because it was a 'hot' vehicle. One which had been well used by one of our teams in Aden, and was suspected of being well known to the opposition. In fact the two bullet holes and several shrapnel holes in the bodywork of the minibus more than convinced me it was very well known to the opposition. However, it gave us independent wheels, and we'd all heard about gift horses' mouths, so we used it to the full – and very handy it was. As we never moved in Aden without a weapon of some kind we felt quite safe in the old bus. We were never attacked anyway.

Talking of minibuses, we were in the middle of a caper near a village up near the Yemen border when a minibus full of people came trundling into the line of fire. A couple of our people rushed out and stopped the vehicle, ordered the occupants out and lined them up, face down, at the side of the road. They were helped into the face-down position by one of the boys putting a burst of automatic fire over their heads.

Imagine our people's surprise when one of the Arabs spoke in a strong 'Brummie' accent, complaining about the noise. It turned out the man had been living in Birmingham for years, worked at Longbridge car plant and had come on holiday to visit his people who lived in the nearby village.

I think a lot of the terrorists in Aden town had got their training from old 'B' movies. They were always making cock-ups which often left them looking stupid. One was about to throw a grenade into a bus full of school children when the driver saw what was going on. He accelerated sharply away, leaving the terrorist struggling to put the pin back in the grenade. Another well-trained crew attacked a small check-point. They drove madly through in a car, dropping a grenade from an open window as they went through. Of course, the grenade rolled and bounced along the road, keeping pace with the vehicle, eventually exploding right where they didn't want it. A lot of good tricks only work on the silver screen.

The operations up country were often frustrating in the extreme. On one operation in particular, the unbelievably slow reactions of some people were hard to take. We were on a job up near the Yemen border, the whole squadron plus other troops were involved, and the job began to 'fizzle' for lack of opposition. One of our helicopters, carrying a couple of squadron people on a recce flight, about three thousand metres away, was shot at by a group of enemy. The opposition used machine-guns and rockets on the chopper, but missed.

As we had just about finished the one job, we expected to be lifted out to close and destroy the new enemy group. Nothing happened. There was a lot of waffling going on – but no one was doing anything! We ground our teeth, and pleaded for the go-ahead to move on the enemy before they could disappear. All to no avail.

It was one hour and twenty minutes before we landed where the enemy had been. By that time they were long gone. Out of play. Over the border into Yemen – probably claiming another resounding victory in their great struggle against British Imperialism. It was that sort of thing which made operations in Aden hard going. There was a strong stench of politicians everywhere. I refuse to believe our field commanders were that bloody thick. It was as if they couldn't wipe their nose without the OK from somewhere.

As usual, the politicians make a hash of something – scream for the Army to get them out of the shit – then meddle with everything the Army does until they make the poor bloody trogs look as stupid as politicians. You don't have to look any further than Northern Ireland to see a prime example of an Army being treated like a pack of fox hounds – forever held on a short political leash!

The politicians never seem to realise it costs men's lives (usually) to show the enemy who is 'boss'. If you don't do it quick – and keep proving it – the enemy will draw courage from your hesitation, bungling or whatever, and any courage on his part will inevitably lead to harder conflict at trog level, with inevitable heavier casualties – on both sides.

The Aden Protectorate was about to be vacated by us, the British, so really any military operations would only succeed in building up the morale of the anti-British element in the long run. They would be the heroes who had 'driven us out' after we left. The whole scene seemed pointless. When 'D' Squadron left Aden for the last time, 18 Troop stayed behind to carry out a long-distance Rover Troop operation. Our vehicles had been sent out to Aden, along with all the equipment and weapons, etc., for the operation. I believe the troop was probably the best and most experienced Rover Troop in the regiment at that time. The planned operation was decidedly dicy in many respects, but we trained hard and were very confident of our ability to pull off a successful job.

In the event, after a lot of hard work, I had to cancel the operation due to half the troop being rushed off on an emergency job to nurse-maid some Foreign Office people somewhere. Some people wanted me to do the operation, using spare clerks, storemen and such from the squadron which had come out to relieve us.

We waited a couple of weeks, hoping to get our men back. When they didn't return, and no one could tell us when they would, I arranged to get the remainder flown back to UK as soon as possible.

It was another instance of the regiment being overstretched, as everyone, military and otherwise, realised the potential of well-trained special forces. At that time the regiment had four squadrons and could likely have found plenty of work for twice that number.

CHAPTER THIRTEEN

Last

A trip to Guyana deserves mention, mostly on account of its different jungle life. 'D' Squadron flew out via Newfoundland and Bermuda, (where I met a few old friends) to Georgetown. We were not long in Georgetown, being quickly organised and off to the sticks.

Getting to the jungle was quite interesting. A hell of a comedown to us 'International Travellers'. We went up the Demerara River on a great rusty metal raft, normally used for bringing timber down the river. It was towed by an ancient, dilapidated tug-boat, which sounded like every 'chug' was its last gasp.

I can't remember how long we were on the raft; it was at least one day. Maybe two days. We found several green scorpions on it, and that didn't augur good for the jungle.

Having reached the end of the line for the river craft, we had to use our flat feet for quite a way before we got into the real 'cabbage patch', passing on the way thousands of acres of sugar cane plantations, source of the famous Demerara sugar, and Demerara rum. Once into the jungle we set up a base camp, then went out in small patrols to check the area and get the feel of a different jungle. Jungle is jungle, there wasn't a lot of difference. I don't remember seeing any attap. Most of the jungle we saw was what we termed 'clean'. It was easy to move through, no problems.

Everyone we had met, local troops and civilians alike, gave us dire warning about the terrible 'bushranger' snake. It was a terrible thing, feared by all who went into the jungle. As far as we could find out, the bushranger was something between a rattlesnake and a python, which usually attacked on sight, without provocation. It had a fearsome bite, more or less tearing its victims to bits. There seemed to be no other animal life in the jungle which presented any threat to life and limb, according to the 'experts'.

The day after setting up the base camp, my patrol was sent south, to go as far as we could (and back) in ten days. There was no rush, we were to take our time, covering a multitude of assessment tasks on the way.

191

On the second or third night we heard the most awesome noise
I've ever heard, just as dusk crept over our curry rice. It sounded
like a dozen huge cats, fighting and screeching at each other. The
uproar came from some distance away. There was no future in
going to investigate – not that any of us cowards were wanting to!

The next day two of the patrol saw two big cat-like animals, which
they decided had to be panthers, or something of that family. The
'cats' were black, and moved very fast. We wondered if the cats
were responsible for the terrible noise the night before. Nearly every
night we were treated to that terrible uproar, at various distances.
Sometimes quite close, like within 1,000 metres. Sometimes very
distant. It remained a mystery until we came out of the jungle, then
we were told the noise was made by monkeys – 'Howling
Monkeys' to be exact.

In the interests of finding out any problems with jungle night-life,
two of us slept on the ground every night, and two slept in
hammocks. I slept on the ground, and every morning I found at
least one scorpion in or under my sleeping bag. Often there were
three or four. They never 'hit' me, but some of them looked a bit
sick after being rolled on in the night.

While still making our way southward, on the third or fourth day
we met an old Indian. He was dressed in a pair of tatty shorts, had
a small pack on his back and carried a large machete in his hand.
We stopped to chat. He told us he was a 'pork-knocker', the local
name for individuals who go into the jungle looking for gold. We
knew a lot of the local people earned a precarious living, hunting for
gold and precious stones which were supposedly plentiful in the
area. In fact we had seen plenty of signs of various types of 'mining'
along our way. In some places old and long-forgotten machinery lay
rusting in the jungle. We saw no 'active' mines. The old Indian
showed us some of the gold he had found and told us he would 'live
good' for a few weeks, then, when the money ran out, he would be
back, always looking for the big find which would set him up for life.
Recognising a true spirit of the jungle we decided to find out about
the terrible bushranger, among other things.

Over a brew of tea the old man explained many of the things
which were new to us, such as some animal tracks, what was good
to eat and what was not. About fish and birds, about plants and
roots. Then we got to the bushranger. He told us the same things
we'd heard before, so we got down to the nitty gritty. Had he ever
been attacked by a bushranger?

Beverly aircraft loading.

Motley crew. Typical of Aden ops.

Awaiting Heli.

'No, I'm still alive, ain't I?'

Had he ever seen a bushranger? 'No.'

Had he ever seen anyone who had been attacked by a bushranger? 'No.'

How old was he? 'Fifty-two years.'

How long had he been working in the jungle? 'All my life – I was born in the jungle.'

About that time the bushranger went the way of many other myths we had punctured over the years. We decided it was invented by people who wanted to keep other people out of the jungle.

One of the most common of the different wildlife we saw in that area was the humming bird. Given time I could watch them for hours. So different from other birds in their way of flight and movement, we could only wonder at the speed of their wings as they hovered to feed.

On the last day we moved south we came to a small clearing around a huge old tree. The place had obviously been used many times as a stopping place. At the bottom of the tree, leaning against it was brown bottle, which gave us some surprise. It was a Bulmers of Hereford Woodpecker Cider bottle complete with the usual label. The bad news, of course, it was empty.

In common with other jungle areas we had worked in, the jungle in Guyana had its share of airborne stings. Bees, hornets and the like. Two or three times the patrol was scattered by angry insects whose nests we had inadvertently disturbed. It was generally agreed in the regiment, a contact with hornets disrupted a patrol far worse than a contact with enemy forces. No matter how experienced people are, the tendency is to bolt in any direction as fast as you can.

The Guyana trip was interesting in many ways to all of us, but we were all glad to return home. Flogging around empty jungle is no more rewarding than flogging around empty mountains.

The last shots I fired on operations with the British Army were fired to warn, not to kill. As is often the case, they were a dismal failure. A woman was walking along a path where she should not have been. I knew she was walking towards a very certain danger. Had it been a man, Pete would have made sure of him with the machine-gun. But it had to be a bloody stupid woman. So I elected to warn her with a well-placed rifle bullet.

The range was rather long but I managed to bounce the shot off the track about three feet in front of her. She stopped, didn't look to right or left, just stood there. Then she started to walk slowly forward again. I bounced another shot just in front of her feet. Again she stopped. Just stood there, stupidly facing the way she wanted to go.

After about half a minute she slowly shuffled forward again. The third shot must have almost hit her feet. She stood perfectly still. Couldn't she take a hint? What a player! God help any poor son-in-law she might have. A few more steps and she would be out of sight. I decided if she went on she could damn well take her chances.

She stood a long time, perfectly still. Facing resolutely where she wanted to go. Not so much as a half glance to left or right. I had put down the rifle and watched her with binoculars.

Then she shuffled slowly out of sight. I cursed all women for a while, then we listened for the sounds of her demise. Pete suddenly said, 'Hey, look!' We all looked. There was the woman, walking slowly back along the track, leading a damn great brown bull, which had obviously been tethered out to graze.

Thinking about it afterwards, I decided the woman had worked it out. Whoever was doing the shooting obviously didn't want to hit her, so – having a perfectly innocent reason to be there – she carried on. She had more bloody nerve than I have. Especially in that land of cheap life.

The last few years of my Army service were spent with 23 SAS, where I did a variety of jobs on the selection and training scene. Passing on to younger men the benefit (I hope) of my hard-earned experience. A lot of time was spent on recce work, in UK, also on the continent, mostly in Germany. I was often away on my own or with one or two others for several weeks. Usually on those recce trips we also had new or different equipment to test, under field conditions, or whatever.

Sometimes, the equipment was very sophisticated, sometimes very nitty gritty. How nitty gritty can you get?

On one particular trip there were two of us, travelling and almost living in a Land-Rover. We were testing various signals equipment, so my companion was an SAS signals sergeant. The Quartermaster of 23 SAS, or some equally silver-tongued gent, had conned Jimmy, my companion, into testing some disposable undergarments, made of paper! The underpants were not (presumably) designed to be sat on all day, travelling rough forest tracks and the like, so, every day, they completely wore out in the area of firmest contact.

Jimmy, much to his credit, and my hilarity stuck to his testing task far beyond the call of duty. He was also a creature of habit.

Every morning, just as first light crept through the tree-tops, surfacing bleary-eyed from my sleeping bag I would be treated to the disgusting sight of Jimmy, shovel over his shoulder, new paper drawers and toilet roll in his other hand, dressed in an Army string vest and the remaining shreds of yesterday's paper drawers, walking directly away from me into the woods.

When you realise Jimmy was almost a carbon copy (in size and looks) of that great comedian Arthur Askey, you get the picture. His straight-faced answer to all remarks, 'Where there is dignity, there is grace.'

Regular troops serving with 22 SAS Regiment, tend to 'look down' upon the SAS Reserve units. Having served with 23 SAS, however, I found many things to be admired in the Reserve soldier. Being only a part-timer, a 'weekend soldier', he cannot reach the high standards of his Regular Army brethren. Nevertheless, the men of 23 SAS could be quite impressive in the field.

As an example of their ability, their success in a NATO Special Forces competition years ago. Two patrols were sent on the competition. They were selected (those able to get two weeks off from their full-time civilian employment) from a squadron of about thirty strong, all ranks. The two 23 SAS patrols were the only part-timers in the competition. The other participants being Regular Army patrols from all the other NATO Special Forces. 23 SAS came first and second in the competition. This either says a lot for 23 SAS – or very little for the rest of NATO.

My main reason for leaving the Army, when I suppose I could have stayed, was to make room for younger men to get promotion, and get the cash they also had earned the hard way. When a senior rank moves out it sends ripples of promotion all down the line. My days in the field seemed to be numbered. I had no ambition to drive a desk, or be classed as a hanger-on.

It was not until the last year or so of my service that I realised I had survived. For most of my Army service I had never thought of coming out. Somehow, deep down, I 'knew' I would not survive. I 'knew' one day the luck would run out. 'He who lives by the sword is very apt to die by the sword.' I only hoped it would be quick, that I wouldn't be another obscene mess, writhing in the mud, coughing my life out.

As a British soldier I was never trained or encouraged to treat lightly the lives of other people. I don't think I was brought up or trained much different to anyone else of my generation. Over the years I have heard a lot of talk and tales of horror associated with people's reactions to the act of taking human life. Perhaps there is something wrong with me, I have never experienced any regret, remorse or any other emotion I can honestly remember, – except relief! Relief that it wasn't me lying there dead or screaming. Relief that I had acted first and fast. Relief that my weapons had worked as they should. Relief I had not betrayed myself or my comrades with any fumbling – physical or mental. In my experience there is no time for worrying about shooting someone when your biggest problem is who will shoot next?

On the other hand, I do not like to see dumb animals suffer. Before I was ever allowed to go shooting in my younger days, my father taught me how to kill animals and birds quickly and painlessly with my hands, so that wounded game could be quickly saved from unnecessary suffering.

Although I know I could still kill men without thought – in the right circumstances – I will probably never again shoot animals or birds for sport. I feel some sort of affinity with wildlife which, after all, is surviving against the odds – and without hitting back as I had to! I see the survival of wild animals, large or small, as living proof there is hope for all survival.

Outside the Army I had no interest in life, so, to a certain extent, it was a great new challenge. My Army experience – all those years of training – was of very little use to the new civilian. The only things I had going for me were my driving qualifications. A Class I Heavy Goods Vehicle driving licence and a Qualified Testing Officer's certificate up to HGV Class I.

People may pause to wonder what kind of man, or animal, is produced by a background like mine. Most of the gory details, and some best forgotten experiences have been left out of my writing. Thinking back over the years, in common with most soldiers, I don't know if I have ever killed another human being. I have seen a lot of men go down, but whether it was my actions which killed them, if they were dead, is open to question. Not many soldiers have the benefit of medical or forensic experts to certify death or its causes in an operational situation. As far as I am concerned, I did what I had to. No more, no less.

If, on any operation, my mother had been looking over my shoulder she may have been considerably shocked, but never ashamed. Judging by the facts I have accumulated over the years I feel sure the British Army is the most humane Army in the world.

I have a deep disgust for military organisations which inflict wholesale suffering upon civilian populations. My simple soldier's logic is left floundering by some ways of the world. During my lifetime many of the political bosses of Germany were hung at Nuremberg for crimes against humanity. Now I see 'political parties' being given credence in political circles while the gutless wonders they represent are guilty of placing bombs in supermarkets and other places full of women and children.

Are the armless, legless, blinded, shattered and dead women and children politically classed as less than human?

Then there are the people who put themselves on those slippery roads which go Left or Right of centre. Have they every stopped for just a few seconds to think what kind of political system makes a man take his whole family aboard a half sinking little boat, into shark-infested, unpredictable seas, just to escape from a system which has taken over his home and country? (Which he has probably never left before!) Have they stopped to think what it is makes people risk death or horrific injuries, chancing the minefields, dodging the bullets, just to cross the Berlin Wall? These decisions to flee a way of life are not made by a few hairbrained individuals, but by tens of thousands of ordinary people. Why?

Common sense is all that's needed to see the facts. How many 'holocausts' do we need before we all realise that 'far left' is as bad as – or worse than – 'far right'? When people start scrambling eastward over the Berlin Wall, and Viet Nam is inundated with boat people from all over the world – I'll admit I'm wrong!

By which time I'll probably be scrambling over our South Coast Wall, to join others in little boats heading for God knows where.

Don't bloody bet on it!!

Glossary

ARMALITE	–	AR 16 American light automatic rifle 5·56mm (·223 inch).
BAOR	–	British Army of the Rhine (Area of Germany occupied by British Forces).
BMH	–	British military hospital.
BREN	–	Type of light machine-gun.
BLITZKRIEG	–	Lightning war (German).
BLIGHTY	–	UK.
BULLSHIT	–	That which supposedly baffles brains –

    (a) By actions, such as polishing, painting, scrubbing, pressing and 'smartening' to a point far in excess of clean and tidy.

    (b) By talking, a load of crap.

CHOPPER	–	Helicopter.
CQB	–	Close quarter battle.
DZ	–	Drop Zone, landing area for troops, equipment or supplies dropped by parachute.
GURKHA	–	Soldier from Nepal, Northern India. Several battalions are part of the British Army.
ETA	–	Estimated time of arrival.
LAST LIGHT	–	Dusk. Sundown.
LMG	–	Light machine-gun.
NAAFI	–	Navy, Army & Air Force Institute (British Forces canteen).
LZ	–	Landing Zone. For helicopters.
IA	–	Immediate Action.
OP	–	Observation point or observation position.
PARANG	–	Machete. Long jungle knife.
POW	–	Prisoner of War.
PT	–	Physical training.
RECCE	–	Reconnaissance.

RNF	–	Royal Northumberland Fusiliers.
RPKAD	–	Resemen Para Kommando Angaton Darat (Indonesian Para Commando Regiment).
RSM	–	Regimental Sergeant Major.
RTU	–	Return to Unit.
RUR	–	Royal Ulster Rifles.
RV	–	Rendezvous. Meeting place.
SANGAR	–	Rock wall, often in a circle, where firing positions cannot be dug into ground.
SAS	–	Special Air Service.
SLR	–	Self-loading rifle (British 7·62mm).
SMG	–	Sub machine-gun.
STEN	–	Type of sub machine-gun.
WADI	–	Valley, gully, chasm, route of river or stream.
·30 CAL:	–	(Point) thirty (inch) calibre Browning medium machine-gun.
·50 CAL:	–	(Point) fifty (inch) calibre Browning heavy machine-gun. Also called 'Point Five'.
36 GRENADE	–	British high explosive shrapnel grenade.
80 GRENADE	–	British white phosphorous grenade.

Index